HEARING THE V
OF GYPSY, ROM/
TRAVELLER COMMUNITIES

Inclusive community development

Edited by Andrew Ryder, Sarah Cemlyn
and Thomas Acton

First published in Great Britain in 2014 by

Policy Press
University of Bristol
6th Floor
Howard House
Queen's Avenue
Clifton
Bristol BS8 1SD
UK
Tel +44 (0)117 331 5020
Fax +44 (0)117 331 5367
e-mail pp-info@bristol.ac.uk
www.policypress.co.uk

North American office:
Policy Press
c/o The University of Chicago Press
1427 East 60th Street
Chicago, IL 60637, USA
t: +1 773 702 7700
f: +1 773-702-9756
e:sales@press.uchicago.edu
www.press.uchicago.edu

British Library Cataloguing in Publication Data
A catalogue record for this book is available from the British Library

Library of Congress Cataloging-in-Publication Data
A catalog record for this book has been requested

ISBN 978 1 44731 357 1 paperback
ISBN 978 1 44731 356 4 hardcover

Cover design by Policy Press
Front cover image: www.alamy.com
Printed and bound in Great Britain by CMP, Poole
Policy Press uses environmentally responsible print partners

Dedicated to our young children and grandchildren:
Arthur, Gabriella, Max, Samuel, Chloe, Megan,
Sophie and Leila

Contents

List of figures and tables

Figures

Tables

Notes on contributors

Thomas Acton OBE is a campaigner for the rights of Gypsies, Roma and Travellers. He is also Secretary of the Brentwood Gypsy Support Group and Patron of the Roma Support Group. Thomas lectured at the University of Greenwich for over 30 years, and was Professor of Romani Studies, and is currently Professor Emeritus, Visiting Professor at the Corvinus University, Budapest and Senior Research Fellow at Buckinghamshire New University.

Susan Alexander is a former National Coordinator for Friends, Families and Travellers. Susan is currently administrator for the Travellers' Aid Trust, the only independent grant maker dedicated specifically to supporting Gypsies and Travellers in the UK.

Neil Ansell is a trustee of Friends, Families and Travellers. He is a former *Big Issue* and BBC reporter and is currently a novelist who has authored the acclaimed novels *Deep Country* and, most recently. *Deer Island*.

Sarah Cemlyn holds Fellowships at Bristol University and Corvinus University, Budapest, having lectured in social work and social policy for 20 years, and worked previously as a social/community work practitioner. Her research addresses equality, human rights and anti-discriminatory practice in social welfare and social policy, with a particular focus on issues affecting Gypsies, Roma and Travellers.

Gary Craig is Professor of Community Development and Social Justice at Durham University. Gary was the world's first Professor in Social Justice when he was appointed at the University of Hull in 2000. He was also founding Fellow at the Wilberforce Institute for the Study of Slavery and Emancipation and led the team working on issues of modern slavery.

John Day was a co-founder of the East Anglia Gypsy Council and former Chair of the Gypsy Council and is from the English Gypsy community. Peter was one of the first Gypsies to work in a local authority Traveller Education Service. Before his retirement John was a community development worker for the Black and Minority Ethnic Network for the East of England Region (MENTER).

Margaret Greenfields initially trained as a lawyer, with a special interest in family law and housing issues. She fairly rapidly moved into legal policy and has worked in the fields of child protection, domestic violence, 'looked-after' children living in 'kinship care' placements and the health, education and social care needs of Gypsy Travellers. Margaret is a Professor in the School of Social Sciences, Primary Care and Education at Buckinghamshire New University. A key research interest is Gypsy, Roma and Traveller communities.

Sylvia Ingmire is Chief Executive of the Roma Support Group and was a founding member in 1998. The Roma Support Group is one of the most established and well-known Roma organisations in the UK and is widely recognised for its pioneering work

Arthur Ivatts OBE is an International Consultant to governments and international organisations, including the EU, UNESCO, UNICEF, Council of Europe, FRA and the Roma Education Fund. Prior to this he was a senior consultant to the Department for Children, Families and Schools (DCFS) and is a former HM Inspector for Traveller Education.

Angus McCabe is Senior Research Fellow with the Third Sector Research Centre, University of Birmingham, where he co-leads TSRC's below-the-radar research, exploring the experiences of small community-based organisations, black, minority ethnic and refugee/migrant groups. Angus has a background in community development work, both in the inner city and in settings on peripheral estates.

Yvonne MacNamara is Chief Executive Officer of the Traveller Movement (TM), a national second-tier community development charity working to raise the capacity and social inclusion of Traveller and Gypsy communities in Britain. Yvonne was a founding member of the TM (then named the Irish Traveller Movement in Britain) and prior to joining TM worked for Irish Travellers through the Brent Irish Advisory Service.

Sarah Mann is Training and Capacity Building Manager at Friends Families and Travellers (FFT), a Brighton-based national organisation that supports Gypsies, Roma and Travellers. Sarah joined FFT in 2007. Her background is in community and environmental work, managing projects and training in the public and voluntary sectors.

Peter Mercer MBE is an English Gypsy and a co-founder of the East Anglia Gypsy Council and former Chair and President of the Gypsy Council for Education, Culture, Welfare and Civil Rights. He is currently chair for the National Federation of Gypsy Liaison Groups. Aside from helping Gypsies and Travellers in the UK Peter has been active on a European level through the International Romani Union.

Iulius Rostas is a Romanian Roma doctoral candidate at Babes Bolyai University of Cluj, Romania, a freelance researcher and Visiting Lecturer at Corvinus University, Budapest. Previously he had roles at the Open Society Institute and the European Roma Rights Centre and has been an expert consultant for the government of Romania (Department for the Protection of National Minorities). Iulius has published several articles on education policies, the Roma movement and Romani identity. He has edited a book for the CEU Press: *Ten Years After: A History of Roma School Desegregation in Central and Eastern Europe* (2012).

Andrew Ryder is a Fellow at the University of Bristol, an Associate Fellow at the Third Sector Research Centre at the University of Birmingham and a Visiting Professor at Corvinus University, Budapest. Prior to this he was Policy Officer to the Irish Traveller Movement in Britain and to the Gypsy and Traveller Law Reform Coalition, and researcher for the All-Party Parliamentary Group for Traveller Law Reform.

Maggie Smith-Bendell BEM has supported countless Gypsy families to gain planning permission on appeal throughout the country, and has taken up the cudgel on behalf of families experiencing harassment and poor conditions on local authority sites. With her brother Robert she established the Romani Gypsy Council in Somerset, and later, with Sally Woodbury, the South West Romani Gypsy Advisory Group. She is a core member of the National Federation of Gypsy Liaison Groups. For a fuller account of her life and work, see her 2009 book, *Our Forgotten Years*, and its 2013 sequel, *After All These Years*.

Siobhan Spencer MBE is a long-term Gypsy activist and leading member of the Derbyshire Gypsy Liaison Group (DGLG). She has also undertaken many planning appeals, built the DGLG to provide a range of other support services and worked locally and nationally with many agencies and services, such as the police, in community-led training and conferences. Through fostering links with other activists, the National Federation of Gypsy Liaison Groups developed as the umbrella support group for many local Gypsy and Traveller groups. She recently completed a law degree.

Natalie Stables is currently chair of NATT+ (National Association of Teachers of Travellers and Other Professionals) Roma Focus Group and is the lead professional for Salford Ethnic Minority and Traveller Achievement Service. She has over ten years' experience of working with ethnic minority children, young people and families, helping to raise attainment and increase awareness of the issues affecting ethnic minority groups in the UK and further afield.

Rob Torkington travelled as a New Traveller for nearly 30 years, and has been a long-standing trustee of Friends, Families and Travellers and was a committee member of the Gypsy and Traveller Law Reform Coalition.

Sally Woodbury is an English Gypsy who became involved with Maggie Smith-Bendell, undertaking planning appeals, liaising with councils and establishing the South West Romani Gypsy Advisory Group. Subsequently Sally has joined work sponsored nationally by the Local Government Association to raise awareness and educate councillors and officials about Gypsy and Traveller culture and the realities of their lives. She has also undertaken Holocaust memorial work, visiting Auschwitz and making a DVD for schools.

Acknowledgements

We wish to acknowledge the assistance of Isobel Bainton of the Policy Press; Angus McCabe and Julie Farrington for reading and commenting on the manuscript; and Alison Gilchrist for her very insightful comments on the manuscript.

Foreword

Gary Craig

Towards the end of the New Labour period of government, the National Equality Panel published a government-commissioned report on inequality in the UK (Hills et al, 2010). Packed with luminaries from the social policy and economics disciplines and based on a wide-ranging data analysis, it made a series of major recommendations addressing inequality across the UK between social classes, genders, ethnic groups and geographies. Compared with what might have been written ten years earlier, the analysis of minority ethnic groups was fairly detailed, although clearly gaps in data remained and some of these are currently being addressed by further research programmes. What the report said – indeed, was able to say – about the position of Gypsy and Traveller people was, however, very limited indeed. Gypsy and Traveller children were noted as falling further behind in terms of attainment at school, largely through an analysis of the Pupil Level Annual Schools Census. Even the size of the Roma, Gypsy and Traveller population was a matter of estimates, ironically, the best coming from the Council of Europe, which suggested that there were perhaps 300,000 (200,000 housed and 100,000 in caravans and thus generally non-sedentary) in 2002.

The National Equality Panel made a few further comments about the position of Gypsies and Travellers in the UK, for example about difficulties in finding site provision that was adequate in quantity and quality, on barriers to adequate employment or on accessing appropriate healthcare provision (drawing on the limited research available, much of it authored by those responsible for this book), but was forced to conclude that, despite such data as was available being 'very striking and of great concern', only the National Pupil Database provided any reasonably comprehensive data. Otherwise, there were huge gaps in the data available on 'other aspects of this community'. What is striking about this and many other reports on minority ethnic groups is that the UK Gypsy and Traveller population is as numerous as, for example, the Bangladeshi UK population, yet the former has been resident in the UK from about 500 years ago, while Bangladeshi settlement in the UK almost entirely dates from less than 50 years ago (Craig et al, 2012). Why this discrepancy? Why are the voices of Gypsies and Travellers not heard, nor their needs adequately portrayed in official data and policy, while those of other ethnic minority groups are beginning to be heard within a much shorter time period (for example the New Deal for Communities in Tower Hamlets investment into Bangladeshi community engagement: Dinham, 2005). This, of course, is not to argue that the Gypsy, Roma and Traveller community should have a greater priority over other minority groups, but that it should have an equal priority in terms of the exploration of its needs and in government responding to them.

The answer to these questions certainly does not lie in the unwillingness of Gypsy and Traveller communities to describe their needs or to respond to the still relatively few research studies that have engaged with them (see for example much of the published work of the editors of this volume; and Neale et al, 2009). What is clear from an analysis of this research and its outcomes, and from much of the material in this volume, is that the reason for the failure of social and economic policy at both national and local levels to reflect an appropriate response to the needs of Gypsies and Travellers lies not with the Gypsies and Travellers themselves (a variant on the tactic of 'blaming the victim' for their impoverishment, so well-used by the current Coalition government) but with the policy process, which, as other minority ethnic groups have found, is riddled with individual and institutional racism and which tends to 'invisibilise' population groups that are not politically popular.

A very good example of this lies in the experience of the national Sure Start programme. This programme was established to give the best possible start to children under 4 years of age and, as might be expected, was largely located in areas of substantial ethnic minority populations. An evaluation of this very substantially funded national programme (Craig, 2007) was highly critical of the national and local approaches to working with ethnic minority populations but saved its most critical comments for the almost complete lack of attention to Gypsy and Traveller children, widely acknowledged to be the most disadvantaged children's group within the UK as a whole. Around 70 local evaluations had been funded; and of these only two had paid any attention to Gypsy and Traveller populations. Hardly surprisingly, the national reporting – and thus the policy and political implications – of this major programme effectively wrote Gypsies and Traveller children out of the policy and political script. At a local level, the growing number of smaller research reports looking at different aspects of the situation of Gypsies and Travellers in relation to the most pressing issues such as health, housing and education have frequently suffered a similar fate at a different point in the policy process, although there are some isolated examples where the findings of local research have been picked up by policy actors. Many of these reports have been directed at individual local authorities and, in general (with some few notable exceptions), they have simply been ignored. Over the past five years the policy process has not managed to turn sensible, well-organised and valid research findings into adopted policies and thus into resource streams.

A bizarrely similar process appears to be emerging within the UK at present in relation to the more recently arrived Roma population. This group is defined by its recent migration status and by its sedentary nature, which, despite its having many issues in common (as well as, in many cases, historically related dialects of Romani), including facing hostility and racism of all kinds in accessing welfare provision, gives it a distinct status from longer-standing Gypsy and Traveller populations within the UK.[1] The Roma population within the UK may now be of the order of 200,000, according to recent research (Fremlova and Ureche, 2011; Brown et al, 2013). While the UK government, under pressure from Gypsy and Traveller interests such as the long-standing Gypsy Council, and from the European Union, has developed Gypsy and Traveller Integration strategies (as have the devolved administrations), it has doggedly refused to develop a Roma Integration Strategy, arguing that this (that is, developing a national strategy) was not the best way to support the integration of Roma. The submission from the UK government to the EU Commission as part of the EU Framework for National Roma Integration Strategies makes it clear that they are effectively excluding the Roma, as defined above, from their discussions. In reality, government conflates and identifies the UK Roma with Gypsy and Traveller people in order to continue receiving funding from the EU to support work for 'Roma' (one of the EU's social priorities). This sleight of hand on the part of government again thus invisibilises this most recent of Romani groups (Parliamentary questions during 2012/13 revealed that the government had no idea of the scope of the Roma population, let alone what its needs were). In the meantime, books such as this can but help to create conditions by which these groups receive the support they deserve by reflecting onto a public stage the issues and needs which characterise these communities. The present book, written and edited by a group of academics and activists who are well known in this territory and who, in many cases, have earned the trust of the communities about which they write, is titled 'Hearing the voices of Gypsy, Roma and Traveller communities' and addresses a major gap in social policy on marginalised groups. It is good to see that the contributions include chapters co-written by community members.

The 12 chapters as a whole provide a spectrum of ideas about ways in which Gypsy, Roma and Traveller communities, and those who support them and work with them, can build capacity (in the current jargon) to represent their own needs. Different chapters look at self-help strategies, the role of representative groups such as the Gypsy Council, support organisations such as the Travellers Aid Trust model (common across a number of areas) and the advocacy organisation Gypsy and Traveller Law Reform Coalition, the role that women activists have played in campaigning organisations and the place for community development as a strategic approach to working with Gypsy, Roma and Traveller communities. Not only does this provide a rich seam of ideas for work with these communities now and in the future, it also reminds us that these communities, despite the often violent racism and persistent exclusion they have had to endure, have always had the capacity to be political actors in shaping their own destiny. What has prevented them from taking a full part in British national life – and continues to prevent them – is that same structural and individual racism they have historically faced. They are not, however, going to go away. The time is long overdue for their voices to be fully heard and accepted; in the meantime, books such as this show us all the way forward.

Note

[1] For a recent portrait of the UK Roma and their history, see www. peer-review-social-inclusion.eu/network-of-independent-experts/2011/ promoting-the-social-inclusion-of-roma.

References

Brown, P., Dwyer, P. and Scullion, L. (2013) *ROMA Source Final Report*, Brussels: European Commission.

Craig, G. (2007) *Sure Start and Black and Minority Ethnic Children*, London: DfES.

Craig, G., Atkin, K., Chattoo, S. and Flynn, R. (eds) (2012) *Understanding 'Race' and Ethnicity*, Bristol: Policy Press.

Dinham, A. (2005) 'Empowered or overpowered', *Community Development Journal*, July: 301–12.

Fremlova, L. and Ureche, H. (2011) *From Segregation to Inclusion: Roma Pupils in the UK: A pilot project*, London: Equality-UK, http://equality. uk.com/Education_files/From%20segregation%20to%20integration. pdf.

Hills, J., Brewer, M., Jenkins, S., Lister, R., Lupton, R., Machin, S., Mills, C., Modood, T., Rees, T. and Riddell, S. (2010) *An Anatomy of Economic Inequality in the UK*, Report of the National Equality Panel, London: Government Equalities Office.

Neale, M., Craig, G. and Wilkinson, M. (2009) *Marginalised and Excluded: York's Traveller Community*, York: York Travellers Trust.

The formation of Gypsy, Roma and Traveller organisations in the UK

1950s
- Society of Travelling People (Tommy Docherty) 1959–Chapter Two

1960s
- The Gypsy Council (Grattan Puxon) 1966 – Chapters Two and Four

1970s
- The National Gypsy Education Council 1970– Chapters Two and Three
- The Romany Guild (Tom Lee) 1972– Chapter Two
- Advisory Council for the Education of Romanies and other Travellers (Plowden, Ivatts and Wallbridge) 1973 – Chapter Three
- The National Gypsy Council 1974 (Hughie Smith) – Chapter Two

1980s
- The national network of local authority Traveller Education Support Services (TESS) - Chapters Three and Eleven
- Derbyshire Gypsy Liaison Group 1987 – Chapter Nine
- The Travellers' Aid Trust 1988 – Chapter Eight

1990s
- Friends, Families and Travellers (Steve Staines) 1993 – Chapters Five and Six
- The Roma Support Group 1998– Chapter Eleven
- The Traveller Law Research Unit 1999 – Chapter Seven
- Irish Traveller Movement in Britain 1999– Chapter Six

2000s
- The Gypsy and Traveller Law Reform Coalition 2002 –Chapter Seven
- The National Federation of Gypsy Liaison Groups 2006 – Chapter Nine

Gypsy and Traveller accommodation policies

Accommodation policies have impacted greatly on GRT community development:

- Caravan Sites Act 1968 – Statist: see Chapter Two (Act only implemented 1970)
- Criminal Justice and Public Order Act 1994 – Localist: see Chapters Five, Seven and Nine
- Housing Act 2004, Planning and Compulsory Purchase Act 2004 and Planning Circular 01/06 – Statist: see Chapters Seven and Nine
- Localism Act 2011 and 'Planning policy for traveller sites' (2012) – Localist: see Chapters Eight and Twelve.

1968 Statist	A statutory duty was placed on councils to provide Traveller sites (council sites on which rents were paid). Approximately 350 sites were developed.
1994 Localist	The duty on councils to provide sites was repealed. Councils were asked to help Gypsies and Travellers to identify and buy land and develop sites. Few councils followed this advice.
2006 Statist/steering centralism	Councils were obliged to assess Gypsy and Traveller accommodation needs. These figures, formed through regional spatial strategies, provided a regional/council target for pitches. The policy encouraged engagement and dialogue with Gypsies and Travellers. Where councils failed to take the required measures there was scope for central government powers of direction.
2011 Localist	Regional pitch targets were abolished. The government has stated that every local authority should already have in place a five-year deliverable supply of sites. However, virtually no local authorities have such a policy in place within their Local Plan. A five-year deliverable supply of sites was meant to be in place by March 2013. The problem is that as a result of a localist agenda there is no longer any power of direction that can be used by the Secretary of State.

List of abbreviations

ACERT	Advisory Council for the Education of Romany and other Travellers
BME	Black and Minority Ethnic
CEE	Central/Eastern Europe
CIR	Comité Internationale Rom
CJPOA	Criminal Justice and Public Order Act (1994)
DGLG	Derbyshire Gypsy Liaison Group
EAGC	East Anglian Gypsy Council
EMTAS	Ethnic Minority Traveller Achievement Service
ERRC	European Roma Rights Centre
FFT	Friends, Families and Travellers
GCECWCR	Gypsy Council for Education, Culture, Welfare and Civil Rights
GRT	Gypsy, Roma and Traveller
GRTHM	Gypsy, Roma, Traveller History Month
GTLRC	Gypsy and Traveller Law Reform Coalition
GTR	Gypsy, Traveller and Roma
IRU	International Romani Union
ITMB	Irish Traveller Movement in Britain
LCTR	Labour Campaign for Travellers' Rights
LEA	local education authority
NATT	National Association of Teachers of Travellers + other professionals
NFGLG	National Federation of Gypsy Liaison Groups
NGC	National Gypsy Council
NGEC	National Gypsy Education Council
NGO	non-governmental organisation
NRIS	National Roma Integration Strategy
RGT	Roma, Gypsy and Traveller
RSG	Roma Support Group
TAT	Travellers Aid Trust
TESS	Traveller Education Support Services
TM	Traveller Movement
WONAFFUNGO	wholly non-autonomous fully funded non-governmental organisation

ONE

Introduction

*Thomas Acton, Sarah Cemlyn
and Andrew Ryder*

This book brings to the fore the voices and activism of marginalised and often condemned communities about whom there is little informed public debate. The editors of this volume take a critical approach to the received wisdom, looking for transformative change, emancipation and self-determination to pursue well-being, social justice and human rights. We are partisan in support of oppressed peoples' self-organisation (cf Fuchs, 2006), and analytical in taking their plight as indicative of the structural fault-lines in the ideologies of the powerful.

This book examines how Gypsy, Roma and Traveller (GRT)[1] communities have produced new, counter-hegemonic responses to marginalisation over the past half-century through mobilisation and campaigning, by traditional leadership, new forms of non-governmental organisation (NGO) activity and community development. Resistance can range from defying pressures to conform by determinedly maintaining traditional lifestyles, to challenging assimilation through innovation and adaptation. This is a moving story of endurance and tenacity, in which some of the most marginalised people in society, including some who do not have literacy skills, have found the resources and strength to offer resistance leading to, or offering a potential for, transformative change.

Location at the margins of society can provide 'spaces of radical openness', removed from the gaze of dominant society (hooks, 1991). Excluded communities occupying marginal space may more readily form an ideology of resistance which is also a mirror to the wider society. Hence, there is much to be learnt about the values and nature of wider society through the eyes of those like GRT communities that are ostracised and excluded.

Answering the 'call to context' issued by one of the founders of Critical Race Theory (Delgado, 1995, p xviii), we present personal stories of adopting new life and political strategies through the authorship of or by edited interviews with GRT community members. These 'thick descriptions' ensure that the subjects of the book and their aspirations are not lost in a fog of abstraction (Geertz, 1973, pp 3–30). Indeed as activist-scholars we contend that knowledge produced on a community's mobilisation should be accessible to those on whom the work is focused and not be hidden away in distant and inaccessible academic publications (Gillan and Pickerill, 2012). All the participants have been invited to review the structure and progress of the chapters within the volume, and divergent views have been charted and reflected on. It is our belief that participatory research centred within movements developed through action and reflection on action ('praxis') (Ledwith and Springett, 2010) can be, to quote Gillan and Pickerill (2012, p 140) 'more worthwhile, perhaps more authentic, than knowledge developed in the academy. This scholarship can actively situate itself against capitalism, corporations and elites and in support of those social movements with which we work.'

This book should be viewed as a companion to the previous study published by Policy Press *Gypsies and Travellers: Accommodation, Empowerment and Inclusion in British Society*, edited by Richardson and Ryder. That book gives a broad overview of social policy and its impact on Gypsies and Travellers, providing something akin to a handbook to help activists and practitioners understand and navigate recent policy changes. This book challenges activists, practitioners and academics engaged in community development or investigations related to it and places such work in a broader historical and theoretical context. We have sought to make the book accessible to a wide range of readers while setting out the links between activism, representation and identity and a series of complex theoretical debates. Activists, practitioners and a growing number of Gypsy, Roma and Traveller PhD scholars are increasingly challenging the existing academic establishment in this field and its scientistic assumptions (for a fuller discussion see Chapter Ten).

Who are the Gypsies, Roma and Travellers?

Over the centuries public attention to Gypsies, Roma and Travellers has fluctuated cyclically according to broader social crises requiring scapegoats. The present moral panic is only the latest recycling of deeply rooted stereotypes (Van Baar, 2011). Newspapers use the language of 'invasion' and 'leeching' in relation to Roma in-migration. The stereotypes occur crudely in programmes like *My Big Fat Gypsy Wedding,* more subtly and in academic guise in policy documents, reflecting institutional and ideological control by power elites in which groups like GRT communities are castigated for real or perceived nonconformity. Sometimes the stereotypes can coexist with the portrayal of resistance, as in the episode of *My Big Fat Gypsy Wedding* set at Dale Farm in the run-up to the evictions.

It is not possible, as many authors try, to specify when the 'old' Gypsy and Traveller populations of the Western European Isles 'entered' Britain and Ireland, since all of these groups, as they now exist, assumed their present ethnic character in the terrible economic and political crises of the later part of the 16*th* and earlier part of the 17*th* centuries, when anti-vagrancy moral panics and legislation led to the intense localisation and consolidation of commercial nomadic groups, who survived only by finding local protectors. Their ancestors may have been varying mixes, of Romani[2] immigrants arriving at the end of the 15th century, Celtic and Anglo-Saxon travelling traders, and stranded sailors, whose linguistic legacies mark in different proportions every 'old' Traveller group in the UK, but who, under the attack of the Poor Laws and the anti-Egyptian laws from the 1550s on, had to hang together or hang separately (Acton, 1979). Whatever they had been in 1500, by 1600, each of Wales, England, Scotland and Ireland had distinct Travelling populations, with distinct sets of dialects, that have retained distinct identities even as they have intermarried and influenced each other. The English and South Welsh Travellers are the most numerous and likely to call themselves Gypsies, though the ethnonym in the English Romani dialects is *Romanichal* (in North Wales it is *Kalé,* though this is now rare). In Scottish Traveller Cant the ethnonym is *Nachin,* and in the Irish Traveller Cant/Gammon *Minceir* or *Pavee.* The most numerous groups are the English Gypsies and the Irish Travellers. Both have traditionally had close-knit family structures centred on bonding social capital (intense social networks which can be inward looking), and because of their history nomadism or the possibility of nomadism remains a strong cultural value in a way that it does not for the mainly sedentary East European Roma. Both prefer work organised around kin groups and self-employment (Ryder and Greenfields, 2010). At the heart of the Traveller economy are concepts of mutualism and collectivity, terms which have undergone a renaissance in recent political discourse (McNeil, 2009). Mutualism and social capital have played a key role in counteracting marginalisation and exclusion for Gypsies and Travellers by creating self-help networks and sources of income and are evident in the strong traditions of family socialisation, which include traditional gender roles as important determinants of group dynamics for work (Ryder and Greenfields, 2010). Such traditions, however, can act as a barrier to participation in formal education, where these traditions, combined with high levels of reported bullying towards this group and a school curriculum which fails to inspire some in this community, have contributed to a low level of participation in formal education (Derrington and Kendall, 2004). This accentuates marginalisation, along with economic, social, ethnic and spatial exclusion (Cemlyn et al, 2009).

Substantial Romani migration from Eastern Europe to the UK and other Western European countries was renewed after the fall of communism in 1989 set free previously repressed anti-Gypsyism. The migrants come mostly from mainly sedentary Romani populations (calling themselves *Roma*) that consolidated in provinces of the former Ottoman Empire or the Kingdom of Poland from the 13th century (Fraser, 1992). Although some, such as the Chergashe, have remained nomadic, the great majority, despite occasional forced migration, have not been nomadic or 'Travellers'. Roma operate within close-knit kin networks in which tradition and gender roles have been important determinants of group dynamics. However, they have a great diversity of language, tradition, culture and religion; as with Jews or Black people, what unites them most is the common experience of racism or anti-Gypsyism, which lumps them together and leads to common actions of resistance and solidarity and exploration of what they do have in common.

Experiences of acute exclusion, combined with an increase in the activity of the far Right in Central/Eastern Europe (CEE), continue (for example, eight Roma were murdered in racist attacks in Hungary in 2009 – *ERRC Journal*, 2009) (Fekete, 2014), prompting many Roma to seek refuge and opportunities in the West, although often racism and exclusion follow them westwards. Growing numbers of Roma businesses and graduates show us that these dreams can come true; but many find that anti-Gypsyism is also strong in the West against both local Gypsies/Travellers and immigrant Roma.

Social exclusion and counting Roma, Gypsies and Travellers

Many Gypsies/Roma/Travellers seek to avoid social exclusion by not identifying themselves as such, and this bedevils attempts to estimate their numbers. Some individuals strongly identify as Roma, Gypsies or Travellers; maybe a quarter of these will even identify themselves as such in the census. Others identify themselves to friends and family only; others keep their knowledge very private indeed. Some discover their Gypsy heritage only when they research their ancestry and meet long lost cousins through the Romany and Traveller Family History Society, and many of course have more than one ethnic heritage. But on the basis of the data we give in Appendix 2, we believe we can be reasonably certain, in this decade, that at any one time there are no fewer than 240,000 people in the UK who normally identify as Gypsies, Roma and Travellers, and perhaps around 350,000 who sometimes do, and never more than 750,000.

Of these, no more than 60–70,000 live in caravans (22–23,000 caravans). Around a fifth of the caravan-dwellers live on unauthorised sites and encampments, three-tenths on local authority sites and half on their own legal sites (CLG, 2009; Ryder et al, 2012). The Gypsies and Irish Travellers who responded to the 2011 Census had the highest proportion with no qualifications for any ethnic group (60%), almost three times higher than for England and Wales as a whole (23%); they were the ethnic group with the lowest proportion of respondents who were economically active, at 47%, compared to 63% for England and Wales as a whole; and they had the lowest proportion of any ethnic group rating their general health as 'good' or 'very good', at 70% compared to 81% of the overall population of England and Wales (ONS, 2014). An earlier Mori survey found them the most reviled groups in society (Stonewall, 2003).

The situation is similar for Roma across Europe (ERRC, 2009). Traditions of trading and entrepreneurialism were largely repressed as communist regimes sought to 'proletarianise' the Roma in (often low grade) industrial employment (Sigona and Trehan, 2010). After 1989 the Roma were the group most affected by economic and structural changes as state-controlled manufacturing and heavy industry where they had been employed was decimated by the market economy. Roma unemployment is often five or six times the national average (ERRC, 2009), and this is compounded by poor accommodation and ethnic and economic segregation (Sigona and Trehan, 2010), especially in the education system, where many Roma have been wrongly placed in inferior 'remedial' learning environments (Rostas, 2012).

In the UK work restrictions applied until May 2011 to A8 (Poland, Slovakia, Czech Republic, Slovenia, Hungary, Lithuania, Latvia and Estonia) and until December 2013 to A2 (Romania and Bulgaria) nationals. These restrictions placed huge obstacles in the way of Roma seeking employment.[3] Many Roma in the UK remain trapped in casual self-employment and earn a fraction of the legal minimum wage, which has consigned them to residence in overcrowded and substandard accommodation (Ryder and Greenfields, 2010).

Mobilisation and resistance through inclusive forms of community development

There is a range of interpretations both of community development and of the crucial constituent but often elusive term 'community', with different underpinning assumptions often operating simultaneously (Taylor, 2003). Normatively, 'community' often carries positive associations such as connection and solidarity, though there can be division and conflict within as well as at the boundaries of communities (Brent, 2009). Used descriptively, it indicates shared characteristics, although this in turn implies boundaries of belonging and exclusion. Community development theorists delineate different descriptive meanings, including community of 'place', of 'identity', and issue-based or 'interest' community, and highlight the shifts within community development prompted by liberation movements to acknowledge intersecting dimensions of oppression beyond class, and internal community dynamics (Craig, 2011; Gilchrist, 2009). Instrumentally, it conveys the political role of 'community' as agent, the active community that is central to community development. While acknowledging diversity and different forms of community, the focus of theorising can default to discussion of place-based community development (Henderson and Vercseg, 2010).

However, GRT 'identity' communities are often geographically dispersed and their relationship with localities is frequently overwhelmingly conflictual (Richardson, 2007), like other minority communities 'delineated by their very status as "other" in relation to the community of locality' (Shaw, 2008, p 29). While this status and the mobilisation of local campaigns that aim to increase this exclusion receive brief mentions in the community-development literature, their position within community development even compared to other minority communities remains generally undertheorised, reflecting currently for Gypsies, Roma and Travellers what Meekosha (2011, p 177) referred to more widely in an earlier era as 'the poverty of articulation of identity issues with community work theory'. A recent exception is the collection edited by Vincze and Raţ (2013) on *Spatialisation and racialisation of social exclusion*, which uses community development theory innovatively, backed up by meticulous ethnographic and survey work, to look at many of the same issues of leadership, action and outsider expertise in Romanian Roma 'ghettos', and examines the relationship of identity issues with the 'mainstream' practice of funded community development workers, which is relatively neglected in the UK (Cemlyn et al, 2009). This book aims to begin filling this gap through the exploration of autonomous community-based action and the work of specialist GRT NGOs, but this also indicates that 'community development', itself an ambiguous concept and practice, has a particularly ambiguous relationship with GRT communities.

Widely accepted definitions of community development include enabling communities as 'active citizens' collectively to exercise power and achieve change, and to contribute to 'civil society', seen as a space between the state and the public within which campaigns and social movements can be active (Henderson and Vercseg, 2010). However, community development straddles many boundaries and uncertainties, including whether or not it is a profession, with its implications of distancing from marginalised communities, or a social movement. With contradictory roots in welfare paternalism, colonial administration and state-sponsored conditionality on the one hand and working-class and social movement struggles on the other, its terrain is continuously contested (Craig et al, 2011, intro; Mayo, 1975). It can be assimilatory and 'technicist', diverting challenges to the status quo, or transformational, supporting struggles for social justice and equality (Mayo, 1998), or both at once. Referring to the conflicted yet mediatory and versatile role of 'community', Shaw (2008) compares 'community as policy', namely a tool of government, and 'community as politics' as a collective public space for deliberation, action and reflection.

The divergence between self-organised social movement activism and professional NGO-based activity pervades this volume, but there is also convergence and synthesis where appropriately supported and inclusive community development achieves collective and individual gains. Progressive community development writers highlight the centrality of values of cooperation, equality, participation, learning and social justice (Popple, 2007), the strengths that come from the versatility of the role and its location (Henderson and Vercseg, 2010), the significance of networking to create links and alliances across institutional and community boundaries (Gilchrist, 2009) and the imperatives of promoting empowerment, challenging power structures and oppressive policy and practice. Ledwith and Springett (2010) and Ledwith and Asgill (2007) take a further step in analysing and challenging sources of knowledge and understanding that impede empowerment, to validate community knowledge, deliberation and reflection as integral to action for change, and build reflective critical alliances across difference, building on the work of Freire, Gramsci and Habermas as we discuss further below.

However, the use of 'partnership working' and top-down community development as tools of government policy, drawing community organisations into governance structures that are framed within a dominant neoliberal agenda, have seen a co-option of much of the deliberative and reflective space that community development from below can create to develop critiques and organise action, particularly by marginalised groups. Emejulu and Bronstein (2011, p 283), reviewing wide-ranging articles across the globe on 'feminisms and contemporary community development' in the *Community Development Journal*, conclude that 'neoliberal policy processes are subverting feminist community development and activism. As the state is rolled back to allow the market to determine welfare provision, this appears to close down the space for radical critique and action – especially from a feminist perspective.' Shukra (2011, p 271) refers to the incorporation of the anti-racist movement into the state in the 1990s, 'to create a process through which potentially militant activists emerging from community action would be emasculated', with those outside the governance framework characterised as 'unrespectable minorities', an assimilatory process heightened in subsequent community cohesion policies (Flint and Robinson, 2008). Kenny (2011) confirms such limitations on community development and argues the need for *visionary* active citizens who can 'scope alternative futures' (p i10), which is a theme throughout this book.

Taylor (2011) refers to groups being 'invited in' to spaces of governance. GRT communities have had to pressure from outside to enter into dialogue with government rather than being invited in. The evidence of this volume indicates that this outsider/marginal status, which is arguably more pronounced than that of most other minority groups apart from asylum seekers, does indeed also provide a source of strength, analysis and resistance to avoid co-option, There are gains to be achieved from working inside partnerships (Taylor, 2011), and GRT organisations, having had to push for entry, are also active in partnerships they choose with government and public services to promote rights for their communities, with mixed success but on-going insights. The relative neglect of GRT community activism within community development theory and practice heightens the importance of this book. It also indicates that GRT community activism can provide lessons for community development more widely.

'Inclusive community development'

The editors and contributors to this book have used the term 'inclusive community development' to signify that they align themselves with a transformational approach while recognising that the resources of mainstream community development have not always been adequately available to GRT communities. It must contain the potential for transformative change in the thoughts and perceptions of individuals and deep structural change in the nature of society. In seeking such change it is important to bear in mind Gandhi's call for us to 'be the change we want to see in the world' (cited in Gore, 1992, p 14). In other words, the process of transformation must reflect the ideals and vision of the change sought. Transformative change is not the preserve of intellectuals but is dependent on the mobilisation of a broad range of groups, including those at the margins, without whom we cannot combat the unfairness of society. But solidarity and empathy can also lead the comfortably-off to commitment to meaningful political change. Thus this book gives insights into the 'practice' of community mobilisation by and with GRT groups by exploring the ideals and vision of the individuals concerned, both external catalysts for change and those within GRT communities. These personal and narrative accounts exemplify and illustrate the arguments of central theorists whose ideas inform community development and social movements, such as Freire, Alinsky, Gramsci and, more recently, Habermas.

The seminal work of the influential Brazilian theorist of community development, Freire, *Pedagogy of the Oppressed*, was translated into English in 1972, marking a new start in grassroots community action, popularising notions of critical pedagogy. This involves deliberation and reflection where communities seek critical consciousness and grassroots mobilisation through trust, dignity, mutualism and reciprocity, and Gandhian ideals of grounding community actions in experience, giving external actions an internal moral basis and gearing the outcomes of external action to promote conscious internal growth, thus creating a community politics of 'integrity and trust' (cf Goswami, 2009). For Freire, the starting point of this journey is critical consciousness leading to a change in the understanding and values of those oppressed and ultimately to their mobilisation for social change.

A contemporary of Freire, Saul Alinsky, reached similar conclusions while working to improve conditions in poor neighbourhoods in the ghettoes of Chicago. His influential work *Rules for Radicals*, published in 1971, articulated his principles on community organisation but also seemed to capture the radicalism of the times, which in the anti-war and anti-segregation demonstrations of America in the 1960s utilised many of the tactics advocated by Alinsky. A controversial feature of Alinsky's approach was to bait and taunt the establishment, which often provoked reactions exposing the worst face of the establishment. This radicalism could, though, sometimes be inflexible and a common criticism was that its zealousness worked against broader alliance building. However, at the core of his message was the need to mobilise communities at the grassroots and for their views and aspirations to be the driving force of campaigns for social justice. As Chambers (2003), an acolyte of Alinsky, has noted, if campaigns and organisations are not rooted in the experiences of communities there is the danger of the 'political' becoming sterile and moribund.

The 'new left' Marxism of the 1970s tried to assimilate such radical community activism through the advocacy of 'organic intellectuals of the working class', a concept taken from the Prison Diaries of the pre-war Italian communist leader Antonio Gramsci, translated into English in 1971. The key idea taken from Gramsci was his notion of hegemonic power, which 'normalises' the ideology of the ruling class so that resistance seems absurd. Counter-hegemonic action required forms of deliberation and education by working-class intellectuals who addressed problems as experienced by the working class, rather than as formulated by traditional ruling-class intellectuals. Gramsci contended that an anti-hegemonic action required alliance building of broad masses of interests, led by organic rather than traditional intellectuals.

Have such ideas survived the hippy countercultural era? The great financial crash at the beginning of the 21st century, and the subsequent election of a former community development organiser from Chicago to the White House, might well make us look at them again; but also compelling is the way they seem to be increasingly urgently rearticulated by Habermas (1984, 1996, 2010, 2011). Habermas advocates a *deliberative democracy*, which can facilitate communicative action and new social movements, seeking consensus and mutual understanding but also forming a counterpoint to the forces of reaction during crises. He argues that citizens and their representatives should deliberate in an environment which is conducive to reflection and mutual willingness to understand the values, perspectives and interests of others and thus show 'empathy', where there is the possibility of reframing their interests and perspectives in the light of a joint search for common interests and mutually acceptable solutions (Lengyel, 2009). One might dismiss this as idealisation of a past bourgeois public sphere of coffee-houses and salons in the age of Enlightenment (Fleming, 2002). However, it does seem that as Habermas complains about 'refeudalisation' and the hegemonic discourse of power elites corrupting civil society, he converges with the previous generation in a call to revitalise public discourse through 'radical democracy', where the people are sovereign (Laclau and Mouffe, 1985; Habermas, 1996).

This bourgeois vision of radical democracy may seem to make little reference to the marginalised (Kellner, 2000) or set out how they will gain the cultural capital to access the forums of civil society (Somin, 2010). But this is precisely the gap in the argument that can be filled by Gramsci's (1971) vision of 'organic intellectuals', whose perceptions of societal injustices spring 'organically' from their marginalised condition. The Roma intellectuals, sneered at as auto-didacts (self-taught community leaders) by the traditional academic elite, have nonetheless succeeded in changing the European agenda. Coalitions which include economically excluded groups as well as those who are excluded on the grounds of race, gender, sexual orientation and disability can deliberate upon solidarity and new transformative notions of social justice (cf Offe, 1985).

'Can' does not mean will. In fact, historically in the UK for Gypsy and Traveller communities most policies of community development and welfare interventions have offered the opposite of 'empowerment' (Acton, 2005). As Mayall (1995, p 43) notes, the British state since the 16*th* century has perceived Gypsies and Travellers as:

> 'persistent and irritating thorns in their flesh ...' on account of perceived 'defiance' of the laws of the land and of contemporary trends to sedentarisation and civilisation.... A common theme underpinning state and wider societal responses is the desire to disperse, contain and, most importantly, to transform.

Powell (2010, p 472) further illustrates how the fate of this minority has often been determined by the power and authority of outsiders, reflecting a '"civilizing" project' that has viewed them as dysfunctional and in need of reform and therapy. Today service providers and third sector community and advocacy groups argue that they have rejected failed forms of paternalism and aspire to inclusive social policy. Yet Powell suggests it is still the case that 'some well-intentioned interventions into the lives of Gypsy-Travellers are unwelcome and assimilationist. If perspectives on what is best for "the community" are derived from normative assumptions based on the empowering potential of dominant social processes such as individualisation and social integration, then they may well be inaccurate or misguided.' In looking at successes and failures, this books sets out evidence as to how far community development with GRT communities can empower and how far it is a new form of 'civilising' project.

As long ago as 2001, Trehan claimed 'NGOisation', with its managerialism and donor-driven agendas, was stifling Roma community mobilisation. In Eastern Europe NGOs are perceived to be directed by a paternalist approach, in which Roma politicians have been corrupted and have forgotten their constituencies and been sucked into wider power games, becoming pawns of the power elite (Kovats, 2003) and that sections of civil society have engaged in what Freire (1972) termed 'horizontal violence', where fellow campaigners become sub-oppressors. Indeed rival organisations fling such accusations at each other with claims of groups belonging to a 'Gypsy Industry' (Ryder, 2011), where securing grants and jobs is the priority.

'Outsiders' as activists or workers within the 'Gypsy Industry' have had an important role to play in community development with GRT communities. Is it possible that despite personally coming from privileged backgrounds such outsiders may still act as Freire-style educators in critical pedagogy? Could some members of the 'Gypsy Industry' still provide technical expertise to support inclusive community development? To answer these questions we need to look at both the tensions and the mutuality between 'insiders' and 'outsiders'.

Since the 1970s members of the Gypsy Industry, like much of the rest of the Race Relations Industry, have sought to measure their own (and condemn others') attempts at inclusivity and empowerment by using Arnstein's (1969) celebrated ladder of participation (Figure 1.1). Can GRT NGOS, whether small ones at stage 8, or larger ones at stages 7 or 6, act as effective goads to state agencies that rarely get beyond stage 4? GRT community group mobilisation is not always inclusive,

Figure 1.1: Arnstein's (1969) ladder of participation

8	Citizen control	**Degrees of citizen power**
7	Delegated power	
6	Partnership	
5	Placation	**Degrees of tokenism**
4	Consultation	
3	Informing	
2	Therapy	**Non participation**
1	Manipulation	

and an elite may play the roles of 'providers' and 'modernisers' and thus may become hierarchical, paternal and discriminatory (Toomey, 2011). But such examples only render more important the aspiration to 'inclusive community development', which builds on existing skills and cultural practices to develop skills, confidence and empathy (Craig et al, 2011) and, as Tritter and McCallum (2006) suggest, turn Arnstein's simple ladder into a complex scaffold, where elite and populist agencies collaborate. As demonstrated in later chapters, hybrid approaches may be required. Sometimes lay knowledge and excluded communities cannot be expected at the outset of community development to grapple with the unavoidable bureaucratic tasks linked with major transformative community development. Furthermore, oppressed people sometimes do not have contextual tools and need external help (Popple, 1994). GRT community development has to navigate a tough terrain of the colonialising agendas of more paternalist forms of community development with limited resources. First steps, even where reliant on external support and with limited forms of empowerment, may lead to a holistic progression, if external support can be balanced and measured against growing community confidence, critical consciousness and aspirations for ownership and control.

In referring to tools and concepts for measuring empowerment we may cautiously adopt what has been termed a 'capability approach', a measurement tool for inclusion and social justice that evaluates 'human outcomes in terms of choices and opportunities that a person faces' (Sen, 1992, p 39ff). Sen, though, has refused to defend 'one pre-determined canonical list of capabilities', and in this spirit we have entered into a dialogue among the contributors of this book as to what 'empowerment', 'participation' and 'human rights' mean for GRT communities. Sen (1999) has also recognised the importance of institutions to development, in the sense that a variety of social institutions, like elected bodies, due process of law and a fair press, contribute to the process of development precisely through their effects on enhancing and sustaining individual freedoms, thus increasing equity and upholding norms and values to achieve social justice. This echoes the approach advocated by Ife (2001) where human rights are discursively constructed through engagement with the situated voices and needs of human beings, and evolve through dialogue and political action. Ife and Fiske (2006) argue that bottom-up community development approaches and more top-down, convention-framed human rights work are potentially mutually reinforcing and complementary.

Community development and cultural, social and emotional capital

A continual theme in the history of GRT communities has been the role of participation in public education and how far state education is a legitimate addition to GRT culture and how far a threat of cultural eradication (Liégeois, 1998). In discussion on community development this book also demonstrates that levels of education have been important factors in limiting or assisting activism.

Bourdieu (1991) and his followers (Bourdieu and Wacquant, 1992) have argued that, since education plays a key role in allowing individuals to access economic, social and cultural capital without which their capability to act in society is constrained, somehow the excluded must crack the education system, without first being cracked by it. They need 'cultural capital' (knowing how the social system works and being able to adapt behaviour accordingly) that enables the privileged versed in the behaviour and the language of the ruling class to accrue 'symbolic mastery' (such as exam success) which translates into wealth and status and thus justifies and rationalises inequality through notions of academic meritocracy. Empowerment for GRT communities through educational success will require inclusive forms of schooling where dialogue and a diversity of learning approaches are practised in the mainstream, if they are to increase the skills and confidence to organise on behalf of their communities and transmit positive images to the wider community. The book offers examples of where a lack of cultural capital on the part of GRT community members is overcome by alliances and partnerships that develop skills and can enable community members to progress up the steps of Arnstein's ladder towards community control.

Cultural capital can be added to what Bourdieu and Wacquant term social capital, which is 'the sum of resources, actual or virtual, that accrue to an individual or a group by virtue of possessing a durable network of more or less institutionalised relationships of mutual acquaintance and recognition' (1992, p 119). But allowing the additional cultural capital may devalue the traditional social capital: as they sang of Yankee soldiers in the Great War: 'How we gonna get them back on the farm / Once they've seen Gay Paree'. Without it, however, we may be left with inward-looking and isolated cultural and community enclaves (Ryder, 2011; Woolcock, 2001).

Such dynamics have at times worked against GRT community mobilisation and contributed to a lack of trust not just towards outsiders but also towards other groups, clans and factions within GRT communities, creating disunity (Rostas, 2012). Disunity can be spawned through disagreements as to the degree to which the community or outsiders are perceived to be in control of a community organisation, but often tensions have emerged over competition for limited resources in the form of grants, power and influence. Despite these difficulties, groups have come together effectively, as is demonstrated in this book.

The cement for these partnerships has often been dialogue and understanding where unity is given time and space to grow, but also nourished through forms of emotional capital (Nowotny, 1981) where strong forms of solidarity and support are provided. Such support can become particularly strong when activists are engaged in battles that seem impossible to win. The hope and inspiration that can be drawn from such friendships and trust are an invaluable resource in community mobilisation.

It should be noted that a prominent feature of successful partnership work is the growing involvement of GRT women in community action. Feminist writers (such as Dominelli, 2006) have explored the important contribution of women and the principles that often inform women's activism, such as working collaboratively and not in hierarchical ways, paying attention to people's experiences and their feelings, linking these personal experiences with political structures and issues. Gypsy and Traveller women activists have made a particular contribution to this way of working and developed further connections, notably through their powerful linking of personal, family, community and political issues, which forms an important feature in a number of chapters in this volume.

In search of empowerment

As this book shows, organisational innovation is possible. Yet, as recently as 1975, a Labour Young Fabian pamphlet by a student who had been a volunteer teacher presented the Gypsy Council and the Romani Guild as necessary, brave, but *unrepresentative* and asserted 'Gypsies have no conception of democracy or representation' (Smith, 1975, p 6). Such an assertion *by a pro-Gypsy activist* shows the hegemony of older racist discourses among outsiders who interested themselves in Gypsies, which constrained debates over how best to help the Gypsies from the 19th century on. The debate was between romantics who wished to conserve Romani culture unchanged and assimilationists such as the philanthropist George Smith of Coalville, who lobbied in the 1880s for a Bill to compel Gypsies and Travellers to attend school. His suggestions were eventually embodied in the 1906 Education Bill, but were cut down, in the Act as passed, to attendance for only half the year for Gypsy children after Dora Yates, a Liverpool student who had joined the Gypsy Lore Society (a folklore and antiquarian group) wrote to her cousin, the Liberal MP Sir Herbert Samuel, advocating the merits of half-yearly attendance to facilitate the continuance of nomadic patterns (Acton, 1974; Okely, 1983).

Although the Gypsy Lore Society cautiously supported the defence of Gypsy encampments by Labour MP Norman Dodds and Liberal MP Eric Lubbock (now Lord Avebury) in the 1950s and 1960s, it remained sceptical of attempts to 'improve' Gypsies and sought to stay out of politics. As Yates (1953, p 161) wrote, 'Gypsylorists have reaped their reward from the publication of their researches and from the fun they have had in pursuit of such specialised knowledge.' Perhaps they suspected that the policy agenda, in which Gypsies had little say, might be to sedentarise them and assimilate them into waged labour, as undoubtedly it was for some of those who voted for the Caravan Sites Act 1968 to provide local caravan sites for Travellers (Okely, 2001; Richardson and Ryder, 2012). The campaign of the Gypsy Council, founded in 1966, took place in the context of the 1968 Act and was only just beginning to lift GRT participation off the bottom rungs of Arnstein's ladder. In the five years after the Act was brought into operation, the GRT community advocacy groups splintered into bitterly opposed factions, perhaps leading the Cambridge student Smith (1975) to channel the Gypsylorist beliefs of the Liverpool student Dora Yates that Gypsies needed protection, not participation.

Today few anti-racists would fall into such a naively racist assertion as Smith's (1975), but this is partly because the landscape of ethnic politics has changed, to a great extent along the lines prophesied by Stuart Hall (1991). Ethnic minorities are not fixed and rigid identities but are fluid and diverse entities subject to change and adaptation. This book in part records how different generations of Gypsies, Roma and Travellers, with different backgrounds and education, have defined their identities and responded to the challenges and exclusions that have confronted them in their lives. These personal life strategies include traditional and 'conservative' approaches based on bonding social capital that have built on some existing community strengths but have often also restricted more formalised community mobilisation or fuelled distancing and reactive and nationalist forms of identity (Ryder, 2011). The book examines the use of ethnic identity in mobilisation and cultural adaptation and the adoption of new and innovative life and political strategies. Feminist readings of Hall (1991), from theories of 'hybridity'[4] to contemporary theories of 'intersectionality', in dialectical interaction with critical race theory, are exemplified by and supportive of the growing number of women taking up new roles as community advocates (Ryder and Greenfields, 2010).[5]

Critical race theory placed a strong focus on the recognition of the experiential knowledge of excluded ethnic communities in defining their exclusion (Matsuda et al, 1993). This was coupled with activist agendas that incorporated commitments to social justice and change and recognition that racism is a central factor in a social order that rests on intersectional oppressions including economic, racial and gender exclusion (Hylton, 2012). Sometimes critical race theory has left a residue that reduces everything to 'race'. Power (2007, p 158) argued:

> Analysing and organising around racial inequality is an entry point into the second step of political race (racial consciousness), in which participants articulate and mobilise around a broader social justice agenda.[6] This second step also entails coalition building with other allies. The third step of political race is to 'experiment with new democratic practices that emphasise inclusiveness, deliberation and problem-solving'.

Academic feminism, promoting the notions first of 'hybridity' and then of 'intersectionality', has enabled us to move beyond the reductionist concept of 'race' in the second and third stages of this coalition building that Power identifies. We hope to demonstrate that reflection, inclusive research, deliberation, skills development, mobilisation and framing[7] that reflect intersectionality are prerequisites that can be combined and utilised as central components in the struggle for social justice.

The possibilities and resources for GRT community action working with and not against the grain of community culture are therefore multiplying as older activists pass on their hard-won skills. The first part of the book (Chapters One to Six) provides a historical overview of GRT community development and activism in the UK since the 1960s, and how community action has interacted with professionally supported community development. In the second part of the book (Chapters Seven to Eleven) we explore important developments such as how the different groups have sought to come together as a social movement. Moreover we discuss in more depth the common problems GRT communities face in capacity and resources, including a critique of the 'Big Society' policy agenda. Another important development dealt with in this section is how the third sector has acted as a trigger for change in gender roles. In addition, Chapter Ten discusses critiques of community development policies for Roma in Europe, while Chapter Eleven details recent growth and mobilisation of Roma communities in the UK, which points forward to the rallying call of our Conclusion on empowerment, the state and redistribution.

GRT community organisation is still, however, fragmented and under-resourced, and consequently often goes unnoticed in broader social policy discourse (McCabe et al, 2010). The National Equality Partnership (2008) observed that there are only around 20 GRT groups on the UK charities register. The fragility of pan-GRT action was pointed out by the Independent Task Group on Site Provision and Enforcement for Gypsies and Travellers:

> Seeking to engage a community that has long been effectively excluded from public life presents its own challenges. Low levels of literacy, the lack of a settled place to live, a mistrust of authority in general and a tradition of keeping things within the community can make it hard to establish relationships within the community. Different community representative groups concentrate on different issues and geographical areas and, in common with groups representing any constituency, may or may not be in agreement on the best way forward. Most will struggle with resources and may have limited capacity to engage with local authorities or central government. (CLG Task Group, 2007, p 54)

The multiple reasons cited for the dearth of organised community development are rooted in exclusion and mistrust and hark back to the first part of the 20th century, when both Gypsylorists and assimilationists saw the political disengagement of Gypsies as inevitable and permanent. Faced with such expectations from authority, it is not surprising 'closed communities' often prefer self-help mechanisms rather than seeking redress and support from mainstream agencies (Shukra, 2011). Within GRT communities disempowerment, distancing and lack of engagement by public bodies have been compounded by low levels of literacy (Cemlyn et al, 2009) and a lack of confidence, what Freire (1972) termed a 'culture of silence'. The rest of this book is about the possibilities of overcoming these obstacles.

Chapter Two: Acton, Mercer, Day and Ryder describe how the Gypsy Council was founded in 1966 as a 'radical' form of community politics triggered by the charismatic campaigner Grattan Puxon. Puxon was an 'outsider' catalyst who threaded family networks and traditions into a coherent campaign that played an important role in raising the profile of Gypsy and Traveller issues. As early participants in the activities of the Gypsy Council, Acton, Day and Mercer are well placed to provide a description of its emergence, linking this development to culture, identity and resistance.

Chapter Three: Ivatts, a pioneer champion for GRT inclusion in mainstream education, describes how, despite early tensions over mainstream education as fears were raised over assimilation and a loss of identity, inclusive support mechanisms were developed, leading to the formation of the Traveller Education Service network within local authorities.

Chapter Four: Acton and Ryder provide a portrait of the late Charles Smith, who was chair of the Gypsy Council, a Commission for Racial Equality commissioner, a local councillor and mayor and a lead activist in the campaign for Traveller law reform. This chapter of the book provides insights into how ethnicity and identity are shifting and fluid constructs and how this quality can in fact be conducive to mobilisation and critical consciousness.

Chapter Five: Ansell with Torkington describes how, during the 1990s, the media and political elite created a moral panic over New Travellers that prompted new restrictions on nomadism in the form of the Criminal Justice and Public Order Act 1994. An overview is given of how campaigners responded to the clampdown against Travelling communities and galvanised themselves into a support and advocacy network.

Chapter Six: McCabe, MacNamara and Mann outline the work of two GRT third sector groups that are professionalised and formalised, offering helplines, service provision and policy and voice projects. Friends, Families and Travellers and the Irish Traveller Movement in Britain (now renamed The Traveller Movement) have sought to contribute towards inclusive community development through developing the skills of community members.

Chapter Seven: Ryder and Cemlyn outline the development of the Gypsy and Traveller Law Reform Coalition, an umbrella group that lobbied the New Labour government to address Gypsy and Traveller exclusion. The chapter outlines how civic engagement tools were used and how this mobilisation and social movement was based on facets of asset-based community development, fusing the old with the new.

Chapter Eight: Alexander and Greenfields describe the Travellers Aid Trust (TAT[8]), which is the only independent grant maker dedicated specifically to supporting Gypsies and Travellers in the UK. TAT has gained invaluable insights and expertise into the practicalities and challenges of GRT community development and how to work with and support groups that can be described as 'below the radar', under-resourced and under-represented.

Chapter Nine: Cemlyn, Smith-Bendell, Spencer and Woodbury reflect on the core role of women in the National Federation of Gypsy Liaison Groups, a key forum for the development of local and regional Gypsy and Traveller groups. The chapter considers the relationship of gender, culture and activism, and how personal and political dynamics interact.

Chapter Ten: Acton, Rostas and Ryder argue that, despite the weaknesses of civil society and its hierarchical nature and subservience to donor-driven agendas, these barriers must and can give way to inclusive community development that can mobilise within Roma communities a dynamic, local and transnational campaign and empowerment network that has transformative power.

Chapter Eleven: Ingmire and Stables outline the problems British Roma face in mobilisation, drawing upon their activist and professional experience and recent literature, but explain how these can be overcome, referring to good practice models in schools and support projects like the Roma Support Group.

Chapter Twelve: Ryder, Cemlyn and Acton conclude that inclusive community development techniques can assist GRT communities at the local, national and international levels, but to maintain participation there are key principles that need to be followed. In the wider policy context of policies of mutualism being promoted in the UK and the ramifications of European social inclusion discourses on Roma issues, community-development approaches steer an uncertain course through dominant neoliberal approaches to globalisation. We argue that the framework of a 'Social Europe', with its call for a renewed and robust vision of the social contract to be introduced alongside radical reinterpretations of democracy and the role of civil society, could be the legitimating charter for the community-development aspirations that resonate throughout this book.

Notes

[1] In some chapters the term GRT (Gypsies, Roma, Travellers) is used, but in other sections the emerging alternative of GTR (Gypsies, Travellers, Roma) is found instead. This reflects some disquiet about the use of the acronym GRT, and a perception held by some that it is a term designed by authority. On the other hand many Gypsies, Roma and Travellers have been prepared to work under the similar acronym of GRTHM (Gypsy Roma Traveller History Month). The debate on collective terms has been in a state of flux. In defence of both acronyms it can be argued that an important and positive

point that stems from the use of both terms is that it encourages Gypsy, Roma and Traveller communities to work together and recognise common traits and experience in this process, although it is important to appreciate the heterogeneity of these communities. In the very final stages of editing this book it became evident that the acronym GTR was gaining momentum in terms of acceptance, as in the development of a UK civil society response on progress within the EU Framework for National Roma Integration Strategies the various community organisations involved seemed to favour the term GTR. What is more, the launch of the June 2014 History Month activities at the Victoria and Albert Museum opted for GTR. It remains to be seen how widely the term will be taken up outside civil society by communities at the grassroots. It should also be noted that one of the lead UK Roma organisations (The Roma Support Group) often uses the acronym RGT (Roma, Gypsy and Traveller) in materials where they are primarily interested in Roma but wish to make points of relevance to all of the various groups.

[2] The Romani language and population probably consolidated among Indian migrants in Anatolia in the 11th century (Matras 2002, p 18).

[3] These restrictions were removed at the end of 2013 but some politicians mistakenly claimed that migrants from Bulgaria and Romania would flood into the UK once they had been lifted. Social security rules have changed, so all new EU migrants face new restrictions on welfare payments. Prime Minister David Cameron claims to be seeking limitations on the free movement of labour in the EU.

[4] Hybridity refers to mixed, fluid and dynamic identities.

[5] Intersectionality explores the means by which multiple oppressions interact and overlap each other, such as class, racism, sexism, disablism and homophobia.

[6] They attempt to define the term 'political race' as a process that begins from the ground up, starting with race in all its complexity, and then proceeds to develop cross-racial relationships through race and with race to issues of class and gender (intersectionality).

[7] Framing involves the perceptions that activists build of injustice to contextualise and understand it and build a challenge and counter-narrative.

[8] Not to be confused with the other TAT, TAT/CLP, the energetic Traveller Advice Team of the Community Law Partnership that has an advice line that any Traveller can ring, and publishes *TAT News*.

References

Acton, T.A. (1974) *Gypsy Politics and Social Change*, London: Routledge and Kegan Paul.

Acton, T.A. (1979) 'The ethnicity of the British Romani populations', *Roma – Journal of the Indian Institute of Romani Studies*, no 11 (formerly vol 4, no 4), pp 43–53.

Acton, T.A. (2005) 'Conflict resolution and criminal justice – sorting out trouble; can legislation resolve perennial conflicts between Roma/Gypsies/Travellers and 'National Majorities', *Journal of Legal Pluralism*, no 51, pp 29–49.

Alinsky, S. (1971) *Rules for Radicals: A Political Primer for Practical Radicals*, New York: Random House.

Arnstein, S.R. (1969) 'A ladder of citizen participation', *Journal of the American Planning Association*, vol 35, pp 216–24.

Bourdieu, P. (1991) *Language and Symbolic Power*, Cambridge: Polity Press.

Bourdieu, P. and Wacquant, L.J.D. (1992) *An Invitation to Reflexive Sociology*, Chicago: University of Chicago Press.

Brent, J. (2009) *Searching for Community: Power, Representation and Action on an Urban Estate*, Bristol: Policy Press.

Bunyan, P. (2010) 'Broad based organizing in the UK: reasserting the centrality of political activity in community development', *Community Development Journal*, vol 45, no 1, pp 111–27.

Cemlyn, S., Greenfields, M., Burnett, S., Matthews, Z. and Whitwell, C. (2009) *Inequalities experienced by Gypsy and Traveller communities: a review* (Research Report no. 12), London: Equality and Human Rights Commission.

Chambers, E. (2003) *Roots for Radicals: Organising for Power, Action, and Justice*, New York: Continuum.

CLG Task Group (Communities and Local Government Task Group) (2007) *The road ahead: final report of the Independent Task Group on site provision and enforcement for Gypsies and Travellers*, London: CLG.

CLG (Communities and Local Government) (2009) *Progress report on Gypsy and Traveller policy*, London: CLG.

Craig, G. (2011) 'Community capacity-building: something old, something new …?', in G. Craig et al (eds) *The Community Development Reader: History, Themes and Issues*, Bristol: Policy Press, pp 273–82.

Craig, G., Mayo, M., Popple, K., Shaw, M. and Taylor, M. (eds) (2011) *The Community Development Reader: History, Themes and Issues*, Bristol: Policy Press.

Delgado, R. (ed) (1995) 'Introduction', in R. Delgado (ed) *Critical Race Theory: The Cutting Edge,* Philadelphia, PA: Philadelphia, Temple University.

Derrington, C. and Kendall, S. (2004) *Gypsy Traveller Students in Secondary Schools: Culture, Identity and Achievement,* Stoke on Trent: Trentham Books.

Dominelli, L. (2006) *Women and Community Action,* Bristol: Policy Press.

Emejulu, A. and Bronstein, A. (2011) 'The politics of everyday life: feminisms and contemporary community development', *Community Development Journal,* vol 46, no 3, pp 283–7.

ERRC (European Roma Rights Centre) Journal (2009) Issue 1, 30 July, Budapest: ERRC.

Fekete, L. (2014) 'Europe against the Roma', *Race and Class,* vol 55, pp 60–70.

Fleming, T. (2002) 'Habermas on civil society, lifeworld and system: unearthing the social in transformation theory', *Teachers College Record,* 27 January.

Flint, J. and Robinson, D. (eds) (2008) *Community Cohesion in Crisis? New Dimensions of Diversity and Difference,* Bristol: Policy Press.

Fraser, A. (1992) *The Gypsies: The Peoples of Europe* (2nd edn), London: Blackwell.

Freire, P. (1972) *Pedagogy of the Oppressed,* Harmondsworth: Penguin.

Fuchs, C. (2006) 'The self-organization of social movements', *Systemic Practice and Action Research,* vol 19, no 1, pp 101–37.

Geertz, C. (1973) 'Thick description: toward an interpretative theory of culture', in *The Interpretation of Cultures: Selected Essays,* New York: Basic Books, pp 3–30.

Gilchrist, A. (2009) *The Well-Connected Community. A Networking Approach to Community Development,* Bristol: Policy Press.

Gillan, K. and Pickerill, J. (2012) 'The difficult and hopeful ethics of research on, and with, social movements', *Social Movement Studies: Journal of Social, Cultural and Political Protest,* vol 11, no 2, pp 133–43.

Gore, A. (1992) *Earth in the Balance,* Boston, MA: Houghton Mifflin.

Goswami, P. (2009) 'A rereading of Gandhi's Satyagraha in South Africa for contemporary community organizing', *Community Development Journal,* no 44 (July), pp 393–402.

Gramsci, A. (1971) *Selections from the Prison Notebooks,* London: Lawrence and Wishart.

Habermas, J. (1984) *The Theory of Communicative Action,* trans. T. McCarthy, Boston, MA: Beacon Press.

Habermas, J. (1996) *Between Facts and Norms: Contributions to a Discourse Theory of Law and Democracy,* Cambridge: Polity Press.

Habermas, J. (2010) 'Germany and the Euro-Crisis', *The Nation*, June 9.

Habermas, J. (2011) 'Europe's post-democratic era', *Guardian*, 10 November.

Hall, S. (1991) 'Old and new identities, old and new ethnicities', in E. King (ed) *Culture, Globalisation and the World System*, Basingstoke: Macmillan, pp 41–68.

Henderson, P. and Vercseg, I. (2010) *Community Development and Civil Society: Making Connections in the European Context*, Bristol: Policy Press.

Hylton, K. (2012) 'Talk the talk, walk the walk: defining critical race theory', *Race, Ethnicity and Education*, vol 15, no 1, pp 23–41.

Ife, J. (2001) *Human Rights and Social Work: Towards Rights Based Practice*, Cambridge: Cambridge University Press.

Ife, J. and Fiske, L. (2006) 'Human rights and community work: complementary theories and practices', *International Social Work*, vol 49, no 3, pp 297–308.

Kellner, D. (2000) 'Habermas, the public sphere, and democracy: a critical intervention', in L. Hahn (ed) *Perspectives on Habermas*, Chicago: Open Court Press, pp 259–88.

Kenny, S. (2011) 'Towards unsettling community development', *Community Development Journal*, vol 46, suppl 1, pp i7–i19.

Kovats, M. (2003) 'The politics of Roma identity: between nationalism and destitution', *Open Democracy*, July 29, www.opendemocracy.net/people-migrationeurope/article_1399.jsp.

Laclau, E. and Mouffe, C. (1985) *Hegemony and Socialist Strategy: Towards a Radical Democratic Politics*, Verso: London.

Ledwith, M. and Asgill, P. (2007) 'Feminist, anti-racist community development: critical alliance, local to global', in L. Dominelli (ed) *Revitalising Communities in a Globalising World*, Aldershot: Ashgate, pp 107–22.

Ledwith, M. and Springett, J. (2010) *Participatory Practice. Community Based Action for Transformative Change*, Bristol: Policy Press.

Lengyel, G. (ed) (2009) *Deliberative Methods in Local Society Research (The Kaposvar Experiences)*, Budapest: Corvinus University Press.

Liégeois, J.P. (1998) *School Provision for Ethnic Minorities: The Gypsy Paradigm*, Hatfield: University of Hertfordshire Press.

Matras, Y. (2002) *Romani: A Linguistic Introduction*, Cambridge: Cambridge University Press.

Matsuda, M., Lawrence, C., Delgado, R. and Crenshaw, K. (1993) *Words that Wound: Critical Race Theory, Assaultive Speech, and the First Amendment*, Boulder, CO: Westview Press.

Mayall, D. (1995) *English Gypsies and State Policies*, Hatfield: University of Hertfordshire Press.

Mayo, M. (1975) 'Community development as a radical alternative?' in R. Bailey and M. Brake (eds) *Radical Social Work*, London: Edward Arnold, pp 129–59.

Mayo, M. (1998) 'Community work', in R. Adams, L. Dominelli and M. Payne (eds) *Social Work. Themes, Issues and Critical Debates*, Basingstoke: Macmillan, pp 160–72.

McCabe, A., Phillimore, J. and Mayblin, L. (2010) *'Below the Radar' Activities and Organisations in the Third Sector: a Summary Review of the Literature*, Birmingham: Third Sector Research Centre.

McNeil, C. (2009) *Now It's Personal: Personal Advisers and the New Public Service Workforce*, London: IPPR.

Meekosha, H. (2011) 'Equality and difference: what's in a concept?' in G. Craig et al (eds) *The Community Development Reader: History, Themes and Issues*, Bristol: Policy Press, pp 171–83.

National Equality Partnership (2008) *Supporting Equality Groups: An Overview of Support to the Diverse Third Sector in England*, London: NEP.

Nowotny, H. (1981) 'Women in public life in Austria', in C. Fuchs Epstein and R. Laub Coser (eds) *Access to Power: Cross-National Studies of Women and Elites*, London: George Allen & Unwin, pp 147–56.

Offe, C. (1985) 'New social movements: challenging the boundaries of international politics', *Social Research*, vol 52, no 4, pp 817–68.

Okely, J. (1983) *The Traveller-Gypsies*, Cambridge and New York: Cambridge University Press.

Okely, J. (2001) 'Non-territorial culture as the rationale for the assimilation of Gypsy children', *Childhood*, vol 4, pp 63–80.

ONS (2014) *Census Analysis, What does the 2011 Census tell us about the Characteristics of Gypsy or Irish Travellers in England and Wales?* London: Office for National Statistics, www.ons.gov.uk/ons/rel/census/2011-census-analysis/index.html.

Popple, K. (1994) 'Towards a progressive community work praxis', in S. Jacobs and K. Popple (eds) *Community Work in the 1990s*, Nottingham: Spokesman.

Popple, K. (2007) 'Community development strategies in the UK', in L. Dominelli (ed) *Revitalising Communities in a Globalising World*, Aldershot: Ashgate, pp 137–60.

Power, J.M. (2007) 'The relevance of critical race theory to educational theory and practice', *Journal of Philosophy of Education*, vol 41, no 1, pp 151–66.

Powell, R. (2010) 'Gypsy-Travellers and welfare professional discourse: on individualization and social integration', *Antipode*, vol 43, no 2, pp 471–93.

Richardson, J. (2007) *Contentious Spaces: The Gypsy/Traveller Site Issue*, Coventry: CIH/JRF.

Richardson, J. and Ryder, A. (eds) (2012) *Gypsies and Travellers: Accommodation, Empowerment and Inclusion in British Society*, Bristol: Policy Press.

Rostas, I. (ed) (2012) *Ten Years After*, Budapest and New York: Central European University Press and Roma Education Fund.

Ryder, A. (2011) *UK Gypsies and Travellers and the Third Sector* (Third Sector Research Centre Working Paper 63), Birmingham: TSRC, Birmingham University.

Ryder, A. and Greenfields, M. (2010) *Roads to Success: Routes to Economic and Social Inclusion for Gypsies and Travellers*, London: Irish Traveller Movement in Britain.

Ryder, A., Cemlyn, S., Greenfields, M., Richardson, J. and Van Cleemput, P. (2012) *A Critique of UK Coalition Government Policy on Gypsy, Roma and Traveller Communities*, Equality and Diversity Forum, www.edf.org.uk/blog/?p=19051.

Sen, A. (1992) *Inequality Re-examined*, New York: Harvard University Press.

Sen, A. (1999) *Development as Freedom*, New York: Random House.

Shaw, M. (2008) 'Community development and the politics of community', *Community Development Journal*, vol 43, no 1, pp 24–36.

Shukra, K. (2011) 'The changing terrain of multi culture from anti oppressive practice to community cohesion', in G. Craig, M. Mayo, K. Popple, M. Shaw, M. Taylor (eds) *The Community Development Reader: History, Themes and Issues*, Bristol: Policy Press, pp 267–72.

Sigona, N. and Trehan, N. (2010) (eds) *Contemporary Romani politics: Recognition, Mobilisation and Participation*, London: Palgrave Macmillan.

Smith, M. (1975) *Gypsies*, (Young Fabian Pamphlet), London: Fabian Society.

Somin, I. (2010) 'Deliberative democracy and political ignorance', *Critical Review*, vol 22, nos 2–3, pp 253–79.

Stonewall (2003) 'Profiles of prejudice: the nature of prejudice in England', in-depth analysis of findings carried out by MORI in May 2003 on behalf of Stonewall's Citizenship 21 project, London: Stonewall.

Taylor, M. (2003) *Public Policy in the Community*, Bristol: Policy Press.

Taylor, M. (2011) 'Community participation in the real world' in G. Craig et al (eds) *The Community Development Reader: History, Themes and Issues*, Bristol: Policy Press, pp 291–300.

Toomey, A.H. (2011) 'Empowerment and disempowerment in community development practice: eight roles practitioners play', *Community Development Journal*, vol 46, no 2, pp 181–95.

Trehan, N.(2001) 'In the name of the Roma? The role of private foundations and NGOs', W. Guy (ed) *InBetween Past and Future: the Roma of Central and Eastern Europe*, Hatfield: University of Hertfordshire Press

Tritter, J. and McCallum, A. (2006) 'The snakes and ladders of user involvement: moving beyond Arnstein', *Health Policy*, vol 76, pp 156–68.

Van Baar, H. (2011) 'The European Roma', PhD thesis, University of Amsterdam.

Vincze, E. and Raţ, C. (eds) (2013) 'Spatialization and racialization of social exclusion.The social and cultural formation of"Gypsy Ghettos" in Romania in a European context', Special Issue of *Sociologia, The Journal of Sociology and Social Work*, vol 58, no 2, Babeş-Bolyai University.

Woolcock, M. (2001) 'The place of social capital in understanding social and economic outcomes', *ISUMA Canadian Journal of Policy Research*, vol 2, no 1, pp 11–17.

Yates, D. (1953) *My Gypsy Days*, London: Phoenix House.

TWO

Pedagogies of hope: the Gypsy Council and the National Gypsy Education Council

Thomas Acton, Peter Mercer, John Day and Andrew Ryder

This chapter provides an account of the formation in the 1960s and development of the Gypsy Council and its successor organisations (Figure 2.1). Most accounts of the origins, trajectories and achievements of Romani organisations concentrate upon the story of how they interacted with state authorities and what result they had upon the overt policy and actions of the local and central state and, more recently, transnational organisations. Over the last 25 years narratives have been set within the banal discourse of the 'NGO'. Although the phrase 'non-governmental organisation' appeared in the UN Charter of 1945 (in a rather different context), the acronym NGO was popularised only in the 1980s, through the abbreviation of the somewhat more euphonious acronym the 'QUANGO', or 'quasi-autonomous non-governmental organisation'. That phrase, first used in 1967, was itself acronymised only in 1969 (Pifer, 1987), but was picked up by right-wing governments, such as the Heath government (1970–74) in the UK as the welfare state staggered under the twin shocks of the oil price rises and the rapid growth in the number of old-age pensioners and sought to outsource welfare provision to independent agencies that it nevertheless had to fund. Acknowledging that they were only quasi-autonomous, however, meant that the government was still held accountable for their performance. Neoliberal discourse swiftly dropped the 'quasi' bit, and reinvented government as the righteous, avenging popular regulator of the agencies that perpetually failed to manage the poor on the budgets they are given. The modern use of the term 'NGO' invites one to consider them only in relation to governments. How strange it is that at the very moment when the last major version of state utopian authoritarianism lost legitimacy in 1989, the neoliberal ascendancy was able thus to appropriate an inverted vision of the ubiquity of the state. Most of the Romani organisations bravely and ineffectually (according to some) taking grants across Europe to cover for the failings of the

Figure 2.1: The Gypsy Council

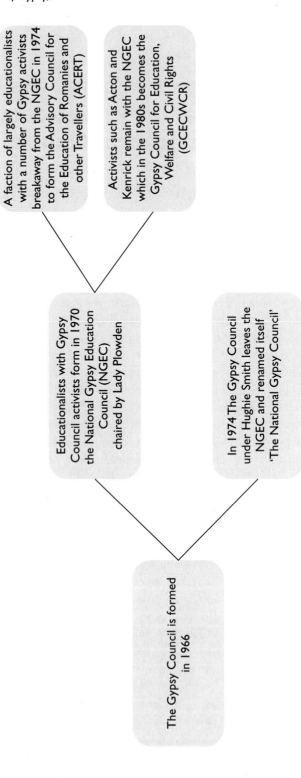

A faction of largely educationalists with a number of Gypsy activists breakaway from the NGEC in 1974 to form the Advisory Council for the Education of Romanies and other Travellers (ACERT)

Activists such as Acton and Kenrick remain with the NGEC which in the 1980s becomes the Gypsy Council for Education, Welfare and Civil Rights (GCECWCR)

Educationalists with Gypsy Council activists form in 1970 the National Gypsy Education Council (NGEC) chaired by Lady Plowden

In 1974 The Gypsy Council under Hughie Smith leaves the NGEC and renamed itself 'The National Gypsy Council'

The Gypsy Council is formed in 1966

welfare state might better be termed 'wholly non-autonomous fully funded non-governmental organisations' (WONNAFFUNGOs).

The Gypsy Council, from its foundation in 1966 down to its local offshoots, and the two Gypsy Councils which dispute the title to be its legitimate successor today, have never been one of these WONAFFUNGOs. The Gypsy Council has never been able to hold on to a grant for more than a few years, and yet its legacy and myth have a secure place in the Romani movement. This chapter will look at it, not as an NGO to be evaluated against a list of organisational tick-boxes, but as a movement of ideas, a political pedagogy that redefined the previously impossible as the possibility and hope of the future. It follows the near-contemporary accounts of Acton (1974), who was part of the nuts and bolts of the Gypsy Council's early years, and Liégeois (1976, pp 133–57), who details the Romani nationalism in France that shaped the thinking of its first secretary, and also the slightly less starry-eyed retrospective account of Grattan Puxon (2000), as well as the personal recollections of the authors. The story of the Gypsy Council is a case study in community leadership and how campaigns can try to remain true to their ideals and avoid the pitfalls of authoritarianism either from donor driven bureaucratisation or/and traditional patriarchal or charismatic leadership.

The key role Grattan Puxon played has to be acknowledged. To what extent, with his elite Westminster School education and training as a journalist, was Puxon one of the 'outsider' catalysts identified by Freire (1972; 1998) as necessary for the process of critical pedagogy? Or was he more of a pragmatic, oppportunistic political adventurer who was able to seize on the experience of Roma, Gypsies and Travellers so as to assist in the birth of something actually transcending the limitations of existing European political discourse? Perhaps the first observer to identify the Freirean character of the Gypsy Council and the links between education and politics was the Swedish teacher Lundgren, whose (2000) report of her 1970 summer with the Gypsy Council does not actually mention Puxon. Nonetheless, Puxon was well equipped to help in the mediation between Gypsies and Travellers and the political establishment, being something of both an 'insider' and 'outsider' himself.

Puxon came from a well-to-do family of Anglo-Irish Huguenot origins. In order to avoid conscription into military service in 1960, he fled to Ireland, sustaining himself as a freelance journalist. He bought a horse-drawn barreltop wagon, as used by the Irish Travellers at the time, and moved alongside Travellers who had flocked to the outskirts of Dublin as agricultural depression hit the countryside, causing an unprecedented crisis of accommodation. Puxon was drawn into their continuous struggles against eviction (Acton, 1974). Many Irish Travellers also fled depressed Ireland for booming Britain, forming an important part of Puxon's support when he eventually followed them.

Puxon's work with Travellers in Ireland reached a high point at a stopping-place near Dublin called Cherry Orchard in 1964–65 and tactics were developed that were to be employed in his work in the UK. The Traveller organisations and Puxon's own rhetoric remained formally non-violent and appealed to the moral authority of the Gandhian tradition. At the same time Puxon pointedly said nothing to undermine the fear of the authorities that desperate individuals, or uncontrollable radical elements among left-wing non-Traveller allies, might become violent.

The Garda were threatening forcefully to evict what had become a large encampment, but through the sheer numbers present the Travellers were able to deter such action. In addition to this Puxon, in a way reminiscent of Alinsky (see Chapter One), was able skilfully to exploit the media attention that the threatened eviction aroused. As Acton (1974, p 156) notes 'The Travellers began to realise that they were not totally powerless; they had the threat of their nuisance value in creating adverse publicity, if nothing else; if they organised, they could reach out for power.'

As part of this strategy Puxon established a series of Traveller schools on child-centred Montessori principles, the first of which, at Ballyfermot, was burnt down by council workmen. Direct action and the creation of media platforms centred on eviction and setting up site schools were prominent features of Puxon's later work with the Gypsy Council after his expulsion from Ireland for allegedly hiding munitions for his left-wing allies in Sinn Fein.

In the wake of Puxon's departure a group of Roman Catholic priests and nuns, aided by wealthy philanthropists, monopolised representation of Travellers' interests in Ireland through a new group, 'The Itinerant Settlement Committee', which arguably side-tracked Traveller activism into endless tame lobbying and charity work, diminishing the voice and control of the Traveller community (McCarthy, 2001). The Gypsy Council that Puxon later founded in the UK was to face similar challenges and dangers. This chapter speculates why, in the UK, movements were not completely co-opted in the same way by outside 'community workers' or state-sponsored WONAFFUNGOs.

The formation and achievements of the Gypsy Council

On his arrival in the UK in 1966 Puxon moved to Kent with his partner, Venice Manley. He forged links with lead activists in establishing the Gypsy Council, of which he was secretary until 1971. Among those who worked with him was Tommy Doherty (the first chair), an Irish Traveller who had founded his own organisation in Leeds. Acton (1974, p 48) describes the mood and sense of optimism that is often evident at the birth of a new movement:

> People who came into that movement at the time were caught up in a great surge of enthusiasm, a feeling of new awakenings and mighty forces stirring, a belief that the persecutions of the centuries could now in a brief space be ended by our efforts.

The first meeting was held in 1966 in a pub in Kent that had a sign proclaiming 'No Gypsies'. Overriding the objections of the landlord made the inaugural meeting itself an exercise in militant resistance to discrimination. The meeting issued a statement the opening section of which read: 'We live in a world in which many hands are turned against us, the Travelling people. Our rights are not recognised and every place is closed to us. But today we have a chance to unite and speak with one voice, to change the world and make it a better place for our children to grow up.' The three central tenets of the campaign were to be: camping sites in every county open to Travellers, equal rights to education, work and houses and equal standing and respect (Acton, 1974, p 163).

An early point of contention was the tension between English Gypsies and Irish Travellers. The core of Puxon's early support in England came from Irish Travellers led by Tommy Doherty and Johnny Connors. Grattan Puxon originally tried to establish the name of the organisation as 'The Travellers' Community', seeing 'Traveller' as a group name used equally by Irish Travellers and English Gypsies.

During the struggle to maintain a stopping-place on a bombsite near Rathbone Market in East London, however, local leader Johnny Brazil put up a notice on a hut that he had put at the disposal of the organisation, saying 'Gypsy Council Office'. Although Grattan Puxon tried to keep the other name even at the foundation meeting, the predominance of English Gypsies ensured that the name 'Gypsy Council' prevailed, and indeed, English Gypsies (Romanichals) rapidly came to play the leading role. Many of the English Gypsy heads of families who flocked to pay the £1 subscription for Gypsy Council membership were inclined to blame the influx of Irish Travellers for the shortage of sites, and this scapegoating was reinforced by newspapers (and writers in the *Journal of the Gypsy Lore Society*) who suggested that Irish Travellers, not 'true Gypsies', were to blame for all the trouble. A Romani member of the Gypsy Lore Society, Cliff Lee, disassociated himself from the Gypsy Council over the issue. Puxon and others, however, including Johnny Brazil, managed to prevail in the argument that Irish Travellers should be included, and indeed Irish Travellers from both Ireland and England were present at the First World Romani Congress in 1971 and have remained in the International Romani Union (IRU), despite objections from Roma nationalists in Europe with a more racist understanding of ethnicity. Despite occasional outbreaks of inter-communal strife, the various wings of the Gypsy Council and the broader Gypsy and Traveller movement that has since developed have largely remained faithful to this concept of inclusivity.

The young may be baffled by the organisational skills involved in running the Gypsy Council when there was no e-mail and many of the activists had no phones and were nomadic and unable to read and write. The campaign kept in touch with local leaders already established in their regions and areas and through visits to Gypsies/ Travellers threatened with eviction who could become *causes célèbres* to win broader support. Success could turn local leaders into national leaders as their confidence and skills increased and they passed these on to others by 'throwing them in at the deep end'. Acton (1974, p 239) recounts this impact upon one activist:

> Puxon ... consciously devoted thought to training individual Gypsies as political leaders, mainly by putting them into situations where they would have to develop leadership skills.... For example, one can cite the case of a Gypsy over fifty years of age.... when he came to London he was in my opinion reliant on the initiative of others in confrontation situations such as evictions ... he suffered ridicule for some time because his only comment to a TV reporter, when one of the demonstrations was filmed, was 'Er ... Grattan 'ere will tell you about it'. A year later I saw the same man [Harry Smith] travelling to strange towns to lead eviction resistance amongst Gypsies whom he had not known personally before and negotiate successfully for sites.

The Gypsy Council was flexible because of the informality of the organisation. It had no written constitution until 1971. This gave it the ability to respond quickly to events but also meant that the more traditional leaders did not have to come to terms with the demands of formal organisation. The campaign remained true to its roots and retained its radicalism by being largely dependent on membership subscriptions and avoiding the patronage and control that powerful donors might have exerted. Thus the liaison/social worker role mapped out for Puxon by Richard Hauser, a philanthropist and early patron of the Gypsy Council, was rejected not just by Puxon but by the lead Gypsy and Traveller activists.

Another important and innovative aspect of the Gypsy Council's activities was the growing participation of women in its deliberations. Often these were the wives of male committee members, like Margaret Lee and Rosemary Penfold. One of the most remarkable, however, was Elizabeth Easton, who joined the Gypsy Council in 1970, when she was just 16 years old. She was working as a junior in a solicitor's office, having left school at 15. Her mother and father, Gypsies from Surrey, had settled in a house when she was 9, and against expectations she passed the 11+ selection examination to go to grammar school, where she was subjected to marginalisation and discrimination.

With another young Traveller woman she joined a Flamenco class at the Mary Ward Centre, a community centre in Holborn that also hosted meetings of a newly formed offshoot of the Gypsy Council, the National Gypsy Education Council (NGEC).[1] After one meeting, Grattan Puxon wandered over to the group of girls in the centre's café sitting in brightly coloured costumes, and told them they really ought to be Gypsies to dance Flamenco. Elizabeth replied "I am a Gypsy". After Grattan had explained the work of the Gypsy Council, she volunteered secretarial help. Thereafter she came every Saturday morning to 61, Blenheim Crescent, where Grattan Puxon had moved into a flat above that of Dr Donald Kenrick. Kenrick supervised her typing, somewhat impatiently, as at the age of 16 she was less immediately competent than the graduate volunteers he was used to. She persisted, and made her mark in the Gypsy Council when she was one of 11 activists who barricaded themselves in a caravan outside Buckingham Palace in 1972. Thomas Acton recalls his surprise when, in the police station, this slight, self-effacing young woman, dressed like a city secretary, used the English Romani dialect volubly to reassure Gypsy men twice her age who were distressed at having been arrested for the first time. After that Elizabeth played a major role in the Gypsy Council and became treasurer of the NGEC.[2] At the same time she returned to full-time education and gained a degree from the London School of Economics. Elizabeth Easton paved the way for later strong, independent women, Sylvia Dunn and Josie Lee, who were Presidents of the NGEC (which eventually renamed itself the Gypsy Council after Hughie Smith changed the name of his organisation to the National Gypsy Council (NGC)).

In the 1960s tension increased over the growing shortage of sites. In 1968 the Liberal MP Eric Lubbuck (later Lord Avebury) was induced by Prime Minister Harold Wilson to add a section on Gypsies to his private member's Bill on non-Gypsy caravan accommodation, in return for government support. The Caravan Sites Act 1968 placed a duty on councils to provide sites for Gypsies and Travellers. The Gypsy Council gave community members a platform to advise on the government's implementation of the Caravan Sites Act, while also having some impact on public opinion by staging protests at evictions and through creative publicity stunts, such as Tom Lee drawing his caravan into Downing Street in 1970.

The high point of the Gypsy Council, for which it is perhaps most noted internationally, was its hosting of the first World Romani Congress in 1971. Brian Raywid, who had moved on from living with Travellers to working as the cook in a private boarding school in Kent, was given permission by the head teacher to hold a conference on school premises. The Comité Internationale Rom (CIR), led by Vanko Rouda in Paris, was trying to organise the First World Romani Congress at the Palais de l'UNESCO in Paris, but running into continual delays. Grattan offered to organise a preparatory meeting in the school (with all the delegates sleeping in the dormitories). A few weeks before the Congress, Grattan Puxon, with the bemused support of the Gypsy Council committee, announced that so many delegates had promised to come that the meeting would be the First Congress. Faced with a fait accompli, the CIR agreed.

Delegates from 17 countries came to the Congress, including from Czechoslovakia and Yugoslavia, both still communist countries, which agreed to send delegations partly because of the Indian diplomatic support arranged by W.R. Rishi, then working at the Indian embassy in London and a personal friend of the Nehru dynasty. At the event a flag and anthem were adopted and various commissions were established that held a few meetings.

Soon after the 1971 Congress, Grattan Puxon, suffering from fatigue and feeling that the Gypsy Council now could and should carry on without him, moved to Shuto Orisare,[3] the Romani municipality adjacent to Skopje in Macedonia. There he worked with local Romani politicians and scholars and attempted to push the CIR to organise a second Congress. Its failure to do so led to the formation of the IRU in 1978 to organise a second Congress in 1979 (although Puxon, writing the statutes of the IRU to gain it recognition as a consultative NGO at the United Nations, backdated its foundation to 1971, an action that caused a dispute with the CIR, still being run in Paris by Vanko Rouda). Thus the foundations for contemporary international Romani politics were laid. The IRU and many of the organisations that attended the first two Congresses still exist, along with a plethora of competitors that would have amazed the pioneers of the 1960s. The new conceptions of group identity and activism that stretched beyond the limits and confines of national identity are still developing.

The Gypsy Council after Grattan Puxon

After Puxon's departure there was some turbulence within Gypsy politics. Tom Lee, who was briefly secretary of the Gypsy Council, founded the Romany Guild in 1972, which supported Lady Plowden's breakaway from the NGEC in 1973 to found a WONAFFUNGO named the Advisory Council for the Education of Romanies and other Travellers (ACERT). The Gypsy Council came to be dominated by Hughie Smith, a business partner of Gypsy Council chair Tommy Doherty. In December 1973 they expelled Roy Wells and Donald Kenrick, who had formed an independent Southern Gypsy Council. The Gypsy Council left the NGEC in 1974 and renamed itself the National Gypsy Council.

After the Gypsy sections of the Caravan Sites Act 1968 were brought into operation in 1970, the outgoing Labour government of Harold Wilson and the incoming Tory one of Edward Heath both informally promised to consult the Gypsy Council before any municipalities were 'designated' as having fulfilled their duties under the Act, provided they did not object to every designation proposed. When the first three designation orders were laid before Parliament in 1972, endorsed by the Gypsy Council, Tom Lee's Romani Guild outbid the Gypsy Council in radicalism by denouncing them, supported by Lady Plowden. Lord Avebury (who had proposed the law while he was still an MP) opposed the designations in the Lords. The government broke off contact with the Gypsy Council (until, later, Hughie Smith's NGC became a favoured negotiating partner for the government).

Whether keeping the negotiations over 'designation' open and reasonable would have made for faster progress under the Caravan Sites Act 1968 is a matter for speculation. The award of 'designated status' (especially for local authorities exempted from provision on the claim that they had no land, or no Gypsies) led to an increase in local authorities' powers of eviction. Designation increased the hardship of those who remained on unauthorised encampments. The duty to provide sites was enforced very slowly, with some authorities never fulfilling their obligation before the Act was repealed in 1994. Not all the sites were well designed, and some were labelled 'reservations' by their residents, partly also because of the draconian management regimes of many and the marginal space on which they were located. The Gypsy Council was blamed by some for these failures of government.

In 1974 it might have seemed as though the legacy of Grattan Puxon had all but collapsed. A majority of the Gypsy and Traveller committee members had defected to the Romani Guild or remained in the Hughie Smith-led NGC. Puxon's approach was only fully honoured in Roy Wells' Southern Gypsy Council and the NGEC, which together were the smallest of the three factions in Traveller politics, easily exceeded in influence and reputation by the Romani Guild/ACERT alliance and Hughie Smith's NGC, which explicitly condemned the radicalism and amateurism of the NGEC (Smith, 1976). It was time, they asserted, for professionalism, for paid staff and to secure the grants to get things done. Grattan Puxon's driven personality might have sustained a dynamic voluntary movement for a while, but sometimes he set too fast a pace and left people behind, working himself and those around him into the ground. Reflecting the demands and pitfalls of such activism, 'Black' Harry Smith told Thomas Acton in 1970 "When I came back from Wolverhampton [from an eviction resistance] my wife asked me for money to go shopping, and I put my hand in my pocket and I didn't have enough. That's when I realised I had to pull back a bit from this Gypsy Council lark, so that would never happen again."

A hypothetical observer might conclude that the Gypsy Council was a centralised entity not having a wider network of branches. The committee members, however, were often prominent within large extended family networks and it was through these activists that links were maintained at the grassroots. However, the problem remains that such 'charismatic' forms of leadership have tended to neglect developing the skills of a younger generation of activists or more widely articulating their views and aspirations. Furthermore, with the death or retirement of such leaders, wide family networks have found themselves somewhat cut off from activism, now no longer being able to look to the political patrons within the family they had once relied on.

Much of the conflict between groups centred on the competition over educational projects (Acton and Kenrick, 1991). Before the Gypsy

Council, and indeed up until the Education Act 1981, many schools openly and legally excluded Traveller children on the grounds that 'they did not belong to the area'. Others operated a laissez-faire 'open door' policy, putting the onus on Traveller parents to register their children and adapt to the system. But this often meant separate and unequal treatment, being taught in segregated units or special classes. For many, school meant merciless bullying by fellow pupils and the denigration of their culture by racist and assimilationist school authorities.

ACERT accused the rump NGEC of being against mainstream educational participation, and arguing that, within traditional Traveller socialisation practices centred on cultural and economic activities, the rudiments of education could be delivered through on-site educational provision. In fact the NGEC was very serious about gaining access to formal education for Gypsies/Travellers without their having to hide or lose their identity and culture.

The immediate result of the ACERT/NGEC split was a huge increase in the number of summer projects, the NGEC being desperate to prove that despite being unfunded it could get more voluntary projects going – and supply a resource package not only to NGEC projects but also to ACERT ones. Meanwhile, however, Hughie Smith's NGC had backed a new coalition of local authorities in the West Midlands, which had appointed C.A. Beresford-Webb to run official outreach to bring children into schools. This, the first large Traveller Education Service, was criticised by the local voluntary (Van-Leer-funded) West Midlands Traveller School. Teachers in the official service formed the National Association of Traveller Teachers (NATT),[4] which became the chief non-Gypsy supporter of Hughie Smith's NGC. Hughie Smith and C.A. Beresford-Webb became the main advisors on Gypsy affairs to the Wilson and Callaghan governments of 1974–79, profiting from the squabbles of ACERT and NGEC and being able to accuse them of being led by non-Gypsy ideologues motivated only by their own sense of self-importance (Wells and Kenrick, 1978).

Paradoxically, a steady stream of refugees from ACERT and the NGC re-energised the NGEC. Tommy Doherty re-defected to the NGEC in 1975. The support of both ACERT and the NGC for the new West Midlands Local Authority Consortium's Traveller Education Service drove the independent West Midlands Traveller School (WMTS) into the arms of the NGEC; from the WMTS came Traveller teaching aides, like Nonna Price, and its charismatic lead teacher, Dick Worrall, who served terms as NGEC secretary and editor of its long-term journal *Traveller Education*. The most important recruit, who remained in both ACERT and the NGEC committees for most of the 1980s, however, was Peter Mercer, a man who, without any original input from national bodies, had founded his own independent East Anglian Gypsy Council (EAGC: its very name shows how the power of the *idea* of the Gypsy Council had spread, partly through the Gypsy Council summer school projects in Wisbech in the 1970s!). The EAGC fought for sites in Cambridgeshire for some of the poorest rural Travellers in the country. Secure in his mastery of this local organisation, Peter Mercer was perhaps the most diplomatic of all the Traveller leaders to emerge in 20*th*-century Britain, always eager to build coalitions with other, sometimes more charismatic, Romani leaders and thick-skinned enough just to shrug off their patronising comments about his humble origins and low status within traditional Romani class structures.

The Peter Mercer era

Mercer had been taken into care as a child when a dog on the site barked at a visiting policeman, and placed first in a Roman Catholic orphanage, and then as a skivvy in a hotel, from which he had to run away to find his family again at the age of 16. A 2013 interview provides some insights into this experience:

> Thomas Acton: I always thought your abduction by the state and fighting your way back to the community gave you an inner steel.
>
> Peter Mercer: I was put into care and taken away from my parents … a lot of this was down to what I am. I had to put up with the Sisters of Mercy .. their treatment of children! … they would come and take you away … I was not a catholic and they baptised me to keep me … I had just turned 8, I saw people come in and go and I would say "When can I go home?", and they would say "When your mum gets a proper home, when she moves into a house". They were sadists … they would cane you for nothing that was their idea of corporal punishment.

His time in the Catholic orphanage and then the army gave him insights into the non-Gypsy world and an ability to bide his time, to build bridges and forge understanding, a skill that served him well in local disputes over stopping-places, his later role as a Gypsy Liaison Officer and chair of the NGEC and later the National Federation of Gypsy Liaison Groups (NFGLG). In this work Peter was sustained and supported in part through his strong working relationship with his brothers-in-law and co-workers John and David Day. John Day commented in an interview in 2013:

> "The relationship of the three of us created the 'three musketeers' thing and to be honest we worked well together because there were three different people with three different ways of looking at things. Peter is a peacemaker.[5] Pete will arrange a deal, we would go in [to a meeting with officials] and me or David ... usually David, would threaten them with all sorts of things ...'We are going to fill the town with trailers!'... and then go to the toilet and by the time we came back Pete had a deal on the table ... it was kind of good cop bad cop."

During the later 1970s Roy Wells, who had dominated the NGEC after 1973, suffered a number of personal and political reverses, especially the NGC's Nobby Penfold being appointed warden of the Wandsworth Council Traveller site, which Wells had won through legal and street battles. Evicted and struggling to run a squatted scrapyard in the shadow of Battersea Power Station, and keep other Southern Gypsy Council activities going, Wells played less and less of a role in the NGEC. Supported by Elizabeth Easton and Donald Kenrick, Mercer assumed the Chair of the NGEC and immediately set about building bridges with rivals. The Romani Guild distanced itself from ACERT and affiliated to the NGEC, Tom Lee was elected to the NGEC committee, and with him Romani Guild secretary Elsie Fisher, who had been the first paid employee of both NGEC and ACERT. Mercer's biggest coup, aided by Thomas Acton, was to assume the leadership and organisation of the UK delegation to the 2nd World Romani Congress in Geneva in 1979, which the Romani Guild and the NGC also joined. Mercer became a fixture in IRU ruling circles and at the 5th World Romani Congress his allies simply ignored an attempt by Charles Smith to have him deselected.

The NGEC also proved itself at this time to be effective in combating infiltration of organisations by Romani supporters of the neo-fascist National Front, led by a covert Holocaust denier, Tom Odley, a community leader on the Edenbridge Travellers site in Kent. They had disguised their fascist connections. As Romani Guild members, they had been appointed to the ACERT Committee and sought election to the NGEC. They began to arouse suspicion through anti-Black racist remarks made to those whom they tagged as potential converts.

One, the Peterborough Travellers' teacher Robbie Britton (who was actually also a Labour Councillor and strong supporter of Peter Mercer), played along with this by corresponding with Odley and elicited letters from him in which he denied the Holocaust and boasted of his connections with prominent members of 'nationalist' (that is, fascist) circles. Enquiries through the anti-fascist magazine *Searchlight* revealed him as a long-standing National Front member and the magazine later published an exposé of him (Searchlight, 1989). Tom Lee expelled Odley and his followers from the Romani Guild. ACERT, however, with more formal procedures, could not just expel Odley; it had to reform its constitution to give it a subscription membership so as to define who had the right, finally in 1987, to vote Odley and his clique off. Once it thus had an open membership, some NGEC members paid subscriptions and joined ACERT, and Thomas Acton stood for election to its committee, becoming the only person in its history ever to lose an ACERT election. He was elected at his second attempt and the war between ACERT and the NGEC appeared to be over.

Under the leadership of Mercer, the NGEC became a broad alliance. Mercer conceived of it as an educational body composed of both Travellers and non-Gypsies, to which any of the independent Gypsy/Traveller bodies could affiliate, such as his own EAGC, the Romani Guild, and the Southern Gypsy Council. When the National Romani Rights Association, an organisation of more wealthy Travellers led by site owner Eli Frankham affiliated, the NGEC was effectively linking all the Traveller organisations except the NGC.

At this stage the NGEC used its formal democracy to balance its factions. Contested elections were held each year using a proportional single transferable vote system, and office holders were regularly rotated, with Thomas Acton, Dick Worrall and Donald Kenrick serving terms as secretary, and Peter Mercer, his chief lieutenant, John Day, Tom Lee and Eli Frankham and their supporters sharing out the other offices and seeing how many of their members they could elect to the committee. Almost every year in the 1980s there were secret ballots (often counted by the nuns from the Irish Roman Catholic Chaplaincy to Travellers based in Oxford). Most election losers accepted their losing gracefully (often being co-opted in consolation). The idea that one could lose the top office but remain an important minority voice, perhaps winning another year, is one of the most important legacies of the Mercer leadership.

Achievements of the National Gypsy Education Council

The most important political victory of these years was the final achievement of the right of nomadic Traveller children to attend school, through an amendment to the Education Act 1981. This was the conclusion of a battle that had been started by Roy Wells and Donald Kenrick in Croydon when the NGEC helped an Irish Traveller girl, Mary Delaney, who was stopping with her family by the side of the road in a caravan. She sued the local education authority for not admitting her to school. In 1977 the courts decided that despite the existence of a 'No-Area Pool' subsidising the education of children deemed not to belong to the area of any authority, local education authorities were under no obligation to accept them. In other words, although since 1906 nomadic parents had been under a duty to send their children to school, the children had no right to be admitted. The NGEC had demanded a meeting with Shirley Williams, the Labour Secretary of State for Education, and she promised, vaguely, to do something about it. Nothing happened, and the NGEC was briefed confidentially by junior civil servants that senior civil servants were arguing that it was not in the public interest to reward families camping illegally with access to schools.

In 1979 a new Conservative government was elected, and the Department of Education agreed to an NGEC meeting with the new Schools Minister, former head teacher Rhodes Boyson. Mercer and Acton recall vividly the deepening frown on the minister's face as Traveller parents told him of their experiences. He turned to his civil servants and said in a soft Lancashire accent, "That's not very naice". He added a clause to the Education Bill abolishing the whole idea of catchment areas and making it illegal for schools to discriminate against applicants on the basis of their place of residence. According to confidential sources, Boyson gained the support of Thatcherite ministerial colleagues by painting it as a measure to boost competition and freedom of choice being blocked by civil servants' restrictive practices. He also refused to sign off the government guidance on the operation of the Act until it made clear the additional rights that it gave Gypsy/Traveller children. It was almost his last act as Schools Minister.

This triumph confirmed the restoration of the reputation of the NGEC. And yet the nature of the campaigns changed radically; for the guerrilla period of voluntary education projects and battles between it and the authorities was also over. Two committed and charismatic HMIs,[6] Donald Buckland and Arthur Ivatts,[7] went around the country persuading local authorities to set up Traveller Education Services that would help bring Traveller culture into schools alongside the children. Hundreds of jobs were created (Acton and Kenrick 1991) and essentially the Freirian and Montessorian principles of the Gypsy Council's insurrectionary educational projects of the 1960s had become official policy through the establishment of a national network of Traveller Education Services.

In the mid-1980s, under Mercer's laid-back leadership, the NGEC was at the height of its influence. The NGEC preserved its independence by being a self-help organisation on a subscription income of around £1,000 a year. It largely left case-work to its affiliates or to ACERT, which did have paid employees. It saw its prime responsibility as being that of lobbying the government and local authorities, and increasingly the message it sent was the same as that of ACERT: that without proper accommodation, educational policy would be frustrated. The NGEC also took an increasing interest in international affairs, becoming effectively the UK representative of the International Romani Union, coordinating delegations to the 3rd and 4th World Romani Congresses and cooperating with Jean-Pierre Liégeois and the work of the Centre de Recherches Tsiganes in Paris, which were also closely linked to the IRU. The positive history of Traveller education after 1981 was among the major factors leading to the most positive ever policies of the EU, the resolutions of the Council of Ministers of 22 May 1989, though unfortunately these were abandoned when the wave of anti-Gypsyism that swept across Western Europe after the fall of the Berlin Wall unleashed pent-up racism. The NGEC, however, became one of the few organisations to offer a positive response and case-work help to the Roma asylum seekers who began to arrive after 1989, and to influence Traveller education services to help them.

Mercer's dominance of the NGEC was ended when he was challenged for the chairmanship and beaten by Charles Smith, whose leadership is discussed in Chapter Four. Mercer accepted defeat with great graciousness and agreed to become President, preserving the breadth and democratic tradition of the NGEC. When, however, Smith persuaded the NGEC to rename itself the Gypsy Council for Education, Welfare and Civil Rights, (GCECWCR), it became one Gypsy organisation among others, with the National Romany Rights Association, the Romani Guild, and eventually the East Anglia Gypsy Council ceasing to be involved when a leading woman officer, Sylvia Dunn, left to form the National Association of Gypsy Women in 1994 after a dispute over the role of the treasurer and was backed in this by

Peter Mercer. The EACG later supported the Derbyshire Gypsy Liaison Group in forming the National Federation of Gypsy Liaison Groups.

Under Charles Smith GCECWCR successfully competed for grants with ACERT and the NGC and professionalised itself; but it left a vacuum in the coordination of lobbying the government, which had eventually to be filled by the Traveller Law Reform coalition. Charles Smith, however, preserved the democratic forms of the Gypsy Council and even recruited Grattan Puxon as a member when he returned to the UK from the United States and became involved in the large-scale struggle at Dale Farm. Even though its dependence on a few key figures was sorely tested by the deaths within a short period of time of Chair Charles Smith and President Josie Lee and the disabling illness of long-term secretary Ann Bagehot, Charles Smith's immediate successor, the Romani artist Daniel Baker, was able to keep the organisation afloat even though its finances collapsed and allow the emergence of a new militantly voluntary leadership by two Gypsies, one from Buckinghamshire and one from Kent, confusingly both named Joe Jones, supported by Councillor Candy Sheridan, her cousin Richard Sheridan (at Dale Farm) and Grattan Puxon. All had been involved in NGEC/GCECWCR activities for a number of years and embodied its traditions by their supreme self-confidence, criticism of past leadership and tendency to fall out with one another.[8]

A new Gypsy politics?

Grattan Puxon cannot be considered as the single catalyst who triggered a growing Gypsy and Traveller awareness of identity and marginalisation through political mobilisation in pursuit of equality (cf Ryder, 2014). He did, however, in the sense of Freire (1972) bring together the pockets of hope that already existed. In other words, Puxon acted as a magnet drawing emerging community activists into the Gypsy Council. But did the experience of Gypsy Council activism actually 'empower' those who became involved?

As Afshar (1998) notes, empowerment is a process that cannot be done for people but has to be experienced by people themselves. Some of the early Gypsy Council activists already had had what Du Bois (1903) describes as double consciousness, understanding of both the dominant culture and those outside at the margins. Puxon galvanised these activists into a national campaign. They were empowered as they came to perceive themselves as being able and entitled to make decisions with a new assertiveness. In the 1970s they challenged Puxon's organisational style and founded new organisations. The Gypsy Council helped to build a sense of community by offering a voice and space to be understood by others, presenting a counter-narrative that could be offered as an alternative to the dominant perspective (cf Delgado, 1988), that could be used to build counter -hegemonic perspectives that combat destructive stereotypes (cf Harper et al, 2009). Puxon was – and is – always on the side of the grassroots against the WONAFFUNGOs, wary of campaigns becoming too allied with service-delivery agendas, and of the danger that efficiency replaces empowerment as the excluded move from being 'decision makers' to 'beneficiaries' (cf Hulme, 1994).

The Gypsy Council may now be only one of a number of Gypsy/Traveller/Roma-led organisations in the UK, just as the IRU is only one of an array of international Romani organisations. They are both conscious, however, of their rich heritage of community action, and not only because both are still involved with the septuagenarian Grattan Puxon and his new ginger group, the April 8th Movement. They know that they are only part of the broader tradition of a pedagogy of hope. Despite divisions, that tradition, and the vigour and numbers of campaigners, were able to prevent the movement as a whole from becoming stale, or controlled by any one clique or individual. Chapter Seven shows how, in the 21st century, the Traveller Law Reform Coalition sought to channel this diverse sea of activism to overcome the disappointments of the early years of the Blair government.

Notes

[1] The 'flagship' summer schools and education work brought the Gypsy Council into alliance with a number of committed educationalists. With Gypsy Council activists they formed in 1970 the National Gypsy Education Council (NGEC) as a registered charity. It was chaired by Lady Plowden, who had led the committee that produced the Plowden Report in 1967,

[2] The NGEC remained faithful to Grattan Puxon's principles of inclusivity, while Hughie Smith's Gypsy Council denounced Puxon and his legacy.

[3] Apart from a brief return visit to the UK in 1973–74, after being expelled from Yugoslavia, Grattan Puxon played no further part in UK Gypsy politics until he rejoined the Charles Smith-led Gypsy Council some 30 years later, after being active in Greece and the United States.

[4] It was effectively colonised by ACERT members in the 1990s.

[5] Though of course he is also a British Army veteran and attended the first Romani wreath-laying party at the Cenotaph, organised by the Romany and Traveller Family History Society.

[6] Her Majesty's Inspectors of Schools.

[7] Who, prior to being an HMI, had been Field Officer for the NGEC and then for ACERT and had, behind the scenes, worked quietly with Thomas Acton to heal the rift between them; they met secretly for dinner at Schmidt's restaurant in Soho.

[8] A humorous observation by Acton.

References

Acton, T. (1974) *Gypsy Politics and Social Change*, London: Routledge Kegan Paul.

Acton, T. and Kenrick, D. (1991) 'From Summer voluntary schemes to European Community bureaucracy: the development of special provision for Traveller education in the United Kingdom since 1967', *European Journal of Intercultural Studies*, vol 1, no 3, pp 20–2.

Afshar, H. (ed) (1998) *Women and Empowerment – Illustrations from the Third World*, London: Macmillan.

Delgado, R. (1988/1989) 'Storytelling for oppositionist and others: A plea for narrative', *Michigan Law Review*, vol 87, pp 2411–41.

Du Bois, W.E.B. (1903) *The Souls of Black Folk*, New York: Penguin Books.

Freire, P. (1972) *Pedagogy of the Oppressed*, Harmondworth: Penguin.

Freire, P. (1998) *Pedagogy of Hope: Reliving Pedagogy of the Oppressed*, New York: Continuum.

Harper, S.R., Patton, L.D., and Wooden, O.S. (2009) 'Access and equity for African American students in higher education: a critical race historical analysis of policy efforts', *The Journal of Higher Education*, vol 80, no 4, pp 389–414.

Hulme, D. (1994) 'Social development research and the third sector: NGOs as users and subjects of social inquiry', in D. Booth (ed) *Rethinking Social Development: Theory, Practice and Research*, Harlow: Longman.

Liégeois, J.-P. (1976) *Mutation Tsigane*, Bruxelles: ÉditionsComplexe.

Lundgren, G. (2000) 'The blond bandit Arthur Thesleff: committed scholarship in early Finnish Romani studies and today', in T.A. Acton (ed) *Scholarship and the Gypsy Struggle*, Hatfield: University of Hertfordshire Press, pp 129–39.

McCarthy, P. (2001) 'Travellers fighting back', in *Red and Black Revolution*, Issue 2, March.

Pifer, A. (1987) 'On quasi-public organisations: whence came the quango and why', Letter to the Editor, *New York Times*, 5 September.

Puxon, G. (2000) 'The Romani movement: rebirth and the first world Romani congress in retrospect', in T.A. Acton (ed) *Scholarship and the Gypsy Struggle*, Hatfield: University of Hertfordshire Press, pp 94–113.

Ryder, A. (2014) 'Snakes and ladders: inclusive community development and Gypsies and Travellers', *Community Development Journal*, vol 49, no 1, pp 21–36.

Searchlight (1989) Editorial: 'Racial Romany gets left-wing platform', *Searchlight*, issue 165, March, p 8.

Smith, H. (1976) *The National Gypsy Council Report* 1976–7, Oldham: National Gypsy Council.

Wells, R. and Kenrick D. (1978) 'Letter to the Editor – a response to Beresford-Webb', *Journal of the Gypsy Lore Society*, 4th series, vol 1, no 4, pp 289–91.

THREE

'Ministers like it that way': developing education services for Gypsies and Travellers

Arthur Ivatts, with John Day

Becoming involved

On reflection, life takes many strange turns, some good, some adventurous, some challenging and some sadly draped in misfortune. In my career journey I was fortunate enough to be blessed with good fortune, adventure and creative challenge.

Having been awarded in 1969 a postgraduate research scholarship by the Social Science Research Council (SSRC), I had to come up with an idea of what I wanted to research. Having previously trained as an art teacher in Wales, I had become very interested in the work of Augustus John and his lifelong fascination with the Romany way of life. Some time later, when I was reading the *Guardian* newspaper in the senior common room at Hull University, I happened to see a small news item about the SSRC wanting more research done on minorities, including 'gypsies'.[1] And so that memory surfaced from my subconscious and my decision was firmly made there and then to research this group of people, about whom I knew virtually nothing.

A further strange coincidence happened to me at roughly the same time. Having qualifications in youth work, I secured some part-time youth work to help keep my bank overdraft in check. The work was in a purpose-built youth wing at a large secondary school on a social housing estate between the outskirts of Hull and Cottingham village. Frequently, while cycling from Cottingham to the youth centre, I used to pass the intriguing scene of a group of Gypsies parked on the grassy verges of rural Middledyke Lane, with all their beautiful bow-topped wagons, horses, dogs and other livestock, together with nearby hedgerows bestrewn with carefully placed washing like brightly coloured patchwork quilts. Families with seemingly many children were sitting around inviting fires. I remember one evening when I returned home, the families had all vanished into thin air and the only trace was the smallest of smoking fire embers surrounded by a ring of grey stones. So, as a keen social anthropologist I had found my community literally on my doorstep and with whom I would work for the following three years.

My research started with the typical 'literature review', together with press searches for relevant material. An interesting news item appeared in the *Times Educational Supplement* in the autumn of 1969, reporting on the work of John Wallbridge in connection to the education of Gypsy and Traveller children and calling for the help of anyone interested. John Wallbridge was a specialist 'remedial' teacher employed by the Inner London Education Authority (ILEA). This call provided me with the significant opportunity to become involved from the start in the developments at a national level. At that time, the emerging Gypsy Council was successfully raising the sensitive issue of the treatment of these communities by the state, local authorities, the media and the majority population. I duly became a member of the Gypsy Council.

Early beginnings

The educational work of the Gypsy Council was covered by two or three Montessori-trained teachers together with some volunteer teachers and assistants. With funds secured for the Gypsy Council Trust (Education), work started in a number of places with outreach initiatives to the many marginalised Gypsy and Traveller communities, most of which were living on unauthorised encampments. A small demountable school was established on a piece of wasteland in the London local authority of Redbridge. These educational opportunities were greatly welcomed by the families and many local Gypsy and Traveller young children attended. Any real interest shown by the local education authority (LEA) was manifest by its absence.

At the same time John Wallbridge was being positive and supportive to the Gypsy Council's efforts, but his interest was focused on education rather than on the struggle for legal sites. He said at one meeting that he had been taking soundings from 'certain authorities' and that there would be funds available for developing educational provision for these communities if a less politically active vehicle could be established that would be independent of the Gypsy Council. Thus, despite many reservations and concerns about a 'gaujo' (non-Gypsies) takeover of the Gypsy Council Trust (Education), the support and active cooperation of the Gypsy Council leadership was finally secured and the National Gypsy Education Council (NGEC) was established. Needless to say, this development was not achieved without a great deal of political wrangling within the Gypsy Council, with many Gypsy and Traveller members feeling that too much control and power had been agreed and taken by the gaujos within the new constitution of the NGEC. The turbulent inaugural meeting of the NGEC on 10 May 1970 was held in George Whitefield Memorial Hall in Kingsway, Holborn (Acton, 1974).

It may well be that these small-scale early developments had arisen, and/or been given confidence, by two important official publications in the 1960s. The more general concerns surrounding Gypsy and Traveller communities had been beautifully highlighted by a powerful research report from the then Ministry of Housing and Local Government, entitled *Gypsies and Other Travellers* (Ministry of Housing and Local Government, 1967). The chapter on education provided a shameful national picture of the almost total exclusion of thousands of Gypsy and Traveller children from the formal education system.

At the same time another government report was published with even greater significance for the development of Gypsy and Traveller education. The Plowden Report, *Children and their Primary Schools* (Plowden, 1967, p 595), provided a further focus on the educational needs of Gypsy and Traveller children. In the opening paragraph of Annex 12, quoted below, the analysis of the educational situation of these children was termed in such a way that specific actions, despite endemic reluctance on the part of governments, local authorities and schools, could be advocated and justified, given the unchallenged authority of the Plowden Report and the acceptance of it by the then Ministry of Education.

The Report stated that Gypsy and Traveller children were 'probably the most deprived group in the country' (Plowden, 1967, p 595). The significance of the Plowden Report to the education of Gypsy and Traveller children was, however, twofold. In a very creative initiative, John Wallbridge set up a meeting with Lady Plowden in June 1970 and invited her to be the Chairperson of the newly formed NGEC. She accepted, and subsequent meetings took place on a regular basis in London. Despite the formidable gaujo presence and dominance at these meetings, there was also usually good representation by Gypsy Council members, some of whom were now also Executive Committee members of the NGEC. Relationships were very cordial and Lady Plowden made every effort to accommodate differing views. She was treated with enormous respect and her generosity of spirit led on more than one occasion to NGEC meetings being hosted at her Kensington home, with many a good lunch enjoyed.

The initial and central divergence of view was linked to the debate on the best place for Gypsy and Traveller pupils to be educated. In the main, the Gypsy Council was concerned that education in maintained schools would lead to a one-way process of cultural assimilation. Most adults in the communities had themselves had bad experiences at school. On the other hand, the majority of professional educationalists in the NGEC, including the Chair, felt strongly that ordinary schools were by far the best place for all children to be educated together. To some extent the advocates of state education were strengthened in their arguments by the developing race relations legislation and the embryo of multicultural educational developments in schools.

As an executive member of the NGEC, I was asked to accept the role of honorary research officer and my first task was to evaluate the programme of National Gypsy Summer Schools. These took place for two weeks in late July and early August in many parts of the country. The NGEC was successful in recruiting volunteer teachers and other helpers to run the various projects. A detailed questionnaire was prepared and sent to all the projects and a final evaluation report was produced in the autumn of 1971. Prior to the summer schools a training weekend was organised in Southwark, which a majority of the volunteers attended. Nineteen summer schools were run as far apart as York, Oxford and Sutton, and ranged from caravan schools to those located in county primary schools. I organised and ran two summer schools in the open air on both unofficial encampments and official sites in East Yorkshire and Hull, respectively.

The formalisation of national developments

With the chairpersonship of the NGEC in the hands of Lady Plowden in 1970, it was not long before small sums of money were marshalled for the cause. An initial small grant of £500 was given to aid the administrative foundations of the NGEC. Later that year a demonstration was staged by the Gypsy Council outside the Ministry of Education in Curzon Street, with Gypsy and Traveller children holding up a banner saying 'We want to go to school'. This event and its press coverage prompted Her Majesty's Inspectorate (HMI) to put Gypsy and Traveller education on the professional radar. At that time HMI advised ministers and senior civil servants on any developments in education that had policy and/or political implications. Staff HM Inspector for primary education Norman Thomas became interested and judged it prudent to find out a little about what was going on. In 1971 a meeting was set up with the Permanent Secretary at the

Ministry of Education, Sir William Pile, and a small group of NGEC Executive members, including Lady Plowden and myself, and HMI Norman Thomas. Sir William told the delegation of once meeting on his journey to work an "old Gypsy woman" who asked him for some tobacco for her clay pipe. The encounter and subsequent interactions led to a mutually respectful relationship between them.

While Sir William smoked his pipe, Lady Plowden, assisted by John Wallbridge and myself, briefed the meeting on the need for the NGEC to find sufficient funds to employ a full-time officer so that positive actions could be put in place. Sir William invited Norman Thomas to follow up the meeting with civil servants to arrange a small grant of £3,000 pa for three years for the NGEC, by then a registered charity. Following this success, arrangements were made to advertise the full-time post of Field Officer and in the summer of 1972 the first NGEC Field Officer was appointed.

I took up my appointment in the autumn of 1972 and moved to London to fulfil my new duties. These were vaguely defined by the Executive Committee and I reported on a regular basis to the Chair and the NGEC general meetings. Despite serious and growing dissent within the NGEC over the deployment of funds, the general strategy was to provide active support on a national basis to the increasing number of Gypsy and Traveller Support Groups and to assist them in the development of educational provision, most of which was voluntary and in the form of caravan or mobile schools visiting both authorised and unauthorised sites. Some caravans were placed on official sites with the approval of the local authority. A few school-type classes were run on a part-time basis in the small rooms or offices of the site warden when sites had a warden's residence or on-site office. The Field Officer's support was in the form of help with resources, funding, training, the curriculum and teaching, networking and general encouragement.

As the work developed the main thrust was to persuade LEAs to take a responsible interest and make some form of provision, including mobile provision with programmes of outreach and on-site visits. Most LEAs found it difficult to allow mobile provision to visit unofficial sites, as it might have been seen as an implicit acceptance of the unlawful occupation of land for which other departments in the local authority were seeking legal redress.

The process of persuasion was made easy on account of the national respect that Lady Plowden had in the world of education, given her mould-breaking report on children and primary education. The rapidly established tactic was that Lady Plowden would in the normal course of events be invited to speak at conferences all over the country and would exploit the opportunities provided in the margins of the conferences to lobby directors of education and chief education officers on what they were doing for Gypsy and Traveller children. The generally honest disclosures of 'very little' were followed up by her description of the work of the NGEC and the offer of the advice and support of the newly appointed Field Officer.

I was then asked to prepare a letter for Bridget Plowden to send to each appropriate director or chief education officer so placated. The letters contained polite expressions of concern with regard to the limited knowledge of, and action on behalf of, Gypsy and Traveller communities, together with the contact details of the Field Officer. It had usually been agreed in the off-the-record discussions at the conferences that the LEA would welcome an 'exploratory' visit by myself, Arthur Ivatts, to investigate and advise on appropriate forms of policy, provision and practice.

The arranged visits usually lasted a couple of days and involved linking up with local voluntary workers and/or Gypsy support groups so that an accurate picture of the actual situation on the ground could be sketched. All the visits involved meeting families and talking and playing with children. Assessments were made of the numbers and ages of the children, location and disposition, living circumstances and access to education. Post-visit reports were written for the NGEC and provided the basis of a further letter from the Chair to the director or chief officer detailing the findings and making recommendations for appropriate actions. The offer of the on-going support and advice of the Field Officer was reiterated and seen as an essential ingredient of any responsible development. This was the start of building the national network of Traveller Education Support Services (TESS).[2] In many cases the small local voluntary actions were formally supported or taken over by the responsible LEA.

The successful pioneering work of the NGEC was significantly assisted not only by the international status and influence of the Chair, but also by the growing realisation of the availability of additional funding provided via the pot known as the 'No Area Pool'. This financial device was the result of cooperation between central and local government. Given that most local authorities would at some stage find themselves presented with unexpected and exceptional budget demands for the maintenance or necessary extension of statutory public services, all local authorities agreed to allocate a percentage of their annual budget from central government to a 'pool' to be tapped as and when necessary for the unpredictable demands that were not usually seen as belonging to the actual area of the local authority. A set of criteria were established and included such items as the cost of accommodating refugees. Interestingly enough, Gypsies and Travellers were also included, as it was erroneously felt that these people did not belong to any one local authority area. The detailed history of their inclusion within the 'No Area Pool' criteria would benefit from research in official papers, but to all those working in the field at that time, not least some LEAs, it was a most welcome surprise.

This reality was increasingly drawn to the attention of local authorities by some activists and Gypsy and Traveller support groups, the NGEC and its Field Officer and, not least, HMI. The word soon spread and initiatives were being confidently taken by LEAs in the knowledge that any political backlash against public funds being spent on 'these communities' could be softened and massaged sufficiently to make it look like the innocent fulfilment of statutory duties. If special and additional provision was made for Gypsy and Traveller children, then 100% of the costs could be applied for from the 'No Area Pool'. If the provision was to be made in maintained schools, then 75% of costs could be recouped. The temptation either to get teachers for nothing or to get four for the price of one was too much for most LEAs to withstand. Provision grew exponentially.

The fragmentation of advocacy

By 1973 there were discernible tensions emerging within the NGEC and a divide was in evidence surrounding a number of issues. There was a continuous debate about state schooling and its potentially damaging impact on minority cultures, with the majority culture being part of planned assimilation into 'majority' cultural milieux. The hostile nature of school environments to Gypsy and Traveller children and young people was graphically described and confirmed in the 1985 Swann Report.

> The degree of hostility towards Romanies' and other Travellers' children if they do enter school is quite remarkable even when set alongside the racism encountered by children for other ethnic minority groups. (Swann, 1985, chapter 16)

The fear that some members of the communities had in relation to sending their children to school was well articulated by John Day when interviewed by Andrew Ryder and Thomas Acton in May 2013.[3]

"My personal educational experiences provided a weird situation. We lived in a house for a long time when I was younger and my early experience was going to school and kind of being the odd one out and very often had to sit in the corner of the classroom with a few wooden bricks whilst the teacher got on and taught the others and … you would get beaten around the playground by the pupils and pushed around the classroom by the teachers and I am talking about the 1950s. When we were on the road we went to school when the truancy officer caught up with us and he'd take us in and then the police would come and move us on and then they would take us out of school and you'd probably only end up being in school for a few hours."

A majority of the Gypsy Council members were still uneasy at the single-minded approach being taken by the influential hierarchy of the NGEC, which was increasingly unequivocal about the importance of Gypsy and Traveller children being given equal opportunities to be educated in state primary and secondary schools. A further on-going dispute focused on the control and use of the increasing financial resources, with reputable donors including the Ministry of Education, the Gulbenkian Foundation, the Joseph Rowntree Trust, IBM, the Carnegie Trust and the Watts Foundation. Financial control in regard to cheque signatories and bank accounts, and decisions on use of the funds, were by this time firmly in the grip of the 'professional educator' caucus within the NGEC.

A divide was also developing between the Gypsy and Traveller members of the NGEC, with some remaining loyal to the Gypsy Council and some increasingly keen to back the 'professional educators' both in terms of their knowing what was best educationally for their children and in terms of the realisation that creditability with the 'establishment' was the best way to access significant resources. The skilful control over meeting agendas ensured that the Gypsy Council's influence on the course of events was increasingly weakened, despite voting guarantees within the constitution. Later in 1973 the frustrations of the Gypsy Council members manifested themselves at a discordant NGEC meeting in which voting rights were being insisted upon by some members of the Gypsy Council, and the exasperated Chairperson closed the meeting early. That same evening the 'professional educators', including the Chair and the Field Officer, together with a group of Gypsies and Travellers, decided to withdraw from the NGEC and to set up a new organisation that would be able to exercise uncomplicated advocacy for the education of Gypsy and Traveller communities. In the home of John Wallbridge the group worked to establish the new body by adapting the NGEC constitution and creating a new name with the acronym ACERT (Advisory Council for the Education of Romany and Other Travellers). An embargoed press statement was drafted and delivered by hand to Reuters in the early hours of the next morning by the Field Officer.

An initial administrative difficulty for ACERT was that it had no funds, since all the donor allocations rested with the NGEC. Immediate action was thus taken the next day through telephone calls to the donor organisations, including the Ministry of Education. Grants to the NGEC were suspended pending further investigations and discussion. I, as the now new Field Officer for ACERT, was given the task of urgently visiting all the donors to explain the circumstances of the split and the need for the redirection of funds to enable ACERT to continue the work initially started within the context of the NGEC. Despite an exchange of solicitors' letters, all of the pending grants were eventually transferred to ACERT and work began to continue as normal, despite the costs of the organisation, including the Field Officer's salary and expenses, being 'bankrolled' personally by Lady Plowden for the best part of nine months. Needless to say, the two organisations were now fierce competitors for funds, influence and truth.

The role of the Ministry of Education and Her Majesty's Inspectorate

The Ministry of Education continued to be supportive and regular meetings were held with officials and HMI. In the summer of 1973 and in the context of an uneasy truce between the two national organisations, HMI organised an in-service training course on the topic of the education of Gypsy and Traveller children under the programme known as 'Teachers' Short Courses'. It was attended by representatives from both organisations as well, of course, as teachers, LEAs and activist organisations. Thirty-seven people attended the first course, which was directed by HMI Don Buckland. HMI Norman Thomas was also present and he made a surprise suggestion to me that at some stage I might be interested in joining Her Majesty's Inspectorate. Given the raw nerves and sensitive politics at the time I was gratified by a very courteous letter that arrived shortly following the course from HMI Thomas, thanking me for my 'wise and constructive contribution to the course'.

Subsequently, I met HMI Buckland every few months to report on national progress. At one such meeting he asked me if I would be kind enough to arrange a visit to a Traveller project school for a very senior civil servant. The visit was arranged to be in Hertfordshire and I picked up the official from the then Department for Education and Science in my old white Morris 1000 saloon. The day was pleasant enough and the civil servant, Mr Peter Litton, expressed considerable interest in the families and the education being provided for the children. He accepted the offer of a lift home afterwards and on the way he said something that has remained with me to this very day. "Arthur, we [the civil service] have always taken the view that it is best that what you do about Travellers is 'nothing'. Ministers like it that way."

Significant progress was made in 1983 with the first HMI publication on Gypsy and Traveller education, which described the models of good and promising policy, provision and practice (HMI, 1983). With this formal HM Stationery Office publication following on from the Plowden Report and the Ministry of Housing and Local Government document, Gypsy and Traveller education was firmly on the agenda of HMI and, by implication also, in theory at least, on the official policy agenda of the Department for Education and Science. In 1983 HMI Buckland was promoted to a Staff Inspector for Physical Education and so I was asked to take over the national HMI responsibility for the education of Gypsy and Traveller communities, a post I held until my retirement in August 1998.

The role of advocacy for the education of Gypsy and Traveller communities was much assisted by the status and influence of HMI. Interestingly enough, I found that I was able to continue the almost identical role that I had developed as the Field Officer for NGEC and, later, ACERT. The work was, however, much more effective, given the power and influence of HMI at that pre-Ofsted time. The continuing debate about separate or mainstream provision for Gypsy and Traveller children was only finally ended by the wise and emphatic statement by Chief Inspector HMI Eric Bolton in a keynote presentation to the HMI Teachers' Short Course in Southampton. HMI Bolton simply said that separate provision was unacceptable, given that all the research and inspection evidence proved that children do less well and are thus seriously and irrevocably disadvantaged by being educated separately.

Apart from continuing to assist HMI Buckland with the Gypsy and Traveller courses under the HMI Teachers' Short Course programme, I was also able to identify at will any LEA and arrange an inspection visit. Most LEAs were very cooperative and provided me with the list of schools that they thought 'Traveller' children attended. I mostly worked alone, but often with HMI Buckland and/or an HMI colleague would ask to do a 'Traveller' inspection with me and this was frequently the case when a new colleague's HMI mentor requested it.[4] The process was to visit all or a sample of the listed schools and to use the evidence to compile a composite report on the quality of the policy, provision and practice. The report was essentially for HM Senior Chief Inspector and department officials and would also be the basis of the feedback to the LEA. In addition to the visits to schools, I always also visited both official and unofficial sites in the local authority area, spoke with families, checked recent local press cuttings and liaised with as many people as possible, including the LEA teams/services responsible for 'multi-cultural' and bilingual educational support, and those too in neighbouring local authorities.

The national inspection and advocacy work continued when I took over national responsibility for the education of Gypsy and Traveller communities. The Teachers' Short Course programme included a course on Gypsy and Traveller education every two years, and the last week-long course in Winchester in 1987 was truly international and had over 250 participants representing all communities including Gypsy, Roma, Travellers of Irish heritage, Fairground/Show people, Circus families, New Age families and Bargee families.

In a determined rolling programme of HMI visits and inspections, all LEAs were targeted, either in relation to models of identifying and reporting on developing and good practice as exemplars that could usefully be publicised and disseminated, or where there were suspicions of poor provision or wilful neglect, often brought to the attention of HMI by 'whistle-blowers' within the increasing national informal network of committed advocates. With the benefit of LEAs having access to seemingly unlimited resources, the national network of TESS was built during this period. In many ways these developments were flying under the official and political radar both at local level and nationally. However, by 1987 there was sufficient official recognition of the work being developed by local authorities, together with an appreciation of the extreme educational needs of the communities, that when the reforms to local government finance resulted in the termination of the 'No Area Pool' arrangements, alternative resources had to be considered. A further strength to the work of HMI was the publication of the Swann Report on the education of minority ethnic pupils in 1985 (Swann, 1985). This report included an important chapter on the education of Gypsy and Traveller children. The positive role of HMI was usefully documented in this report and was very much in contrast to the role of civil servants, which received a less than enthusiastic caricature betraying the reality of the assumption that 'Ministers like it that way'.

Role of the Department of Education and Science and Her Majesty's Inspectorate

At the time of its termination date the 'No Area Pool' was allocating £15 million a year to local authorities for running their pioneering TESS. HMI encouraged the department's officials to flag up serious concerns with ministers about the importance of continuing this essential work and, not least, ensuring that the political complications of hundreds of increasingly specialist teachers becoming suddenly redundant and unemployed did not surface in the national media. By this time there was certainly no shortage of seriously committed people who would no doubt have obliged.

The response to this crisis situation that HMI had been warning about ever since the local government finance reforms were rumoured was, rather belatedly, to insert an additional section into the then 'Great Education Reform Act' of 1988. Section 210 introduced a new Specific Grant entitled 'Grants for the education of travellers and displaced persons'.[5] It is possible, given my memory of those events, that ministers were never formally consulted on the specific grant proposal, but if they were it is more likely that the terms 'displaced persons' and 'refugees' and 'international UN Convention duties' would have been pushed to the front of the argument. I was asked to draft this section of the Act and the draft went to and fro between HMI, Pat Masters, who was the senior department official at the time, and the parliamentary council drafters, who would keep sending back revised drafts asking, "Is this what you are meaning? Does this form of words convey accurately what you want to happen in practice?" Involvement in this fascinating process later led on to my drafting the Circular issued shortly after the 1988 Act became law. The first suggested section 210 grant allocation within the department was for £3.5 million, but after much jumping up and down by HMI, given the shortfall between this derisory figure and the £15 million paid under the 'No Area Pool', this sum was increased to £5.5 million. Within a couple of years the annual allocation had reached £8.5 million. A key breakthrough was that the legislation ensured that grants were for 'persons' rather than school-aged children and so adult members of the communities could be beneficiaries. In addition, the Circular secured that Gypsy and Traveller children were to have 'unhindered access to mainstream education'. This was the end of any special and/or separate provision and, in addition, it allowed LEAs to bid for any policy initiative that was judged to address any 'hindrance' to access to mainstream education and happy and successful learning. Thus, bids could include the cost of outreach to families, transport to school, books and materials, uniforms, dinner money and in-service training.[6]

With the forceful and strategic encouragement of HMI, the vast majority of LEAs set up a bespoke service despite there being no statutory obligation or other formal and/or specific direction from national government. By 2007, the UK had undoubtedly achieved the most comprehensive structure of best educational practice in Europe for these hitherto marginalised and excluded communities. Sadly, the UK government could never be persuaded to share this with other countries, despite international commitments to do so. It was also to be regretted that, from the day that the new specific grant for 'travellers and displaced persons' came into force, it came under attack both by the media and afterwards by ministers and some civil servants. The death by a thousand cuts and the accompanying administrative change proposals were always part of wider reforms in government and departmental policy. Each time, HMI argued strongly that the 'ring fencing' of the specific grant was essential, as the politics surrounding Gypsy and Traveller communities was so hostile that without central government 'ring-fenced' funding programmes, TESSs would eventually lose the fight for local financial resources. This advice to department officials usually fell on deaf ears and no one civil servant senior enough who was hearing the voice of HMI was willing to defend an 'exceptions policy' to ministers. Subsequent developments proved HMI right and within the decade following 1990 nearly all central government funding streams were eroded to the point of extinction.

Despite this story of significant achievements in securing against all the odds substantial sums of public money for the education of despised people, it has to be said that it was achieved by the efforts of HMI, which has a statutory duty to tell the truth without fear or favour, and a number of wise, just and committed civil servants who appreciated the reality of the prejudice and official discrimination faced by these communities and were thus determined to see justice done in the name of equality. The names that stand out in this regard are Pat Masters, Robert Mace, George Anderson, Annabel Burns and Sheila Longstaff. However, our joint efforts seldom managed to get ministers to make firm public statements about the rights of these children to a good education. Many, many attempts were made to get ministers to make a firm statement that racist bullying towards Gypsy, Roma and Traveller children and young people in schools must stop.

The same disappointment was experienced in regard to the school curriculum, which was never formally inclusive of Gypsy, Roma and Traveller culture, history and languages. The importance of this was well illustrated in a comment by John Day in his interview previously referred to:

> "Travellers need to be in the curriculum and the schools that need that the most are the schools that don't have Travellers. It is a massive belief of ours that the only way we will get on is if people know more about us."

The nearest thing to curriculum inclusion was when Sheila Longstaff took forward the ideas and work of Rocky Deans (Brent TESS) and Peter Saunders (Leeds TESS) by formally initiating the 'Gypsy, Roma and Traveller History Month' (GRTHM) each year in June. Sheila Longstaff somehow found sufficient funds to launch this policy in 2008 with a fanfare event in the House of Lords with Lord Adonis (Schools Minister) and Lord Avebury presenting prizes to all the Gypsy, Roma and Traveller children and young people who had entered and won a national poster competition. Sadly, the initial enthusiasm and commitment died when Sheila Longstaff moved to another post in the department. Subsequent civil servants perceived the political dangers for ministers of the initiative and quickly closed down the department's involvement and funding allocations. In comparison with the department's decades-long involvement and commitment to the 'Black History Month', it is a shameful and unacceptable reflection of racist discrimination against Gypsy, Roma and Traveller communities. It is good, however, that many TESSs, local authorities and some international organisations still recognise this event and mark it in some celebratory way or another.

Community participation and involvement: 'hearing the voice'

In the early days relating to the pioneering work of the NGEC, the involvement of Gypsies and Travellers in the advocacy process was marked by a determination to see access to basic education brought to their communities, to receive recognition and respect and to secure social justice. Their voluntary efforts were often stimulated and steered by the work of well-informed gaujo activists like Mr Grattan Puxon, Dr Donald Kenrick and Dr Thomas Acton. However, there was less certainty about what the orientation and direction of policy, provision and practice should be when considering suggestions put forward by non-Travellers. As a result, some Gypsies and Travellers agreed that maintained schools were unwelcoming and hostile environments for their children, and others, despite their reservations about racism and non-inclusivity in schools, still favoured mainstream education as the route to equality of treatment.

The splitting of the NGEC and the establishment of ACERT saw these differences of view publicly expressed to some extent, with some Gypsies and Travellers siding with the NGEC and others willing to throw in their lot with the clear intentions of ACERT and the stressed importance of securing access to ordinary maintained schools.

It was clear, however, that although most initiatives within organisations were promoted and directed by gaujo professional activists, they were at the same time acutely aware of the importance to organisational credibility of having the active participation of Gypsy and Traveller members. Although opportunities were always provided for open and frank discussions within meetings and other gatherings, the 'voice of Gypsy and Traveller communities' was far less influential on policy, provision and practice decisions than was that of the professional educationalists. In subsequent years this situation slowly changed, and especially as a result of TESSs and schools developing such excellent listening relationships with local Gypsy and Traveller families.

Perhaps one of the most positive developments was the formal employment of Gypsy and Traveller adults within TESSs. Many TESSs were very successful at recruiting and training young people from the communities to work in schools as Learning Support Assistants (or similar roles/titles) and as educational welfare officers linking with families over issues of attendance and welfare. To some extent these posts provided positive role models for the children and contributed significantly to the erosion of prejudiced attitudes on the part of some teachers and non-Traveller parents.

This development did so much to boost the trust and confidence of families in their local schools, as well as giving a foothold to career development for the Gypsy and Traveller people involved. However, a number of difficulties were experienced with these developments. Although a very few of the employed members of the communities had fully qualified teacher status, most were employed and deployed in capacities that might have been viewed by some as 'low status'. Many of the members of the communities involved in these capacities frequently found themselves exposed to racist attitudes in schools from both staff and non-Gypsy and non-Traveller pupils. In addition, many would complain that their access to in-service training was sometimes restricted and that schools too frequently saw their role as being 'just for the traveller pupils', rather than accepting and appreciating them as full professional team members. A further complication was associated with the credibility and confidence that such employees had while working within their own communities. Again, John Day comments graphically on this point:

> "I am not really the person to judge it but it was a double-edged sword because it put a Traveller input into what was happening in education but it created a wedge between me and the community ... as an education welfare officer I had the power to prosecute people for not going to school. How could I prosecute my own people when I knew about all the prejudices in school that kept them out of school in the first place? What I was successful in doing was changing the role of that [post], locally and nationally, I was instrumental in the role of moving to non-prosecution and moving it towards becoming school liaison officers as opposed to educational welfare officers."

Sadly, listening to the voice of Roma, Gypsy and Traveller communities in UK schools, local authorities and central government was short lived. Now we are faced with an international crisis of the world not listening to the 15 million voices of these communities and majority populations led by their politicians, and much of the mass media treating them as if they were nuclear waste as opposed to human beings. If Gypsy, Roma and Traveller communities want to effectively and decisively confront this ubiquitous abuse by government and majority populations, then they have to access and stay in high-quality education in order to gain the necessary tools for such a battle.

Notes

[1] Note the lower case 'g'. The *Guardian* has amended its ways in recent years, which is in contrast to the tabloid press, which wilfully continues to use the disrespectful lower case 'g' for Gypsy and 't' for Traveller, despite both these groups being covered by the Equalities legislation (2000) and their inclusion as minority ethnic groups.

[2] Support services for Gypsy and Traveller communities carried different titles in different authorities. Most were known as 'Traveller Support Services'. The application of the title of Traveller Education Support Services (TESS) was formally introduced by the Department for Children, Schools and Families

in 2007 by the senior civil servant responsible for this area of work, Sheila Longstaff.

[3] John Day was a lead regional activist in East England and member of the Gypsy Council from the 1970s (see Chapter Two) and was one of the first community members to be employed in a Traveller Education Service.

[4] Newly appointed HMIs at that time were allocated an HMI mentor for one year as a kind of professionally supported induction and probationary period.

[5] It should be noted that at the time the terms Gypsy and Traveller were not capitalised by the state, a failure that still occurs today on the part of public bodies and the media.

[6] Education (Grants) (Travellers and Displaced Persons) Regulations 1990, SI 1990/306 Circular 1090.

References

Acton, T. (1974) *Gypsy Politics and Social Change*, London: Routledge and Kegan Paul.

HMI (1983) *The Education of Traveller Children*, London: HMSO.

Ministry of Housing and Local Government (1967) *Gypsies and Other Travellers*, London: MHLG.

Plowden Report (1967) *Children and their Primary Schools: A Report of the Central Advisory Council for Education (England)*, London: Her Majesty's Stationery Office (HMSO), Annex 12.

Swann Report (1985) *Education for All: The Swann Report*, London: HMSO.

FOUR

Charles Smith: the fashioning of an activist

Thomas Acton and Andrew Ryder

Charles Smith, then chair of the Gypsy Council, reflected in an interview with Sarah Cemlyn in 1997 as to how the Gypsy Council had fared while being involved in a local authority panel to deliberate on Gypsy and Traveller matters:

> Charles: ... It took us 20 years to get onto their panel. We kept asking to be involved in the decisions that were being made about Gypsies. They never spoke to us. We was allowed to go and watch but not participate. And they eventually thought it was a good idea to have a Gypsy on there and the power started to change slightly and we did get a seat on there..not voting but like an advisory seat – but when we gave advice and it wasn't what they wanted to hear, it was goodbye.

> Cemlyn: What did they do? Did they stop sending the minutes or..?

> Charles: No. They still send us the minutes and..give us some money. Not very much, about a 200 quid donation..I think they thought they'd bought us basically.

> Cemlyn: Did they just say you can't come anymore?

> Charles: Well no, they threatened us. They said if you're not in agreement with our sort of policies and things like that, you know, we can't..we won't be able to guarantee you get the money anymore. So we wrote back and said, well you can stick the money because we're not bought that cheaply. And then that didn't work so they decided they couldn't have us as representatives because we didn't represent every single Gypsy in the country. So I argued that

they [councillors] as a political party did not represent every single person in the county of XXXX so how can they sit there and make decisions. And they didn't like that. I was basically an 'uppity nigger' and they didn't like it. You're not allowed to have an opinion. They wanted someone to say yes, it's a very good idea and then they could go away and say they'd consulted with the Gypsies.

The above exchange reflects the tenacity of the late Charles Smith, and also a determination that was evident throughout his life to avoid tokenism and to secure a meaningful say in decisions affecting his community. Charles, as much as any Gypsy Traveller in the UK before or since, achieved that goal. Charles was chair of the Gypsy Council, a Commission for Racial Equality commissioner, a Labour councillor and mayor and a lead activist in the Campaign for Traveller Law Reform. This chapter seeks to give the reader insights into the factors and personalities that fashioned Charles as an activist and in the process will try and form a series of conclusions as to the lessons that can be learnt and conclusions drawn for other emerging activists among GRT communities. Before this we seek to avoid losing Charles' essence and message in a fog of abstraction and analysis and let Charles speak directly to the reader by reprinting in full his inaugural speech as Mayor of Castle Point, and later a poem by Charles. This 'thick descriptive' and narrative approach also stems from a desire to avoid adopting an 'authoritative voice' and to provide an account of a life lived that can reflect multiple realities and alternative interpretations (cf Okely and Callaway, 1992, p xi).

The first Romani mayor in the United Kingdom: inaugural speech of Mr Charles Smith as Mayor of Castle Point 2002

If you will allow me, I'd like to explain a little of myself and how I have come to be standing here, as Mayor of Castle Point. Born in Rochford, after ten days moved to my Granddad's tailors shop in London Road, Hadleigh, lived in Hadleigh until I got married, moved to Thundersley and apart from the times my wife and I travelled round to the horse fairs and so on, I have always lived here. My father was born over the top of the family shop in Notting Hill and first came to Thundersley, Hart Road, in the 1930s when it was not much more than a little rural village.

My mother was born in a bender tent pitched behind the family's horse drawn caravan in a pea field at Cold Norton, and her family have lived around this part of Essex longer than anyone can remember. So I consider myself to be a true local lad, born and bred.

If someone had said to me when I left school that one day I would be the Mayor of the Borough, I would never have believed it. In fact my Housemaster told me on the day I left, "I give you six months out in the real world and you'll be in prison." I'm pleased to say his prediction was not realised. From that, you can take it my time spent in the local educational establishments was neither one of much pleasure nor one of great educational achievement.

You soon find out when you start school if there is anything different about you, even if you didn't know yourself, and it wasn't long before I was informed that "Your Mum's a Gypsy." After telling my Mum, as I had no concept at five what a Gypsy was, my Mum told me this, "Remember you are as good as any of them, and probably better than many," and told me to sing this little song when they made such remarks. First let me tell you the meaning of one of the words in this little rhyme for those of you who don't speak Romani; Gorgia, meaning non-Gypsy, it can be derogatory or not, depending on how it is used, just like Gypsy. So, here goes, "Gorgia bred, Gorgia bred, half-starved and nearly dead, poor little Gorgia bred". It worked well with the five and six year olds leaving them standing there with their mouths agape, I'm only thankful that no one asked me what it meant as I thought Gorgia bred was something like ginger bread. Unfortunately it did not work with the teachers and the more subtle actions of the adults left me with a full understanding of prejudice and racism by the time I left school at fifteen ... If you experience this type of prejudice for whatever reason it can have a big effect on the way you interact with the world, some people will withdraw into their shell, keeping their head down, never confronting people, whilst others may bear resentments and end up hating the world, looking out only for themselves. Others choose to try and change things, some through writing, art or education, some through politics, which is what I decided to do, and having now been actively involved in politics for over twenty-five years, I know you can change things; unfortunately, it often takes twenty-five years to do it, as I am sure many of you have realised.

One of the people who has influenced me most in my political career has been Thomas Acton, Professor of Romani studies at Greenwich University, whose company we have the pleasure of tonight; he convinced me to join the Labour Party. I don't intend to go on too long, but would just like to warn you how he works. After becoming involved in working with the Gypsy Council, Thomas, about four others and myself attended a public meeting where a site for Gypsy people was to be debated. The room was packed to capacity with about 500 people; to say they were anti would have been polite. The usual views and stereotypes were fully expressed with much vigour from the local residents. Thomas, lacking any sense of extreme danger, stood up and spoke with his usual eloquence, in favour of the site, its would-be occupants and proceeded in dispelling their misguided prejudices and stereotypes, to much heated booing, hissing and varied insults to his person. Someone then shouted out "There's no Gypsies got the guts to be here." "Oh yes there is," said Thomas sticking the microphone in my hand and urged me to speak to these enraged residents. With the call from the irate and heated throng of "Come on let's hear what you've got to say for yourself," I was directed to the front of the hall.

At this point the microphone stopped working but the people called for me to speak up and some laughed at me, as some still do, but as I spoke they listened. I told them that the land on which their houses were built was land that Gypsy families had camped on for hundreds of years. Some of these families still lived in the area in houses and bungalows, the same people they bought their turf from or who had landscaped their gardens, and this site was for their relations who had kept to the travelling lifestyle, but needed a base to return to, as the places they used to camp on no longer existed, being covered with those same houses and factories. At the end of the day, the site was only for six families; families not unlike themselves, struggling to earn a living and support their families, nor indeed the Gypsy families already living among them whom they did not seem to realise were Gypsy people at all, despite all their perceived stereotypes. When I had finished I received a round of applause and many people came and spoke to me after the meeting. I realised then that you could change people's way of thinking by talking to them, having knowledge of your subject and explaining it.

Of course, people who make the decisions don't always want to talk to the people those decisions affect. National issues like the Poll Tax and the Criminal Justice Act, where public opinion was virtually ignored, and local issues such as the selling off of the place where I live without consultation, was what finally made me get involved by standing for Council.

Something all politicians must do is learn to listen, and not just to themselves ...As politicians, I think it is our job to make people feel that they are valued members of society, and can achieve their full potential as citizens. No one should be left sitting at the edge bearing resentment and feeling excluded.

We must always strive for inclusion, openness and equality, and an open fair democracy is the best way to achieve this with everyone feeling able to participate, without fear of prejudice or discrimination.

I once had the pleasure of spending an afternoon with the actress Miriam Margolyes, who was visiting the Save the Children Fund Gypsy support office in London. We were going out to meet some Gypsy families living around the area. The Save the Children Fund officer said to Miriam that she would be showing her what prejudice means today, to which Miriam replied, with one of the best comments I have ever heard, "Darling, I'm fat, Jewish and a lesbian, what can you show me about prejudice?" This made me realise that if people want to, they will always find a reason to discriminate against you, and I hope as a Councillor I have helped in some way to have reduced prejudice and exclusion in this Borough and as your Mayor will continue to promote the inclusion and participation of all our citizens.

I am very proud to be standing here today as Mayor of Castle Point, a place I care passionately about, and I shall endeavour to work hard as your Mayor with all the people of Castle Point, and I thank you for this honour you have bestowed upon me.

First published by the European Roma Rights Centre – 10 July 2002

Three years after making this speech Charles finally succumbed to the leukaemia that he had been battling for a number of years. The final years of Charles' life were nonetheless highly productive, coinciding with two key developments. One was that the New Labour government from 2002 started to consider the need to address the Traveller site shortage. The second and less positive development was the intense media and political campaign directed at Gypsies and Travellers. In both of these events Charles was a prominent and robust defender of Gypsy and Traveller interests. Possibly one of the most important aspects of this work was finally getting the Commission for Racial Equality (CRE) to engage with Gypsies and Travellers after years of perceived neglect. This new engagement led to the landmark report by the CRE *Common Ground*, which chronicled Gypsy and Traveller exclusion, a report that Charles helped to guide. It also led to the CRE joining with the Gypsy and Traveller Law Reform Coalition to lobby the New Labour government, which indeed led to significant progress. Acknowledging Charles' contribution, the then CRE Chairperson, Trevor Phillips, said in tribute to Charles following his death: "Since his appointment as a CRE commissioner in April 2004 his contribution and insight to the Commission's work on Gypsies and Travellers, as well as other spheres of work, has been invaluable. In particular he reconnected the CRE with Gypsy and Traveller communities" (Press Association, 2005).

During this period of intense political activity his leukaemia had started to return and his doctors had advised him to avoid stress and anxiety but Charles ignored this advice and was active in the political and media fray until the very end, both literally and physically. Typical of Charles' eye for the ironic and propensity to challenge authority, he stipulated that he was to be buried on the plot of land for which he had unsuccessfully sought planning permission over a number of years. This was indeed where Charles was buried: the local authority was happy for a dead Gypsy to be buried beneath the land but not for a live one to live on that land.

Extracts from *Guardian* obituary, 14 November 2005, by Thomas Acton

Charles Smith: Gypsy activist, poet, and film-maker, he once ran a successful antiques business

[Charles] joined the National Gypsy Education Council, of which I was secretary, in the early 1980s. He came to two meetings at which he said nothing, but at the end of the second meeting, he pulled out a sheaf of fair bills from a pocket. He had written an autobiography entirely in pencil on their backs. Edited extracts giving a wonderful ethnographic description of Stow Fair from the traders' viewpoint appeared in the journal Traveller Education, and Charles was finally convinced that he was not illiterate, as his old headmaster had told him.

He went on to publish two volumes of poetry, *The Spirit of the Flame* (1990) and *Not all Wagons and Lanes* (1995). He also collaborated with the late Jeremy Sandford on a film about the Gypsy Council, presented by David Essex, and went on to make his own elegiac film *Footsteps in the Sand* (2004) about the Gypsy festival of Saintes Maries in the south of France. He always claimed he learned to speak in public when we went to a public meeting about building a Gypsy site in Southend, and one of the antis shouted out: "Have any Gypsies bothered to come?" And I pointed to him and said: "There's one here," leaving him no choice but to make a speech.

Gypsy politics were in some disarray in the 1980s. The old Gypsy Council, founded in 1966, had splintered into a number of organisations, including the National Gypsy Council, led by Hughie Smith, and the National Gypsy Education Council. Charles was elected chair of the latter in 1990, and soon guided it to shorten its name to the Gypsy Council. This sharpened a long-standing feud with Hughie Smith, who said he was life president of the only authentic Gypsy organisation, and eventually sued Gypsy Council members for libel. Charles took a certain glee in refusing to give in, and winning the case and extracting £14,000 in costs. Since the Gypsy Council could not afford lawyers, all the work had been done voluntarily by Gypsy Council members reading up law books; most of these costs were donated back to ensure that the Gypsy Council remained an open, democratic, membership-based organisation.

This victory over the old Gypsy politics opened the way for new alliances. None of the Gypsy organisations were going to give way for each other, but they were prepared to work together, especially after being traumatised by their failure to make any dent in the Conservative 1994 criminal justice act. This repealed the 1968 caravan sites act (which had placed a duty on councils to provide sites), and was left intact in 1997 when the Labour government suddenly discarded those shadow ministers, such as Peter Pike, who had studied the Gypsy brief in opposition.

Charles and the Gypsy Council became core members of the newly created Traveller Law Reform Coalition. It did a lot of solid research that stopped ministers making uninformed comments about Travellers and began to influence policy making, especially the Housing Act 2004. Charles' own appointment to the Commission for Racial Equality was another indication that the disastrous marginalisation of the 1990s was being overcome.

He faced his prolonged final illness with great courage, working normally, with interruptions for chemotherapy or bone marrow transplants, until nearly the end. His marriage had broken up some years previously, and he was cared for by his devoted friend and former fellow Labour councillor, the Gypsy Council treasurer, George Wilson, who survives him, as do his father and mother, Charles and Peggy, his sisters Peggy-Jane and Elaine, and his son, Charles.

Many of Charles' poems dealt with the prejudice that Gypsies and Travellers suffered, but also the vibrancy and diversity of Gypsy and Traveller culture.

Identity: a poem by Charles Smith

What do you see
When you look at me?
Am I the Gypsy
You've read books about?
Am I the Traveller
You heard talk about?
Will you see the folki
Not in the books?
Will you judge my cousins
Just by their looks?
Will you know the Gypsy who lives in your street?
Or the one in the butchers who serves your meat?
What of the midwife who helped at the birth of your son?
Her parents were Gypsies so she must be one

Then there's the old lady who tends all the graves
She preaches the Bible and claims Jesus saves
You will recognise her son who calls with a bell
The other one's a teacher, you won't know him so well
On a stall in the market or shop in the High Street
It might be a Gypsy who owns it who you might regularly meet
It could be your postman, milkman or priest
Busman, mechanic or waiter serving you a feast
So next time you down us, don't just look at a few
Because we are all around and we're looking at you too
And you are not so perfect to be calling us names.
(Taken from 'Not All Wagons and Lanes' by Charles Smith, 1995)

In the foreword to the book *Not all Wagons and Lanes*, Charles outlined what the message being conveyed through this poem was:

> The Gypsy community of this county does not spend all its time hunting rabbits or going to Appleby Fair; we don't sit round the camp fires all day telling old folk tales while we make pegs or paper flowers. Now the truth is, just like everybody else, we are involved with today's modern world. I fear that if we spend too much time living in the past we shall miss what is really happening today and if we do that we just entrench ourselves into the stereotypes that many in the non Gypsy society want us to. (Smith, 1995)

Some reflections on Charles Smith

Why did Charles feel so passionately about taking a stand towards prejudice and yet feel it imperative that his community did not become weighed down and stifled by conservative and static notions of what it means to be a Gypsy and Traveller? Compiling this chapter on Charles Smith, reading his prose and poems and reconnecting with an old friend has been a strange, difficult yet uplifting process. It is difficult to be objective about a friend and important mentor. Looking at his life through a sociological lens, however, raises a number of important questions. C. Wright Mills (1959) contended that sociology draws on the interaction between biography and history, in other words the connection between individual experiences and societal relations. Looking at the trajectory of a human being like Charles Smith we can uncover the processes which shaped his life and what made him identify himself as a member of various groups, including Gypsies, and what made him, nonetheless, unique. In such an endeavour one has to navigate the complexity of personal history, psychology and human agency in shaping motivations.

Looking at what makes a person become an activist, Harré et al (2009) after interviewing eight New Zealand long-term political activists suggest that they went about creating their lives through 'identity projects'. Projected forms of identity can in fact be seen as by-products of heritage and life history and take shape through action. Those actions are shaped by 'community' (a sense of responsibility for the well-being of the people to whom one belongs and by whom one feels valued), 'efficacy' (a feeling that new challenges can be met) and 'integrity' (living according to core values). All of these themes can be traced in Charles' actions.

Like a surprising number of those who identified as Gypsies and Travellers born in the post-war period Charles, was born into a family of mixed ethnicity, his mother being of Gypsy descent and his father being non-Gypsy, a tailor who catered to Gypsy businessmen. Moreover, like many such Gypsies, he was raised in a house. Others of his time and age assimilated or hid their ethnicity or felt a sense of shame. It has been noted that forms of judgemental gaze present profound and powerful forces for 'change'. For example, working-class individuals can be compelled to reject their culture and aspire to middle-class culture (Tyler, 2011). The same processes have been played out with Gypsies and Travellers, with many highly conscious of the prejudice their neighbours and peers hold towards them, leading to many hiding their identity or renouncing it and assimilating. The negative value judgements about the history, heritage and perceived behaviour of Gypsies and Travellers, combined with intense bouts of persecution and assimilation, have created not only a powerful change agenda on GRT communities but a sense of collective trauma within this community. As Alexander et al (2004, p 1) suggest: 'Cultural trauma occurs when members of a collectivity feel they have been subjected to a horrendous event that leaves indelible marks upon their group consciousness, marking their memories forever and changing their future identity in fundamental and irrevocable ways.'

As is evident in Charles' voice in this text, the 'judgemental gaze' was something that Charles had to grapple with throughout his life. Charles noted in his mayoral address how his school housemaster predicted he would end up in prison. During this period Charles was indeed alienated from school and felt he was not literate. This adolescent stage of Charles' life could be labelled as one of disenchantment and alienation, where the values and approved goals of mainstream society seemed to hold out little chance of success for him (cf Merton, 1996). Agnew's (1985, 1992) general strain theory of institutional and societal alienation suggests that these negative emotions and general rebelliousness lead to a search for alternative, oppositional values. It was during this time of confusion and searching that Charles initially flirted with the far Right politics of the National Front, which seemed to support independent small businessmen against the establishment. Disillusion set in when a National Front march attacked a Traveller site in Deptford. A more mature understanding of business interests led him towards mainstream Conservatism, and the neoliberal version of it espoused by Margaret Thatcher in the 1980s. That spirit of enterprise, entrepreneurialism and independence attracted many Gypsies and Travellers, until they were alienated from Conservative politics by the introduction of the Criminal Justice and Public Order Act in 1994. As Charles' political awareness became more refined through his association with the Gypsy Council and his love of poetry, the strategies he adopted departed radically from those of his youth.

Charles' journey towards more progressive politics was further propelled by the conflicts which his growing activism brought him into, often with Conservative councils and councillors opposing sites. However, defiance of the 'gaze' of the mainstream was something that, from Charles' mayoral address and its reference to his self-defence in the face of school-yard taunting, was evident at an early stage. As this recollection indicates, this pride in his identity was due in part to the encouragement of his mother, and also his father, and their desire to remain connected to and celebrate aspects of Gypsy culture, which included visits to fairs and family events and spending time visiting Gypsy relatives, especially those hop-picking in Kent along the Medway river, which could be reached by the small yacht Charles' father had bought.[1] It should be noted that other Gypsy and Traveller children respond to the taunts of the playground and adult life in a range of life strategies, which tend through the vicissitudes of time to become less confrontational. What makes Gypsies and Travellers like Charles exceptional, though, is the fact that they take this celebration of identity into the public sphere, in the case of Charles as an activist, leader and poet. For Charles, prejudice seemed to fuel his determination to make a stand, but this strength was also bolstered by a sense of growing confidence in his own efficacy.

Despite his apparent failure at school, Charles was able to assume challenging and complex political roles. This confidence may have stemmed from the fact that after leaving school he entered into the

Traveller economy and established himself as a successful trader at traditional Gypsy and Traveller fairs. As Acton's obituary notes, at the first Gypsy Council meetings that Charles attended he was a passive participant but, as was typical of Gypsy and Traveller learning practices, moved from observation to doing. In developing his political skills Charles was indebted to the support of his long-standing aides Ann Bagehot, the secretary of the Gypsy Council, and its treasurer, George Wilson. Charles' personal journey of innovation and adoption of new skills, practices, alliances and relationships within and outside of the community disposed him towards 'bridging' forms of social capital (Putnam, 2000) that rejected reactive, insular and conservative forms of Gypsy and Traveller identity. This capacity for change and cultural borrowing was in part attributable to his mixed heritage and life history within and outside the boundaries of tradition. Most prominent among these acts of departing from tradition was living with George Wilson, who became his partner after the break-up of his marriage. This caused some anger and tension among the more traditional sections of the community but it should be noted that, by and large, most of the groups were prepared to continue to work with Charles and his funeral was attended by more conservative members of the community as well as the more culturally progressive.

No culture is static and held in suspended animation. Culture and identity are continually subject to change. It is something that can evolve and, in extreme cases, fundamentally redefine social boundaries and relations with others (cf Anthias and Yuval Davis, 1992). However, identity is increasingly seen as fragmented and fractured (cf Hall and Du Gay, 1997, p 4), but is also fluid and dynamic in a process that has been termed 'new ethnicities' (Hall, 1991), where mixed marriages, neighbourhoods and cultural experiences create new forms of identity that differ from those of the generation that came before them, leaving in their train an imprint reflected in new tastes, views, aspirations and even outward appearance. Charles, like many of his contemporaries, had had experiences differing from those of older or more traditional members of his community. Minorities are defined by the boundaries negotiated and defined by people on both sides, and sanctions and restraints for behaviour outside the group code (Barth, 1969). Unity and 'imagined community', which divides the world into 'us and them', is in part maintained, and ideologically reproduced by a whole system of 'border guards' or what could be termed 'identity managers' that categorise people as members or non-members of a specific collectivity, and are linked to specific cultural codes or styles of dress and behaviour, and customs and language. At times it was the opinion of some of these more 'conservative' identity managers that Charles was not in fact a 'true' or 'proper' Gypsy. A host of reasons would be presented such as his mixed parentage, lifestyle choices and having lived in a house.

However, Charles was sceptical of such conservatism and rationalised that at the heart of Gypsy culture was innovation. It may have been this belief that drove Charles to improve and increase his skill sets and hence the influence he could exert on behalf of his community, and also fuelled a defiance not only towards prejudice but also towards the excessive restraints of tradition. In this sense Charles can be seen as an exemplar of the notion of 'new ethnicities'. As Tyler notes: 'the production of new ethnicities facilitates inclusive notions of belonging that challenge and reformulate essentialist accounts of nationhood, identity and difference. Thus new ethnicities include a diverse sense of who we are and where we come from, whereas the notion of respectability serves to reproduce fixed classed distinctions and hierarchies of belonging' (Tyler, 2011). It may be deceptive to imagine that this is a new phenomenon, as ethnic groups have always adapted and embraced new practices and made them their own, but in a globalised and multiracial society such processes may have become more pronounced.

Charles was driven by a firm sense of moral outrage. He had a strong set of convictions that echoed the assertion of Harré et al (2009) that constructing a strong personal integrity is an important factor in the formation of activists. Charles, like all of us, was not perfect. Charles could be impatient at the pace of change set by those within his community or those around him in campaigns for Gypsy and Traveller equality. This impatience could sometimes manifest itself in anger and scorn and a forceful manner that could alienate some supporters and reduced the breadth of the Gypsy Council leadership, so that some accused it of having become primarily a platform for Charles rather than a broad alliance of activists. Charles' work in the Gypsy and Traveller Law Reform Coalition, however, demonstrated his propensity to work with others. For a period during the life of the Gypsy and Traveller Law Reform Coalition, Charles was Ryder's line manager in his capacity as the development worker. Ryder considers Charles to have been one of the best managers he ever had. It was, however, one particularly stern rebuke from Charles to Ryder that led Ann Bagehot, then Secretary of the Gypsy Council, to confide that Charles, who had been struggling with leukaemia for the best part of a decade, felt he had a limited time to make a change. According to Ann, he wanted to use that time to help his community but that time was finite and he was keen to see change and progress and could thus become frustrated when he felt mistakes were being made.

Ryder's reactions on the interaction of his own life-course with that of Charles are an attempt at reflexivity where emotions and biases are considered in the process of 'understanding' and 'interpretation' (Alldred, 1998). In the process of 'reflexivity' the writer needs to consider the impact of their own 'life story' in the writing of biography. Indeed as Okely (1992) notes in an academic context, 'the personal is theoretical', a notion that stands in contrast to the established academic tradition, which demotes and devalues the personal and allows the writer/researcher to consider the consequences of our relations with others, whether they be conditions of reciprocity, asymmetry or potential exploitation. Reflexivity can be seen as counter to positivist academic approaches. Commenting on this Okely (1992, p 23) argues that the 'reflexive I of the ethnographer subverts the idea of the observer as impersonal machine'. Hence, we as observers have our own particular biases, backgrounds and histories, and it is through these prisms that the reflections on Charles Smith must be weighed and evaluated.

Below, Acton and Ryder reflect individually on their relationship with Charles and how their own life histories shaped interactions and perceptions.

Reflection

Reflection by Ryder: Charles' frustrations with me (cited above) were perhaps born out of several factors. Charles sometimes expressed concern about me moving too quickly and not carrying others in the campaign with me. This was also a criticism that Charles levelled at Grattan Puxon (see Chapter Two). On reflection I can see that Charles was right; Grattan and I were fired by a conviction to do the right thing but this was combined with a sense of immediacy which could be disempowering to the community. Another point of irritation for Charles was my then initial inclination to a New Labour political agenda, which made me at times counsel a more conciliatory approach to the powers that be. However, Charles was aware more than me that centuries of vacillation and compromise had left Gypsies and Travellers at the margins and that in the 21st century delays and prevarication were no longer excusable. Under Charles' mentorship I hope that my political beliefs returned to earlier conceptions I held in my youth as to what socialism meant. In the final year of his life Charles failed to renew his Labour Party membership in protest at the leadership of Tony Blair.

Reflection by Acton: As the editor of Charles' first published writing, and the man who first proposed his election to the National Gypsy Education Council

(NGEC) executive, I had a ringside seat at his remarkable political development and achievements. As Charles moved beyond our collaboration in the 1980s, he grew critical of me and Donald Kenrick and others involved in the earlier phases of the Gypsy Council because we had not attracted larger levels of funding. He actually wrote to me to say that if I and Kenrick had pursued a different strategy, the NGEC could have had premises and employees much earlier. I replied that Kenrick and I were the people Gypsies came to when they *couldn't* raise the money to challenge the authorities. Inevitably the vision of the Gypsy Council was diluted by donor-driven agendas and began to lose the commitment and drive of unpaid activists and membership subscriptions. The agenda to lobby the government was subverted by the pressures of pursuing individual cases. I appreciate that Charles' aspiration was based on a sincere desire to offer more professional support and assistance, but in that drive there was the danger that the Gypsy Council would be consumed by a service agenda and managerialism and in the process cease to act as a stimulus and network for debate and action among Gypsy and Traveller activists. This role was taken over first by the Traveller Law Reform Coalition and then the National Federation of Gypsy Support Groups, which cooperates with the currently reviving Gypsy Council.

Charles felt that a well-resourced and staffed organisation could offer professional and comprehensive support. However, the reality was that the Gypsy Council was in an interim stage, being largely run by the unpaid activism of Charles, Ann and George. Unfortunately the wider committee and membership became too dependent on these core workers and, following Charles' death and the subsequent ill health of George and Ann, much of the bureaucratic structure that they had assembled quickly unravelled.

Charles followed in the footsteps of a number of other dynamic community leaders like Tommy Doherty, Eli Frankham and Tom Lee, all of whom, alongside Charles Smith, can be viewed as what Crook et al (1992) have called 'exemplary figures' – those whose militancy and activism makes them a beacon for social struggle. Charles' life, however, may be more of a harbinger for the dilemmas of future generations of activists, given the personal conflicts he experienced between tradition and innovation in lifestyle choices, alliances and political strategies and his desire to develop modern and efficient organisation. Whether the course he chose to steer in terms of activism was the most effective or transformative is at the heart of the discussion that threads through this book.

In Memoriam

In memory of Ann Bagehot MBE (1944–2014) former Secretary of the Gypsy Council who recently passed away – a strong and valiant fighter for Gypsy, Roma and Traveller communities who will be remembered with great affection.

Note

[1] Charles, when he became a father, took great care to immerse his son, Charles Smith Jnr, in Gypsy traditions, encouraging him to visit the fairs and Gypsy Council meetings and developing his own market stall business.

References

Acton, T. (2005) 'Gypsy activist, poet, and film-maker, he once ran a successful antiques business', *The Guardian*, 13 November.

Agnew, R. (1985) 'A revised strain theory of delinquency', *Social Forces*, vol 64, pp 151–67.

Agnew, R. (1992) 'Foundation for a general strain theory of crime and delinquency', *Criminology*, vol 30, pp 47–87.

Alexander, J., Eyerman, R., Giesen, B., Smelser, N. and Sztompka, P. (2004) *Cultural Trauma and Collective Identity*, Berkeley, CA: University of California Press.

Alldred, P. (1998) 'Ethnography and discourse analysis – dilemmas in representing the voices of children', in J. Ribbens, and R. Edwards (eds) *Feminist Dilemmas in Qualitative Research: Public Knowledge and Private Lives*, London Thousand Oaks, New Delhi: Sage, pp 56–78.

Anthias, F. and Yuval Davis, N. (1992) *Racialised Boundaries*, London: Routledge.

Barth, F. (ed) (1969) *The Social Organisation of Cultural Difference*, Bergen, Oslo: UniversitetsForlaget.

Crook, S., Pakulski, J. and Waters, M. (1992) *Postmodernization: Change in Advanced Society*, Cambridge: Polity Press.

Hall, S. (1991) 'Old and new identities, old and new ethnicities', in E. King (ed) *Culture, Globalisation and the World System*, London: Macmillan, pp 41–68.

Hall, S. and Du Gay, P. (1997) *Questions of Cultural Identity*, London and Thousand Oaks, CA: Sage.

Harré, N., Tepavac, S. and Bullen, P. (2009) 'Integrity, efficacy and community in the stories of political activists', *Qualitative Research in Psychology*, vol 6, no 4, pp 330–45.

Merton, R.K. (1996) 'A life of learning', in R.K. Merton and P. Sztompka (eds) *On Social Structure and Science*, Chicago, IL: The University of Chicago Press, pp 339–59.

Okely, J. (1992) 'Anthropology and autobiography: participatory experience and embodied knowledge', in J. Okely, and H. Callaway (eds) (1992) *Anthropology and Autobiography*, London: Routledge, pp 1–28.

Okely, J. and Callaway, H. (1992) 'Preface', in J. Okely and H. Callaway (eds) *Anthropology and Autobiography*, London: Routledge, pp ix–xii.

Press Association (2005) 'Gypsy Rights Campaigner Dies', by Caroline Gammell, PA Deputy Chief Reporter, 8 November, see http://news.bbc.co.uk/2/hi/uk_news/england/essex/4418106.stm.

Putnam, R.D. (2000) *Bowling Alone: The Collapse and Revival of American Community*, New York, NY: Simon and Schuster.

Smith, C. (1995) *Not all Wagons and Lanes*, Avely: Essex County Council.

Smith, C. (2002) *The First Romani Mayor in the United Kingdom*, inaugural speech of Mr Charles Smith as Mayor of Castle Point published by the European Roma Rights Centre, 10 July 2002, www.errc.org/cikk.php?cikk=919.

Tyler, K. (2011) 'New ethnicities and old classities: respectability and diaspora', *Social Identities: Journal for the Study of Race, Nation and Culture*, vol 17, no 4, pp 523–42.

Wright Mills, C. (1959) *The sociological imagination*, New York: Oxford University Press.

FIVE

Friends, Families and Travellers: organising to resist extreme moral panics

Neil Ansell, with Rob Torkington

Who are New Travellers?

This chapter seeks to give insights into the early development of the support group Friends, Families and Travellers, which began to organise around the needs of 'New Travellers' in 1994, but in the 21st century has put its experience and expertise at the service of the whole GRT community. Its transition, from its original name 'Friends and Families *of* Travellers' (1996) to its present name 'Friends, Families *and* Travellers', perhaps encapsulates the transition from an 'external' help and support network to an organisation that places a greater focus on community participation.

'New Travellers' built a very specific identity and image during the 1960s, something that was rather more than the trickle of individuals and families into commercial nomadic lifestyles as opportunities arise, such as itinerant workers following the agricultural seasons such as the hop picking in Kent, or various recycling opportunities that arose during the Industrial Revolution. In time, some of these people have assimilated into the existing Gypsy and Traveller communities. But over the course of the past couple of generations, this trickle turned at times into more of a steady stream, motivated in part by economic changes and also in part by ideology.

The mostly young people in this movement, in the literal sense of the term, have often been called New Age Travellers (Lowe and Shaw, 1993; Stangroome, 1993), though seldom by themselves, as this term was more of a media construct. The participants were more likely to refer to themselves as New Travellers, or more likely just as Travellers. Here we shall use the name New Travellers, to distinguish this group from the traditional communities. There has been very little integration and they have remained quite distinct from the Gypsy and Irish Traveller communities, who have tended to regard them with suspicion. While traditional Travellers tend to travel in extended, multi-generational family groups, New Travellers, at least in the earlier years, have generally chosen to travel in quite large groups of unrelated individuals and nuclear family units, with the vast majority being of a similar age, typically from the late teens to early thirties. This is of course a generalisation – there will be some who do not fit this pattern. It is also worth noting that there is a small proportion of New Travellers who claim Gypsy ancestry, whose parents or grandparents have settled into housing and who claim to be returning to their nomadic roots, and an even smaller number who are from the traditional communities themselves but have been expelled or left and subsequently found common cause with the New Travellers. The fact that the New Travellers are sometimes seen as having emerged out of the 'hippy' movement of the 1960s and are suspected of a rejection of family values, of sexual immorality, of being irreligious and of drug use, has also led to on-going suspicion from the traditional communities, who often have more conservative views and keep New Travellers at a distance through a fear that they might be a negative influence on their own young people. Though this depiction of New Travellers is a stereotype, it is not without some truth – New Travellers will themselves tell you of the harm they have seen caused to their peers by drugs, and of the losing battles they have fought to keep their own sites drug free.

New Travellers first came to public attention in the 1970s, in association with the development of the free festival movement. Young people began to acquire live-in vehicles in which they could move freely from festival to festival, and for some this became a more permanent arrangement and a lifestyle (Earle et al, 1994). These early New Travellers were relatively few in number and did not attract huge public awareness. This all began to change from the beginning of the 1980s. Political changes saw a rapid rise in unemployment, particularly among the young, while at the same time housing benefit restrictions on the under-25s made it increasingly hard for young people to move away from the family home and strike out on their own. It was a time of rapidly rising youth homelessness, and many saw taking to the open road as a rational choice. These new arrivals were largely from the punk generation; rather than the hippy sensibilities of the earlier New Travellers, they held to a more confrontational and politicised do-it-yourself ethos, and often originated from the urban poor rather than from the middle classes. This group, in rejecting society, found themselves rejected by society in turn, and gained little public sympathy. Sibley (1997, p 228) asserted that, unlike Gypsies,

> New Age Travellers conjure up no romantic associations.
> They cannot claim exotic origins....The ascription covers a
> loose grouping of people ... who have decided to travel or,
> if sedentary, to live without many of the material comforts
> of mainstream society....An image of dependency combines
> with popular associations ... to create a pariah group.

These rapidly rising numbers on the road had an increasing visibility,
exacerbated by the tendency of some among them to travel in much
larger groups than traditional Travellers; most notably the 'peace convoy',
which regularly travelled in groups of over a hundred vehicles. The free
festival circuit still remained very much a part of the New Travellers'
year, with festivals such as the Green Gathering at Glastonbury
attracting thousands. These festivals served a similar function for the
New Traveller movement to that which horse fairs traditionally had
done for Gypsies – as a centre for economic activity, as an opportunity
for widely dispersed nomadic groups to re-establish old contacts and
make new ones. A seemingly safe space of resistance (Willis et al, 1993)
enabled a counter-cultural resistance to dominant values (in the sense
of Cohen, 2002) and served as the locus for nascent activism within
the community, with the distribution of cheaply produced fliers and
newsletters, some of which became well established; perhaps the best-
known example is *Festival Eye* magazine, which was launched in 1996.

Of all the free festivals in the circuit, though, the key event in the
Travellers' year was the Stonehenge Free Festival. There had been
gatherings at the summer solstice at Stonehenge every year since
1974, and each year they had grown larger. By 1984, the numbers had
swelled to an astonishing peak of maybe 100,000, and the government
of the day determined that this would no longer be tolerated. As Andy
Worthington (2005, p 5) claims, 'Behind this rationale, however, there
was also a strong desire to decommission the whole of the travellers'
(sic) movement, which had become increasingly politicised throughout
the early 1980s.' Painted as folk devils in a moral panic in the media,
New Travellers, and Gypsies generally, were deemed to be a lawless
and anti-social threat (Richardson, 2006), and were made the excuse
for a series of attacks on civil liberties, especially through the Public
Order Act 1986 (Kenrick and Bakewell, 1995) and Criminal Justice
and Public Order Act of 1994 (Greenfields, 2008).

These laws can be seen as marking the failure of a resistance that was
often more romantically symbolic than practical, offering what Cohen
(2002) describes as 'magical solutions', like taking drugs or mods and
rockers fighting, not logically or actually connected to the source of the

problem or confronting the material base of subordination or sustaining an organised challenge. Perhaps the goals of many of the New Travellers did not go far beyond wanting to get on with their own lives in peace, but their very existence began to be seen as a threat to the 'status quo' and to generate symptoms of a 'moral panic' (Hetherington, 2000). As Karner (2004) puts it: 'Voluntarily opting-out, "deciding to travel" and to shop for no more than the essentials may be the ultimate ideological affront against the dominant social order in times of postmodernity.' After the dispersal of the 'Peace Convoy' near Wakefield in 1984, the regrouping of Travellers to go to Stonehenge for the 1985 summer solstice seemed to provoke a decision by the authorities that they had to be prevented from going ahead, at any cost.

On 1 June a sizeable convoy of New Travellers (around 140 vehicles containing perhaps nearly 500 men, women and children) was heading towards Stonehenge when they were intercepted by a force of 1,300–1,400 riot police drawn from six different police authorities, plus the Ministry of Defence. In the events that followed, many of the Travellers sustained injury, and many of their live-in vehicles were destroyed. Publicity at the time was extremely hostile to the New Traveller movement, and the events of the day were widely misreported. 'Stonehenge hippies attack police' was the headline in the *Mail on Sunday*. While there have been many other conflicts between police and New Travellers, before and since this event, the 'Battle of the Beanfield' remains notorious, and subsequent investigations have largely exonerated the Travellers from blame and found the conduct of the police disproportionate. Five years after these events, 24 people arrested at the beanfield went on to successfully sue the police for false imprisonment, assault and destruction of property (Worthington, 2005).

Nonetheless, legislation was put in place in 1986, the Public Order Act, which would make the continuance of the Stonehenge Free Festival a virtual impossibility and would create further legal barriers which would render the furtherance of a nomadic lifestyle an increasing challenge. According to Worthington (2005, p 212), the biggest impact came from

> its notorious 'anti-hippy' clause 39, which edged closer to the criminalisation of trespass. Under the new clause, which applied to scheduled monuments (including Stonehenge), 'land forming part of a highway,' and agricultural buildings, the police were enabled to arrest two or more people for trespass, provided that 'reasonable steps have been taken by or on behalf of the occupier to ask them to leave.' In

addition, the previous requirement of arrest under these circumstances – damage to property – was amended to include the use of 'threatening, abusive or insulting words or behaviour' and/or the presence of 12 or more vehicles.

It is undoubtedly the case that a proportion of the first wave of New Travellers saw which way the wind was blowing and gave up their adopted lifestyle at this time, or moved abroad (Dearling, 1998), but there was a new generation coming of age and ready to take their place, and the overall number of New Travellers continued to grow rather than diminish.

The late 1980s saw the arrival of a new type of dance music, closely associated with the arrival of a new drug, ecstasy, and the modus operandi of party promoters on this music scene was to organise large-scale outdoor events of which the public would be informed only at the last possible moment. To some extent, the New Travellers found common cause with the rave generation, with some sound systems being closely linked to Traveller groups, though they were not always the most comfortable of bedfellows. The New Travellers generally had some sense of not deliberately provoking landowners and of respecting the land, while the ravers, parachuting in with no longer-term plan than to dance, drink and take drugs for a day before returning home, had no such scruples. In the corridors of power, however, the two problems were increasingly being seen as largely inseparable.

Events finally came to a head at Castlemorton Common in 1992. In May of that year, thousands of New Travellers and ravers were travelling to the annual Avon Free Festival, the largest annual gathering since Stonehenge. Avon and Somerset police launched Operation Nomad to stop them getting there. Pushed out of the area, they gathered at Castlemorton Common in the Malverns, and there began a week-long party that attracted 20,000–40,000 people (depending on whom you ask).

The event attracted a huge amount of publicity. Simon Reynolds, in his history of rave culture and electronic dance music, wrote that 'during the next five days of its existence, Castlemorton will inspire questions in Parliament, make the front page of every newspaper in England and incite nationwide panic about the whereabouts of the next destination on the crusty itinerary' (Reynolds, 1999, p 167).

'New age travellers? Not in this age! Not in any age!'

In the wake of Castlemorton the government pinned the blame squarely on the shoulders of the New Travellers, with then Prime Minister John Major giving a vitriolic speech in which he essentially vowed to bring the movement to its knees and stated: 'Society needs to condemn a little more and understand a little less. New age travellers? Not in this age! Not in any age!' Prior to this he rationalised his logic on the matter:

> There's another problem we are dealing with – the illegal occupation of land by so-called 'new age travellers' ... They say that we don't understand them. Well, I'm sorry – but if rejecting materialism means destroying the property of others, then I don't understand. If 'doing your own thing' means exploiting the social security system and sponging off others, then I don't want to understand. If alternative values mean a selfish and lawless disregard for others, then I won't understand. Let others speak for these new age travellers. We will speak for their victims. (Major, 1992)

This public opprobrium was translated into legislation, the draconian Criminal Justice and Public Order Act (CJPOA) of 1994. While parts of this Act were targeted squarely at the rave generation – outdoor parties were made effectively illegal by Section 63(1)(b), which outlawed the performance of 'sounds wholly or predominantly characterised by a succession of repetitive beats' – it also made the pursuit of a nomadic lifestyle a near impossibility. It repealed the Caravan Sites Act 1968 and gave the police wide-ranging new powers of near-instant eviction from public places. The 1968 Act had placed a duty on local authorities to provide pitches on Traveller sites according to local need. Although flawed – after 26 years in force, there were still many councils that had yet to fulfil their obligations – it was seen as better than nothing. Since the repeal of this Act, pitch availability on local authority sites has become as rare as hens' teeth. Greenfields (2008) calculated that

> in 2005, a homeless Gypsy/Traveller at an 'unauthorised location' (both self-owned sites without planning permission and roadside encampments) would wait on average 27 years to access an authorized site at the then-current rate of site provision.

While the CJPOA claimed primarily to target relatively new alternative youth cultures, its impact on traditional Travellers was overwhelming, with them being placed in a Catch-22 situation where unauthorised camping was increasingly being criminalised, while the supply of authorised pitches almost came to a full stop. Greenfields (2008) asserts:

> The three options available consisted of settlement into housing; residence on unauthorized roadside sites, (risking both the punitive criminal justice system and experiencing racist abuse and physical violence like broken windows in caravans or threats to burn out their caravans from passers-by or locals who did not want 'gyppos' or 'pikies' living near to them); or to purchase and develop (usually as part of an extended family group) an 'unauthorized' site.

There was widespread dismay at the implications of the CJPOA, leading to the establishment of the organisation Friends, and Families of Travellers (FFT). As the name indicates, this started life as a fairly informal support group of relatives and supporters of New Travellers. There was a small office in Glastonbury, in the New Travellers' heartland of the West Country, run by founder-member Steve Staines, a former soil scientist and teacher, not a New Traveller himself but with close relatives (son and granddaughter) who were travelling, and a loose network of support groups around the country. Staines describes the rationale for the start of his activism:

> a group of Travellers had been occupying a redundant council farm in Somerset and were evicted – one of the Travellers who briefly resisted was manhandled by the police and ended up in hospital. I had told TV about the eviction in the hope that TV presence would calm things a bit … I rang the police at the end of the school working day (I was working as a teacher then). I spoke to the local inspector in charge of the eviction who told me that the Travellers had asked the TV crew to leave. Later talking to my son I learnt the reverse was the case. Later, looking at a newspaper which contained photos of the eviction my granddaughter pointed to the police and said 'bad man, bad man'. The contradiction with what I was supposed to be teaching 10 year olds at school about the police was glaring. These incidents conspired to make me think that there was

a need for an organisation to give support and help to the mostly harmless Travellers.[1]

Staines (2008) describes the early activities of FFT:

> I was very worried about what was going to happen to my granddaughter, a 'New Traveller', if she got caught up in the nasty evictions the [CJPOA] Act promised. We set up [FFT] to start lobbying. Luckily, we linked up with the Public Law Project in London, which specialises in judicial review work. We managed to work together in bringing forward a successful judicial review [the Wealden Judgement] in 1995, which meant that local authorities had to investigate the situation of people and make assessments of their safety before they were able to make a decision to evict. That sometimes slowed the whole process down. FFT took off from there.

In an interview that Staines gave to Sarah Cemlyn in 1997 he outlined FFT's views on inclusive forms of development and the need for local authorities to enter into dialogue and partnerships with Gypsy and Traveller communities:

> "Rather than going in, seeing a problem and going in with a solution which they impose, which I've seen too often ... they should be looking at ways of fostering some sort of community organisation development within the sites they have. This is particularly related to council sites and enabling people to take control of their lives.... bureaucracy is notoriously bad at dealing with real issues ... the people on the ground know what the issues are. They just need help to define the issues..and finding their own way out of problems."

At the time such an approach was innovative; little consideration was being given to issues of empowerment in a service context. It was a stance that became more pronounced in FFT's later work with service providers (see Chapter Six).

Another innovative feature evident in FFT's founding ethos was to protect the right to travel for all who chose it: 'We seek to end racism and discrimination against Gypsies and Travellers, whatever their ethnicity, culture or background, whether settled or mobile, and to protect the right to pursue a nomadic way of life' (FFT mission statement, from www.gypsy-traveller.org). This all-inclusiveness meant that, in spite of its New Traveller origins, FFT would eventually be campaigning as much on behalf of Gypsies and Irish Travellers as it was for New Travellers. The decision to accept and work with all Travellers based on acceptance of 'self-definition' was justified by Steve Staines as follows:

> "self definition ... it's the only way to go ... otherwise you spend all your time as I do in so many local authority working parties – deciding who we're actually talking about and who we're not talking about and what they are responsible for..it's a waste of time. It's a taxonomic device devised by those in power to disempower those with without power.... you label them (separately) and disempower them." (Cemlyn interview, 1997)

It took time for FFT's inclusive approach to be accepted by Gypsies and Irish Travellers who had survived for generations by keeping a relatively low profile, and could hardly be blamed for feeling that the new arrivals, with their high visibility and huge public gatherings, had brought down a whole heap of trouble on their heads in the CJPOA.

Activism within the New Traveller community was hindered by the fact that almost all live with the insecurity of being on unauthorised encampments, although some may have had greater access to education in their earlier lives than many in the traditional communities, and they may have stronger links with the settled community because of their backgrounds. Many activists among Gypsies and Irish Travellers also come from among those who have settled into housing, or are at least on secure sites. It is not easy to engage in planned action when you don't know where you will be living next week. Also, perhaps many New Travellers, seeing the world from an anarchistic or individualistic perspective, have an innate resistance to organisation.

The arrival of FFT, although in its early days it was very unstructured and had chronic funding problems, was an avenue through which New Travellers could engage. Initially there was a lot of direct contact with the client base, with activists constantly travelling around the South of England visiting sites and being there for evictions and planning appeals, which were important points of interaction with those being assisted by FFT. The FFT newsletter was also a valuable resource for people on sites when it was handed out, as it had useful contacts and relevant legal articles (often written with the help of Chris Johnson, who later set up the Travellers' Advice Team). One source of help that gave FFT immediate and at times challenging insights into life on the road was the 24-hour helpline that fed into case-work and later advocacy work. Sometimes calls would be received in the middle of the night or at the crack of dawn and the FFT worker staffing the phone would need to counsel and guide a Traveller through their legal rights in the middle of an on-going and generally traumatic process of eviction.

As FFT grew there was a need to focus and develop its case-work and advocacy and attract greater funding, which thus entailed more formalised organisation. Susan Alexander, an initial volunteer, then paralegal worker, and then replacement for Steve Staines as National Coordinator of FFT in 1998, played an important role in this transition, as did the decision to relocate FFT's centre of operations away from Glastonbury to Brighton.[2] In Glastonbury FFT was becoming a drop-in centre for local homeless people and being distracted from its core role through drug- and alcohol-abuse alleviation work, taking away from the core work of the organisation. With the setting up of the Robert Barton Trust (RBT) in Glastonbury, FFT was able to disengage from this work (as no one else had been providing anything like it until RBT was set up) and relocate. The South-West still held large numbers of new Travellers, around Bristol and, in particular, throughout Dorset and Devon. Susan Alexander (personal communication) recounts the rationale for the move:

> Leaving the South West was a difficult decision and the move was criticised by some who felt that it would leave a serious gap in provision. The move was in part justified by the fact that the Children's Society continued to have a significant presence in the area and that Brighton had established agencies already working with street homeless and those suffering from drug and alcohol issues and that FFT, which was developing a reputation for national policy input, would benefit from being closer to London. The move to Brighton meant that FFT was able to tap into a far greater pool of volunteers with professional skills and it was there that Emma Nuttal, Zoe Matthews and Avril Fuller were recruited as volunteers and eventually engaged as core members of staff. The move also facilitated the recruitment of professionals such as Neil Ansell (then a professional journalist) and Marc Willers (a barrister) onto the Board of Directors. Without the support offered me in the early days in Brighton by these volunteers and a stronger management

committee, the organisation would have folded. All of this was critical in helping the organisation develop from the small under-staffed, under-managed and under-resourced organisation it was, into the professional and well managed organisation it is today.

Alongside the changes in structure and organisation there was also a shift in the focus of the organisation's work; when it began, the vast majority of its clients were New Travellers – now these represent less than a quarter of its casework clients. Though in the early days this change arose as bridges were gradually built with the Gypsy and Irish Traveller communities, it is also noticeable that there has been a significant decline in the numbers of New Travellers on our roadsides.

Rob Torkington has been a dedicated director/trustee of FFT since 1997 (for much of this time travelling to meetings in Brighton or London all the way from Scotland) and also served for some time as a trustee of Travellers Aid Trust (see Chapter Eight) and a representative on the Traveller Law Reform Coalition. His background is that he began to travel full time in 1990 – although he had long been on the fringes of the scene, and had been close friend to some of those present at the 'Battle of the Beanfield' in 1984. Summing up the origins and development of FFT, Torkington argues: "We [FFT] really were a bunch of hippies doing our best in those days. Now we are a professional organisation with a structured workforce." In the following edited extracts from an interview, Rob Torkington describes his experiences of travelling, motivation to become an activist and experiences of the early days of FFT.

Edited interview with Rob Torkington (interviewed by Neil Ansell)

Rob describes moving into and out of nomadism: Towards the later '80s, the car and tent were replaced with a 25 year old converted out-patient ambulance. My partner and I finally took the plunge in about 1990, we disposed of most of our possessions, moved into the ambulance, and headed off to the nearest festival. Once at an event, it was easy to make friends and then move on with a small group of people. It was also easy to find out where the next festival would be, and where sites were.

I had a dream of living in Scotland, so after a summer of some festivals and many confrontations with the police, we moved up to the Highlands via a network of established sites. This was very beautiful, but a very, very hard way of life. Living so close to nature, we were particularly affected by the fact that daylight diminishes to as little as 6 hours per day, and there is an awful lot of wooding and water fetching to be done in that time! I parked up on a site in a lay-by on the West coast, and a few hundred yards further down the road were some 'Scottish Gypsy Travellers'. They used to walk up to us to do business, and cups of tea were shared on both sites.

The first time I arrived on the West coast was early one November. We stopped at Raspberry lay-by for one night on our way up north, but the occupants insisted we stayed a couple of days for their bonfire party at the weekend. On the night of the party, a white Transit minibus suddenly arrived and started disgorging stocky young men with cropped hair. They were so clearly Gypsy boys and my initial assumption was they had come for a bit of bother. I was about to start banging on people's doors and shouting a warning, when I realised that they had brought their kids with them, a barrel of beer and a big box of fireworks! It was a bit of a culture shock for me, having just come up from the south of England.

Later I moved to rural Lincolnshire, again on small sites, mostly green lanes, and stayed in the same area for 10 years. Our sites were all low profile, and we would get at least 3 months before eviction, often a year plus. In this time, I got a poste-restante address and a 'respectable' job, including government security clearance. Over that time, most of my small group of friends moved on and I spent the last few years living alone on green lanes. I always enjoyed my double life as a responsible maintenance engineer on a military site by day, and a dirty hippy by night!

My hard work was eventually rewarded by the offer of a big promotion and a move to my beloved Scotland. I saw this as a new chapter in my life, and took the difficult decision to sell my beautiful Vickers trailer and move into a house in 2010.

Rob describes his activism – I first found out about FFT in 1996 when I met Viv (Vivian Hughes). She travelled around in an old ambulance visiting ancient sites/hill forts and looking for crop circles, and wrote the spares file for the FFT newsletter which, as well as being an interesting and amusing chronicle of her travels, was also an invaluable list of names and phone numbers for Traveller friendly scrap yards and the like. Anyone who has ever owned, let alone travelled in a classic vehicle will know how hard it is to keep the things running. Remember that at the time, most people did not have mobile phones or internet access.

Whenever I saw Viv she told me I should get involved with FFT, so the next year I travelled down to the AGM at Oxford. I had been having a pretty torrid time lately, with numerous evictions and underhand tactics, and at times illegal actions by the Police. I was overwhelmed to meet all these well-meaning and dedicated people. None of them were Travellers, but they were fighting really hard for MY human rights! I wasn't sure how much I had to offer, but I started attending meetings and contributing what I could.

My earliest activism was entirely based on self interest, although when I did manage to secure a small concession for my efforts, my immediate neighbours usually benefitted as well. I had brushed up on my legal knowledge .... I was always careful not to be too cocky when dealing with the police, but I often got the feeling that I actually knew more about the particular laws affecting my situation than they did! In the early days, I gained more moral support from FFT than actual practical help. I slowly learnt enough about the law that I could pass on simple advice to the uninitiated. I learnt enough about my rights that I can calmly but firmly request what I am entitled to. I went from feeling powerless and marginalised to feeling empowered. This whole experience of activism has helped me develop personally too. I would never have believed that I could address a crowded hall at a conference, or sit on a stage at a festival and give a workshop on planning issues. I don't know how much of a lasting impact I have made on the Traveller activist scene, but I know what an impact it has made on me!

FFT has come a long way since the little office in Glastonbury with Tony Thompson (a longstanding volunteer and stalwart of FFT) sleeping under the desk. When we first got the Community Base office in Brighton it seemed huge. Funding was so tight that one summer we ran out of money completely, and Alex (Susan Alexander then full time worker) had to sign on the dole to keep going.

We relied on individuals, or small groups who had managed to get hold of a little bit of information to aid self-empowerment. Letters were written by hand and dole money was saved up for paper, envelopes and stamps. Despite the lack of resources, our self-empowerment did sometimes pay dividends. On one occasion in the Highlands, the police started using the Criminal Trespass Act (Scotland) against us, apparently at the request of Highland Regional Council, whose land we were occupying. We managed to make contact with a sympathetic independent councillor, who invited the whole of the site to a full meeting of the council in Inverness. He made a rousing speech in Gaelic and we all cheered. The rest of the councillors applauded politely, despite not appearing to have understood any more of the speech than we did! The police action stopped abruptly, and we got our pictures on the front page of the Scottish Guardian!

(FFT in its early days) was certainly closer to the grass roots, and could offer at least moral support to anyone suffering any sort of crisis. There was someone on the end of the phone 24 hours who could be contacted in a crisis, but again this was largely moral support, and it is perhaps debatable exactly what real practical help could be offered. Although there was some casework carried out, there was also a lot of 'signposting' to other organisations. This service became less essential when Community Law Partnership came along and the Traveller Advice Team was on hand to offer 'pukka legal' advice when it was required.[3] Today FFT is a more professional and effective organisation in many other ways. Casework is carried out in a structured and well resourced manner. There is effective monitoring of outcomes, and the data gathered then feeds into our policy development and campaigning.

After Susan Alexander left, two Directors were appointed but did not remain in post long creating huge instability. We had no national coordinator and I would work away on my laptop every lunchtime and evening trying to keep the organisation going supporting the Office Manager Emma Nuttall who worked way beyond her hours to keep the organisation running. This was very satisfying at the time, and I got a lot of adrenalin out of it, but it was not really sustainable. I am very happy with the way the organisation, and my own personal role, have developed. We have both matured! Now I just sit on a well-structured democratic board and ratify the decisions of a competent and professional director (Chris Whitwell).

The impact of FFT

FFT emerged as a response to the State's attempts to clampdown on a counter-culture and nomadic forms of lifestyle. The State's response with new draconian laws and surveillance presented a significant development with wider implications for civil liberties and traditional lifestyles (O'Brien, 2009). The forces ranged against New and other Travellers in this period of growing enforcement by the State were immense and the success FFT enjoyed in relative terms was always going to be limited. Counter-cultures are not characterised by mass membership or formal organisations and the propensity for 'magical solutions' where angst and resistance take 'blind alleys' and false turns invariably saps the potency and challenge that a counter-culture can generate. During its early period FFT was confronted with difficult dilemmas: should it remain a loose and more informal support group or incorporate itself into the formalised third sector and access funding and staff. In the course of time the latter direction was taken, which has had clear implications in terms of the bureaucratic structures and approaches that have had to be adopted to sustain new directions. Reflecting this change as was noted in the introduction the name was changed from Friends and Families *of* Travellers to Friends, Families and Travellers in 1998 just before Steve Staines ended his role as Director and signified the fact that Travellers were playing a more active role within FFT and that it was felt the organisation should strive to empower and involve community members. These new strategies though in the opinion of the governance, staff and membership of FFT can be justified, for instance it has made some contribution in further understanding and alliances between New Traveller and traditional Traveller communities as reflected by its mixed Traveller staff team but also clientele. It can also be justified in the sense that it has enabled the organisation to give more professional and meaningful support in its case and outreach work but also an incisive input into national advocacy and policy change which in its own way still presents a strong and critical challenge to social injustice. Reflecting on these transitions Rob Torkington notes:

> I think that the 'radicals', if that's what you wish to call us, have matured. We are focusing on our skills, and making best use of them. Many of us have good educations, even to degree level, and we are using our intellectual abilities to good effect. In the old days, when we felt powerless and rejected by society, it may have felt empowering for some to throw a brick at a riot shield, even if such an action seldom has a positive outcome. These days, it feels even more empowering to engage in debate through a framework where our views can be heard by central government and we can contribute to real change'.

Notes

[1] Personal communication to authors by Steve Staines in 2013.

[2] Steve Staines had kept FFT going for a number of years through his energy and determination and eventually succumbed to what activists term 'burn out'. Although he needed to recuperate he was later to return to FFT and become its planning officer, playing a key role in monitoring the New Labour government's Regional Spatial Strategies and plans for site provision.

[3] The Travellers' Advice Team operates a legal advice helpline and is part of the Birmingham Community Law Partnership based in Birmingham.

References

Cohen, S. (2002) *Folk Devils and Moral Panic: The creation of mods and rockers* (new edn), London and New York: Routledge.

Dearling, A. (1998) *No Boundaries: New Travellers on the Road (outside of England)*, Lyme Regis: Enabler Publications.

Earle, F., Dearling, A., Whittle, H., Glasse, R. and Gubby, Y. (1994) *A Time to travel? An introduction to Britain's Newer Travellers*, Lyme Regis: Enabler Publications.

Friends, Families and Travellers (1996) *A Travellers' Guide*, Glastonbury: FFT.

Greenfields, M. (2008) 'Gypsies, Travellers, and British land conflicts', *Peace Review: A Journal of Social Justice*, vol 20, no 3, pp 300–9.

Hetherington, K. (2000) *New Age Travellers: Vanloads of Uproarious Humanity*, London: Cassell.

Karner, C. (2004) 'Theorising Power and Resistance among "Travellers"', *Social Semiotics*, vol 14, no 3, pp 249–71.

Kenrick, D. and Bakewell, S. (1995) *On the Verge: the Gypsies of England*, St Albans: University of Hertfordshire Press.

Lowe, R. and Shaw, W. (1993) *Travellers: Voices of the New Age Nomads*, London: Fourth Estate.

Major, J. (1992) Leader's speech, Conservative Party Conference, www. johnmajor.co.uk/page1208.html.

O'Brien, M. (2009) 'Still on the road? Technology and historical perspectives on counter-cultural policing', *Information & Communications Technology Law*, vol 18, no 3, pp 285–96.

Reynolds, S. (1999) *Generation Ecstasy: Into the World of Techno and Rave Culture*, London: Routledge.

Richardson, J. (2006) *The Gypsy Debate: Can Discourse Control?*, Exeter and Charlottesville: Imprint Academic.

Sibley, D. (1997) 'Endangering the sacred: Nomads, youth cultures and the English countryside', in P. Cloke and J. Little (eds) *Contested Countryside Cultures*, London: Routledge, pp 218–31.

Staines S. (2008) 'Scientist, teacher, activist', *Inside Housing*, 19 December, www.insidehousing.co.uk/scientist-teacher-activist/6502364.article.

Stangroome, V. (1993) *Investigation into Policies, Priorities and Resources Available to New Age Travellers: The Hippy Convoy*, London: privately published by the author.

Willis, P. with James, S., Canaan, J. and Hurd, G. (1993) *Common Culture: Symbolic Work at Play in the Everyday Cultures of the Young*, Milton Keynes: Open University Press.

Worthington, A. (ed) (2005) *The Battle of the Beanfield*, Eyemouth, Berwickshire: Enabler Publications.

SIX

Building bridges, shifting sands: changing community development strategies in the Gypsy and Traveller voluntary sector since the 1990s

Angus McCabe, with Yvonne MacNamara and Sarah Mann[1]

Introduction

Fonseca (1996) said that Gypsies are a people who live outside history; an odd statement – given the impact of history, particularly on European Roma. This chapter refutes such an a-historical approach, by using case studies of two organisations, the Traveller Movement (TM) and Friends, Families and Travellers (FFT). In Chapter Five, the early phase of FFT was explored; this chapter explores its further development together with that of the TM, both of which rank among some of the most established and formalised Gypsy, Roma and Traveller (GRT) third sector groups. This chapter places community and voluntary sector development in the Gypsy and Traveller community in a wider policy and practice context. In doing so it explores the role of both organisations in 'building bridges' – within and between communities, between Gypsies, Travellers and 'mainstream' services and between these communities and the policy-making process.

Bridge building has, however, taken place in the 'shifting sands' of political and economic change. This applies at two levels. Over the last two decades, commentators have noted substantial intra-community 'shifts', namely, the collapse of the traditional Traveller economy, and also higher (though still limited) levels of educational attainment and a debate within the community about gender roles (Ryder, 2012). At a macro-political level, following the banking crisis of 2008, and particularly following the change of government after the 2010 election, there has been retrenchment, with cuts to local authority budgets and, with austerity, some would say, a dilution in commitments to equalities agendas (Centre for Local Economic Strategies and Centre for Local Policy Studies 2012).

One should not exaggerate the change in the climate within which FFT and TM have evolved and currently work. There are also striking continuities in public attitudes, the persistence of discrimination against Gypsy and Traveller communities and continuing media hostility. At another level there have been policy continuities: the Coalition government's Localism Act (2011) bears more than a passing resemblance to the 'double devolution' and Communities in Control (2008) agenda of the New Labour administrations. Linked to this is the political interest and at least rhetorical, as well as limited financial, support under New Labour for community empowerment (prior to the 2010 election) and, under the Coalition administration, for social action. But perhaps the most striking continuity is the position of Gypsy and Traveller communities in terms of social exclusion, poverty, ill health and morbidity rates, as consistently attested in research over the past two decades (Cemlyn et al, 2009) as well as in the earlier chapters of this book.

The present chapter explores the changing roles and character of FFT and TM in terms of promoting inclusive community development within Gypsy and Traveller communities at three levels: individual, group and policy/national voice and influence. It draws not only on a general review of the literature in this field but on the archives of, and conversations with staff from, both organisations.

The Traveller Movement and Friends, Families and Travellers: short histories

Ryder (2011) argued that there is a distinct Gypsy and Traveller third sector – or at least sub-sector – characterised, and at times united, by responses to the extreme exclusion of the community. Similar arguments have also been put forward in terms of the wider Black and Minority Ethnic voluntary sector: 'united' in the face of racism and discrimination (Ware, 2013). However, reflecting on the histories of the Irish Traveller Movement in Britain (ITMB, now the Traveller Movement) and FFT (summarised in Table 6.1), there are striking similarities.

Both started out as semi-formal unincorporated associations founded by charismatic individuals. Both moved to achieve a legal status (either as Registered Charities and/or Companies Limited by Guarantee with Charitable Purposes) relatively quickly. This enabled them to access funding, initially from grant making trusts and, in the case of

TM, through the Irish Government's Dion Fund. A period of struggle, with one worker/volunteer support, was followed in the mid-2000s by expansion, driven by committed staff and management boards, an expansion made possible by the plethora of short-term funding initiatives under New Labour, whether Area Based Initiatives, capacity-building programmes (for example, Capacity Builders), directly funded by government or channelled through the Big Lottery Fund (Reaching Communities, BASIS and so on). This expansion, and accompanying diversification of funding sources, has enabled both organisations to also diversify the range of services offered and activities undertaken.

However, as noted, there has been a reliance, in common with other locality and community of interest voluntaries, on short-term and ring-fenced or single-cause funders. With the ending of these funding regimes both FFT and TM have become vulnerable financially. This has been exacerbated not only by the reduction in financial resources available to the sector post 2010, but by the 'watering down' of the equalities agenda by the Equalities Act 2010 and the subsequent reduction of the importance placed on Equalities Impact Assessments, which has contributed to issues of race inequality 'no longer being on the agenda' and the voice of equalities organisations becoming more marginalised (Ware, 2013).

The Traveller Movement

TM defines itself as a 'national policy and voice charity' that acts as 'a bridge builder, bringing the Traveller communities, service providers and policy makers together, thereby stimulating debate and promoting forward-looking strategies to promote increased race equality, civic engagement, inclusion, service provision and community cohesion' (Greenfields, 2011, p 9). TM has a well-established track record of active policy development, campaigning, community engagement, training and awareness raising and social cohesion work and participates in all national consultations with regard to Gypsy and Traveller issues. TM changed its name in 2013 from Irish Traveller Movement in Britain so as to reflect its commitment to inclusive partnership work with all groups. Among policy practitioners and experts working in the field of Gypsy, Traveller and Romany (GRT) studies it is widely acknowledged that ITMB [now TM] 'punches above their weight' and has a track record for engaging in 'innovative practice' (Greenfields, 2011, p 9). Among its activities the TM has:

- developed a training and capacity-building programme and opportunities such as an (on-going) health-awareness and advocacy programme for Traveller women leading to Level 2 NVQ qualifications for participants and support for developing local groups;
- produced policy and research papers and submissions on consultations on accommodation, health, education and employment and advocacy platforms where community members can articulate their concerns to policy makers. This includes events in Parliament and the annual TM national conference and advocacy and social justice campaigns;
- held the first Irish Traveller Cultural Symposium at the Hammersmith Irish Cultural Centre and produced a range of materials, including DVDs, to increase awareness of Irish Traveller culture and history. TM has been an active participant and voice, since its inception, in the Gypsy Roma Traveller History Month;
- engaged in negotiations over the Dale Farm Traveller site campaign and is coordinating, with Homes and Communities Agency funding, a plan for a new site for residents who were evicted.

Friends, Families and Travellers (FFT)

The history of FFT from its foundation in 1993 to its status in 2010 as a formally constituted charity with a permanent office and a salaried staff of 19 is given in Chapter Five. Like TM, it has moved from working with one section of the GTR community to a more general brief, with over 50% of FFT's work undertaken with English Romany Gypsies, 30% with Irish Travellers and less than 20% with new Travellers and others, for example Scottish Travellers and Roma. Interestingly, as with TM, the majority of both paid staff and interns/volunteers are women. Key activities include:

- an advice and information unit providing case-work, advice and information to Gypsies and Travellers directly, either by phone or by outreach work to sites;
- providing training and awareness-raising seminars to mainstream agencies within the voluntary and statutory sectors;
- in Sussex, community support, health and well-being outreach services;
- mentoring local self-support groups to empower individuals, families and communities; working with young Gypsies and Travellers to help them to overcome the barriers to inclusion that they experience

and to participate more fully within mainstream society;research, in partnership with academic institutions, into insecure accommodation and its impact on health;participation within wider equality and diversity groups and fora to ensure a more just and equal society.

According to Chris Whitwell, the Director of FFT, the case-work and service delivery plays an important role in informing its advocacy work.

> "We work at national, regional and local levels. At local level we do case work [and] outreach, which is really about supporting Gypsies and Travellers into accessing the services that they need. At national level we are still very much a campaigning and policy influencing organisation setting out how to change the agenda. ... the important strength of the organisation is the way that the case work data that we get both at the local level ... [via the National Helpline] where we pick up a lot of cases from all over the country ... informs the policy and campaigning work. There is a direct relationship between the grassroots service provision and the strategic work that we are doing." (Ryder and Greenfields, 2010, p 141)

Gypsy and Traveller community development in context

It is interesting to note the disconnection between the literature on Gypsies and Travellers and the 'mainstream' of community development writing. While there have been some 15 recent articles in the *Community Development Journal* on the European Roma (reflecting the Journal's international focus) only two in the past 20 years make direct reference to Gypsies and Travellers. The first of these relates to Traveller communities in Spain (Garriaga, 1994) and the second to the challenges of participatory research with Gypsy and Traveller communities in the UK (Brown and Scullion, 2010).

While a tradition of direct community action has existed within Gypsy and Traveller activism (see for example the campaigns of the early Gypsy Council in the 1960s and recent Dale Farm campaigns which still continue despite the 2011 eviction – Chapter Two), it has been argued that community development subsequently became depoliticised (Powell and Geoghegan, 2004; McCabe, 2010) and was used, for example, in regeneration programmes and, for Gypsies and Travellers, what could be deemed as 'civilising' integrative programmes

Table 6.1: Traveller Movement (formerly Irish Traveller Movement in Britain) and Friends Families and Travellers: a short history

Date	Irish Traveller Movement in Britain/Traveller Movement	Joint Initiatives	Friends, Families and Travellers
1993			FFT established by New Travellers and their families and supporters to challenge the Criminal Justice and Public Order Bill 1994
1995			Becomes a Company Limited by Guarantee (3597515)
1999	ITMB set up Prominent agencies were Brent Irish Advisory Service (BIAS) and the London Irish Women's Centre and Action Group for Irish Youth		FFT shortlisted for a human rights award Relocates office from Glastonbury to Brighton Funding from Comic Relief and the Tudor Trust enables employment of five members of paid staff
2000	ITMB secures Dion funding (Irish in Britain) from Irish government Becomes a Company Limited by Guarantee Comic Relief funding secured Employs one worker (remains a single-worker project till 2006)		
2001			Annual turnover approximately £50,000
2002		2002 Gypsy and Traveller Law Reform Coalition (GTLRC) founded, jointly managed by ITMB, FFT and Gypsy Council	Pioneering Sussex Traveller Women's Health Project
2003	Charitable status secured		Expansion of case-work and national helpline
2004		GTLRC wins Liberty Human Rights Award	Cyber Pilots children's interactive website
2005			New director appointed Becomes a Registered Charity
2006	Becomes an organisation independent of BIAS Employs second worker	GTLRC disbands	Big Lottery Funding secured
2007	Inaugural annual conference Traveller Advisory Group formed		Equality and Human Rights Commission funding secured

Date	Irish Traveller Movement in Britain/Traveller Movement	Joint Initiatives	Friends, Families and Travellers
2008	Capacity Builders funding secured for wider organisational development work Expansion of work into education projects and community-development training Birmingham office opens		Big Lottery-funded Reaching Communities Programme commences: assertive outreach, cultural awareness training, case-work, representation and recruitment of Gypsy and Traveller staff Children in Need funding secured
2009	Capacity Builders funds Traveller Women's Community Development Project		One of 27 national organisations funded under the government's 'Tackling Race Inequalities' programme Co-authors report commissioned by Equality and Human Rights Commission on inequalities faced by Gypsies and Travellers
2010	Traveller Economic Inclusion report launched Department of Health (DH) funding secured to undertake health and well-being project		Paid staffing increases to total of 19 posts, including 9 from the Travelling communities
2011	End of Capacity Builders funding PQASSO (quality kite mark) secured Develops internship programme and European Union policy work Media monitoring work commences Expands work into Gypsy and Traveller planning and accommodation work.		Annual turnover approximately £500,000
2012	Winner of the All Party Parliamentary Group (APPG) Award for maternity care education and health project Presents evidence to Leveson Inquiry		
2013	End of DH health and well-being funding Establishes New Horizons Project for 15- to 24-year-olds Employment Training and Education Project Secures Joseph Rowntree Foundation funding for campaigns work Name changed to Traveller Movement		Big Lottery-funded Reaching Communities Programme ends but funding continues from a wide range of sources Increase in earned income

by charities and agencies that adopted a rather paternalistic approach to community development in the 1970s and 1980s in their work with these communities (Ryder, 2011). In some cases community development became a form of conflict management or, even, customer relations between local authorities, housing associations and so on and 'the community'. Subsequently, under the Coalition government, the terms 'community development' or 'community engagement' have been dropped in favour of a version of the American model of 'community building', popularised by Minkler (2005), and a rhetoric of social action.

The introduction to this book examined accusations that such forms of community development just created jobs for a non-GTR 'Gypsy Industry' that was bolstered by just a few community members who were the victims of 'NGOisation' (Trehan, 2001). Such perceptions have often impeded opportunities for projects to forge meaningful links with the Gypsy and Traveller communities that they serve and highlight the inherent dangers when projects do not create valid roles and a sense of ownership for community members, and so render almost impossible the transformative role that Hope and Timmell (1984) see as central for community workers.

However, the examples presented in this chapter challenge the paternalistic condescension that sees GTR communities as stuck for ever on the bottom rungs of Arnstein's (1969) 'ladder of participation', showing that the community itself can have a growing and meaningful role in the governance and direction of those organisations speaking 'for' or 'with' Gypsies and Travellers.

Developing skills and knowledge: effecting change

FFT and TM have attempted, using different strategies, to effect change at five different levels: the individual, organisational, the community, 'mainstream' agencies and in the policy arena. They share a model of working (summarised in Figure 6.1). And a value that has guided their work is: 'nothing about us without us'.

Organisational practice

Although established with limited Traveller input on formal governance, both FFT and TM have sought to increase the say and direction that the communities have in the organisations. This is in part achieved through a range of engagement mechanisms as well as training and employment. TM has developed an innovative way to increase Irish and wider Traveller involvement by establishing an Advisory Group

Figure 6.1: Models of working

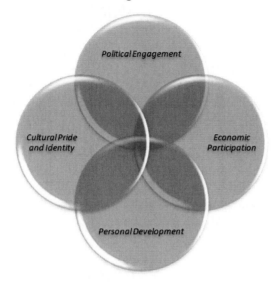

Source: Friends, Families and Travellers

that informs and directs the broad campaign and policy work of the organisation. This is separate from the Board of Trustees. Some Irish Travellers had sat on the Board but were frustrated with the increasingly bureaucratic nature of meetings as the organisation grew and developed. Experienced community members remain on the Board but new participants in the organisation join the Advisory Group and, as they gain experience and an overview of the organisation, they can join the Trustees' committee. Approximately half the Trustees are Travellers.

Another important means of involving community members in the organisation (and preparing them for employment) is through paid sessional temporary internships in the organisation: through participatory research projects, diversity training for service providers, community liaison and cultural promotion. Community member training has also taken on greater importance with, for example, TM offering Level 2 Community Development courses for Travellers from which it is hoped participants can derive a greater understanding of, and seek employment in, the third sector (Greenfields, 2011).

Approximately half of the trustees and staff at FFT come from different Traveller communities. This trend has extended both the organisations' knowledge of the communities they serve and the effectiveness of campaigns and outreach. As Sarah Mann (training manager at FFT) notes:

"It's not so much the external credibility but a recognition of the need to have Traveller staff to be working with Travellers ... one of my colleagues, she's Romany Gypsy; she lived on the road all her life. She started as a volunteer on the Health Project with FFT and then six years ago she started working with us as an outreach worker. Now, she can walk onto an unauthorised encampment and start talking to people immediately and start a conversation immediately. That [involvement] shortcuts the trust-building work to such an extent, to not have that in the organisation can be difficult if you're doing outreach work."

Chris Whitwell, Director of FFT, elaborates on this point, and also on the merits of mixed staff teams and the intercultural learning environments that are created:

"Any structure, any organisation that proposes to work on behalf of a community, needs to be fairly representative of the community which it's working on behalf of. You wouldn't expect a women's organisation to be staffed by a bunch of men making decisions about what's best for women. I guess it is the same with Gypsies and Travellers except that ... the traditional Traveller community is often coming from quite a low base of engagement with mainstream processes.... we benefit from having a mix of Gypsies and Travellers and non-Gypsies/non-Traveller staff. They learn from each other. Quite a lot of staff that don't come from a Traveller background learn obviously about culture and customs of the Traveller community and the staff from the Traveller community are learning about mainstream processes and structures." (Ryder and Greenfields, 2010, p 153)

Community impact

TM and FFT are both influenced by intercultural principles within community development. As Yvonne MacNamara, TM Director, notes:

"it is very much about working *with* the community. It is not about going in and changing a community, it's about equipping a community to make choices and informed decisions.... Travellers will often use the word 'dilute' and declare 'We don't want to be diluted'. Which is a pretty strong word, but ... that's about heritage and culture which is slightly different. I think when you go in and you give a community support and education around preserving who they are, it strengthens them. So there is no need to use words like dilute, you won't be diluted [assimilated]. You are strong in who you are."

Innovation and adaptation, built around cultural identity, is a matter of pressing concern for the traditional Traveller communities as new regulations, a shortage of sites and a decline in the traditional employment sectors mean that for some sections of the community the 'Traveller economy' is in crisis. Hence, there has been a need and demand to explore and take new directions (Richardson and Ryder, 2012). Yvonne MacNamara discusses further the implications of this 'sea change':

> "They want something better. There's a huge acknowledgement within the community about moving a little bit more towards education. That's definitely a sea change. People realise that actually their traditional lifestyle is becoming redundant; we're living in an era of huge austerity. A lot of the men are out of work, the women are having to go out and try and earn a crust more and they're finding that particularly difficult because there's no history of this in recent times. When I say work I'm talking about going in to the kind of labour market and the waged work. So there's a huge shift there and people are acknowledging that, which is probably why we have a lot of Travellers coming to us who want to come on our internship programme, because we've a waiting list for the internship programme. Now I know if we'd tried to do that internship programme maybe ten years ago ..."

Thus third sector involvement in organisations like FFT and TM has not only encouraged Gypsies and Travellers to develop new skills, but also developed bridging forms of social capital in situations where they work with, liaise with and form alliances with non-Travellers. Thus third sector involvement is playing a growing role in intercultural change where innovations in community roles and perceptions are being gradually mediated and transformed into gender roles, work patterns and engagement with outsiders.

Individuals

New challenges for third sector community groups like TM and FFT can sometimes create cultural and gender tensions: the 'tugs' and 'pulls' that can present difficult choices and conflicts for individuals as traditional conceptions of identity collide with the new. In both organisations the majority of paid staff, interns and volunteers are women. In the past pressures on female members of the community about the roles and expectations of more traditional members led to some being unable to participate in the third sector or withdrawing. Yvonne MacNamara recalls: "There were some situations where male family members would tell me 'I don't want you letting her out, I don't want her going to any meetings! Are there men working there?' My reply would be 'What do you honestly think, we keep a stack of men inside the cupboard or what? Do you know, if she's to grow and develop I have to send her out to meetings, I am not keeping the girl inside in the office.'" However, Yvonne noted that there had been some significant changes since that time. "We have moved on and experience such issues less frequently now. Women are gaining more ground. Through the community development training and the internship scheme, we have noticed a real change. All the women participating, including young married women, were supported by their husbands and family and encouraged to develop their careers and education, and many have now moved on to further employment." So there is evidence that attitudes are changing, but it is an area that will continue to need concerted action in the future.

As Sarah Mann notes with regard to the example of the youth work organised by FFT, individual change can come about through apparently simple interactions, but the implications can be profound:

> "One of the top changes we identified as resulting from our work with young people was extra socialisation as in meeting together in a group and going to other places and seeing what other environments were like. Being able to go up and talk to a stranger and ask, can you show me the way to the loo or can I have something? With young people who've perhaps spent all their lives in one tiny area on a site and never gone off for any other reason, whose parents were, quite reasonably, fearful about their children being exposed to mainstream culture because what experience they had of this was very poor, they were afraid for their children getting abuse or discrimination, so finding a safe

way for those young people to come together and make
friends is what we have sought to do."

Building bridges with services

Gypsies' and Travellers' access to services has traditionally been an arena
for the exclusion they suffer, overt racism and discrimination on the
part of service providers, coupled with cultural misunderstandings.
This has been compounded by the self-exclusion of the community,
which stems from a fear of racism and or wider cultural fears as to the
influence that external institutions might have on identity. Bridging
and mediating these divides is thus a challenging and sensitive task but
is one to which both FFT and TM believe they can make important
contributions. Both TM and FFT are committed to mainstreaming
the needs of Gypsy and Traveller communities. Yvonne MacNamara
outlines this goal:

> "in order for us to develop and sustain ourselves and to grow
> as an organisation and individuals, we need to mainstream.
> Because service provision is not for one community out
> there, service provision should be for everyone. So if
> Travellers need to access healthcare, I'm not looking for
> them to set up a specific, specialist, healthcare service for
> Travellers or specialist schools. To me that is almost like an
> apartheid system ... we would describe ourselves as bridge
> building and bringing the Traveller communities together
> to stimulate that kind of debate and engage with service
> provision through that route."

TM and FFT have been active in a range of awareness-raising campaigns
aimed at influencing service providers and decision makers. Through
training and the production of other materials they have sought to
improve the understanding and knowledge of services like health,
education, the police and emergency services, among others, about
Gypsy and Traveller communities. A key dimension of this work has
been involving community members. Among the projects TM has
coordinated was the 'Maternity Project', where TM joined forces with
the Royal Free Hospital's maternity team. The aim of the project was
to educate both staff and Irish Traveller service users about what to
expect as they commence the 'maternity journey' and pass through the
health service system. The project stemmed from 'Pacesetters', which
aimed to facilitate service users to influence the service provided (Van

Cleemput, 2012). Irish Traveller women were able to work with staff on cultural awareness-training and to produce a Maternity Care and Irish Travellers information pack. The project won an award from the All-Party Parliamentary Group on Maternity for 'Best example of involvement of service users in the development and delivery of maternity services'.

FFT departs somewhat from the TM stance on services by being willing to take on the role of service provider. One of the projects FFT coordinates is the Travellers Sussex Outreach Team, part of the Sussex Traveller Health Project. The team is made up of two well-being community development workers and five outreach support workers who provide support, advice and signposting to around 500 Gypsies and Travellers each year across Sussex. Gypsies and Travellers are supported in a number of areas including housing, welfare, health, well-being, adult social care, families and young people, work, education and community engagement.

Within this work there has been a combination of practice, research and activism. The team has been involved in research that explored Gypsies' and Travellers' access to primary care, finding that the majority of primary care staff across Sussex had very little knowledge or awareness of Gypsy and Traveller culture and how this impacts on access to services (FFT, 2010). Sarah Mann outlines how such work can challenge exclusion and how a service-delivery role can inform and shape advocacy and policy change:

> "I can think of several cases where part of the role of the worker is to stand up for and challenge the service and that's part of how our case-work, outreach work feeds into the campaigning policy work ... So we had a GP surgery where they turned away somebody because they had a common Irish Traveller surname. They said, 'We're not taking any more people with that name.' So we challenged it, so the client wanted that but also we then took it to a higher level and were able to take it up through the system to challenge that policy. Then that case, with consent, goes into briefing papers and training for the mainstream organisations. So no, it's not a sticking plaster, if there's a problem with that service then challenging that and if necessary taking that up as high as it needs to go is needed. With the GP registration issue we've also taken it up to health commissioners, to the clinical commissioning groups and to the anti-fraud department of the NHS, who gave out guidelines to GPs

which are partly working against people without postcodes being able to register."

Advocacy

FFT and TM both engage in advocacy and campaign work. A key dimension of this is to bring into the centre of campaign work issues they have identified through case-work or through community dialogue. This involves articulating community concerns into policy papers, submissions and briefings and also creating campaign platforms where community members can have opportunities to engage directly with policy makers. Through their involvement with FFT and TM some community members have progressed to having direct input into policy fora. One Irish Traveller participant describes the impact of the health awareness and advocacy programme:

> "I have increased confidence to encourage other people to do the same [engage with community activism]. I feel I can talk better to people. I can use the confidence I got from doing the course to pass on the information and skills I learned on the course to the Travelling community. I have met new people and have stayed in contact with them after the course was finished. People come to my sister (who was also on the course) and me to ask us questions about how to get access to health services, planning information and we are now able to give them contact numbers, information and to help them, however we can." (Greenfields, 2011, p 29)

For some, the journey of activism has been profound in terms not just of the changes for individuals but also of the influence and reach of activism. One notable campaigner was the Irish Traveller Tom Sweeney, who lived on the Westway Traveller site, directly under the Westway flyover. Despite having no formal education and being unable to read and write Tom became Co-Chair of the TM and frequently met government ministers and gave interviews on the national news. An important vehicle for Tom's activism was the GTLRC, which focused on lobbying and policy change at a national level. Both the ITMB and FFT were among the founders of the GTLRC and, together with the Gypsy Council, line-managed and helped to lead the project on a rotating basis. This sharing of responsibilities reflects a deep commitment on the part of TM and FFT to partnership work and the concept of 'strength in unity', which (given some of the divisions between different Traveller groups and competition for ever-scarcer resources) is not always easy to maintain. TM and FFT would argue that they have striven to be fair in their dealings and operations in the wider GRT social movement, and also to build links beyond its traditional confines. Sarah Mann outlines how partnership and collaboration is a core value in the work of FFT:

> "Where we can work in partnership we will and, although FFT's good at getting funding, we don't want to build a power base in that way ... Given the challenges of the environment we're working in ... I think that's why it's important we're linked, we're not trying to work alone. Our Director (Chris Whitwell) has taken quite a strong line of linking FFT in with other equality bodies, other BME groups, other BME Networks and Forums to fight those issues on a common basis. And, what that's helped to do is also get the BME groups to include Gypsies and Travellers in their challenges. You always used to hear, even till quite recently, BME *and* Gypsies and Travellers.'

TM has contributed to such alliance building through its coordinating role in the Gypsy Roma Traveller History Month (GRTHM) project. The National Association of Teachers of Travellers coordinated the project and a grant from the Department for Children, Schools and Families. The project (2009–11) enabled GRTHM to become more firmly embedded not just among GRT but also within the wider community, in schools and libraries.

TM and FFT have also been vocal champions for the needs of Roma communities to be recognised in the UK and for their interests to be drawn within and promoted by the Gypsy and Traveller and now Roma 'social movement'.

Looking to the future

All the main political parties entered the 2010 general election proposing that citizens themselves, whether as individuals or communities, should participate more in the delivery of public services (McNeil, 2009). This agenda is, and will continue to be, influential in policy and service spheres. The rhetoric of greater community empowerment could be viewed as one that will be beneficial to Gypsy and Traveller communities. McCarthy has noted the dangers inherent in excluding Travellers from decision-making processes on social policy:

> Policy decisions that fundamentally affect Traveller lives are constantly being developed without any input from the Traveller community. Policy decisions reflect the cultural norms of the settled community. How these decisions will affect Travellers is never considered. Without knowledge of this distinct lifestyle, policy decisions cannot be sensitive to their needs. (McCarthy, 1994, p 28)

Although 20 years old, this statement still holds truth and it has only been in recent years that GRT community organisations like FFT and TM have been able to make 'inroads' as a result of some more inclusive social policy and also, most importantly of all, through community mobilisation. However, there is a fear that austerity and reduced funds will have negative consequences for GRT organisations. In a study of the third sector in the North West of England, Davidson and Packham (2012) noted among third sector groups that 78% said they had been affected by local authority cuts in funding, and that 51% said it was likely that as a result their group would close within the next three years. These regional findings have been replicated in other studies of BME organisations (Lachman and Malik, 2012) and such trends are evident in the GRT third sector. A number of projects have closed, are near to closure or have laid off staff. Sarah Mann gives insights into the funding pressures now faced by groups in the present environment.

> "Do you know, it's really difficult sometimes to see beyond the next year and the next funding deadline. We're certainly going through a period of that at the moment, of 'getting through', which I think is distracting from our long-term vision. But, I don't think it's changed in that our headline is equality of access and no discrimination. Those haven't changed. The amount of attention that we give to developing, to continuing to develop our vision is necessarily compromised by having to focus more and more on funding."

As has been noted in this chapter, community development can be a powerful and potent tool for transformative change. However, in some cases, in particular with regard to excluded minorities like Gypsy and Traveller communities, there are limits to what can be achieved without corresponding state action to challenge inequalities and promote flexible and inclusive services. There is a danger that austerity coupled with reduced financial support will see the progress in equalities over the last two decades substantially weakened. The foundations that have been laid and good practice developed by the GRT third sector may be extremely difficult to build up again if lost and, in the process, local and national government and services will lose an important ally in ensuring that the rhetoric of empowerment, inclusion and the prospect of social mobility is translated into reality for one of the most excluded groups in society. The alternative to the dialogues developed by TM and FFT over the past decade would be to return to, and draw on, the communities' traditions of self-help, but this could be at the cost of increased social, economic and cultural isolation.

Note

[1] The chapter was drafted through interviews with Yvonne McNamara (Director ITMB) and Sarah Mann (Training Manager FFT) and analysis of their annual reports and business plans. Angus McCabe has a background in community development and facilitated the deliberative process by prompting lines of enquiry and posing some key questions to develop new insights.

References

Arnstein, S.R. (1969) 'A ladder of citizen participation', *Journal of the American Institute of Planners*, vol 35, pp 216–24.

Brown, P. and Scullion, L. (2010) '"Doing research" with Gypsy-Travellers in England: reflections on experience and practice', *Community Development Journal*, vol 45, no 2, pp 169–85.

Cemlyn, S., Greenfields, M., Whitwell, C. and Matthews, Z. (2009) *Inequalities experienced by Gypsy and Traveller communities: A review* (Research Report no 12), London: Equality and Human Rights Commission.

Centre for Local Economic Strategies and Centre for Local Policy Studies (2012) *Open for All? The Changing Nature of Equality under Big Society and Localism*, Manchester: CLES and CLPS.

Davidson, E. and Packham, C. (2012) *Surviving, Thriving or Dying: Resilience and small community groups in the North West of England*, Manchester: Manchester Metropolitan University.

Fonseca, I. (1996) *Bury Me Standing: The Gypsies and their journey*, London, Vintage.

FFT (Friends, Families and Travellers) (2010) *Fair Access for all? Gypsies and Travellers in Sussex, GP Surgeries and Barriers to Primary Healthcare*, Brighton: FFT.

Garriaga, C. (1994) 'Community work with Gypsies and communities in conflict', *Community Development Journal*, vol 29, no 2, pp 151–7.

Greenfields, M. (2011) *The Irish Traveller Movement in Britain Traveller Women's Community Development Programme, A Social Return on Investment (SROI) Evaluation*, London: ITMB.

Hope, A. and Timmell, S. (1984) *Training for Transformation: A Handbook for Community Workers* (rev edn), Harare: Mambo Press

Lachman, R. and Malik, F. (2012) *West Yorkshire Public Sector Cuts: The Impact on the BME Voluntary and Community Sector*, Bradford: JUST West Yorkshire and University of Leeds.

McCabe, A. (2010) *Below the Radar in a Big Society? Reflections on Community Engagement, Empowerment and Social Action in a Changing Policy Context*, Birmingham: Third Sector Research Centre.

McCarthy, P. (1994) 'The subculture of poverty reconsidered', in M. McCann, S. O'Siochain, and J. Ruane (eds) *Irish Travellers: Culture and Ethnicity*, Belfast: Institute of Irish Studies, The Queens University, pp 121–9.

McNeil, C. (2009) *Now It's Personal: Personal Advisers and the New Public Service Workforce*, London: Institute for Public Policy Research.

Minkler, M. (2005) *Community Organising and Community Building for Health*, Piscataway, NJ: Rutgers University Press.

Powell, F. and Geoghegan, M. (2004) *The Politics of Community Development*, Dublin: Farmar.

Ryder, A. (2011) *Gypsies and Travellers and the Third Sector* (Working Paper 63), Birmingham: University of Birmingham: Third Sector Research Centre.

Ryder, A. (2012) *Hearing the Voice of Gypsies and Travellers: The History, Development and Challenges of Gypsy and Traveller Tenants and Residents' Associations* (Working Paper 84), Birmingham: Third Sector Research Centre.

Ryder, A. and Greenfields, M. (2010) *Roads to Success: Routes to Economic and Social Inclusion for Gypsies and Travellers*, London: ITMB.

Trehan, N. (2001) 'In the name of the Roma? The role of private foundations and NGOs', in W. Guy (ed), *Between Past and Future: The Roma of Central and Eastern Europe*, Hatfield: University of Hertfordshire, pp 134–49.

Van Cleemput, P. (2012) 'Gypsy and Traveller health', in J. Richardson and A. Ryder (eds) *Gypsies and Travellers: Accommodation, Empowerment and Inclusion in British Society*, Bristol: Policy Press, pp 43–60.

Ware, P. (2013) '*Very Small, Very Quiet, a Whisper*' – *Black and Minority Ethnic Groups: Voice and Influence*, Birmingham: Third Sector Research Centre.

SEVEN

The Gypsy and Traveller Law Reform Coalition

Andrew Ryder and Sarah Cemlyn

Background

In this chapter we discuss to what the extent the Gypsy and Traveller Law Reform Coalition (GTLRC) can be seen as a social movement within the framework already drawn in Chapter One from Freire, Gramsci and Habermas. The GTLRC was an umbrella group of Gypsy and Traveller organisations that came together in 2002 as the culmination of a campaign for more sites, a campaign that had begun as the failure of the Blair Labour government to honour its promises in opposition became apparent. This earlier pledge to address the shortage of sites came about in part because of the lobbying of the Labour Campaign for Travellers' Rights (LCTR), which was launched in 1986. Hertfordshire County Councillor Martin Hudson, Paul Winter, Tommy Doherty, Peter Saunders, Bristol Councillor Jenny Smith and the Sheffield Gypsy Traveller Support Group with Acton and Charles Smith formed the nucleus (Hudson, 1987). The LCTR gained the energetic support of Peter Pike MP (shadow minister) but Blair did not include him in the government. This led to Traveller issues being sidelined in the first phase of the Labour government. As the LCTR imploded in shame, in a series of conferences the founders of the GTLRC protested against the injustice of a lack of sites and evictions, demanded human rights for Gypsies and Travellers, challenged hostile, inaccurate and stereotyped media reporting and engaged with policy makers to promote law reform. As a social movement it was indeed 'a reaction to social problems, an expression of fear and dissatisfaction with society as it is and a call for changes and the solution of problems' (Fuchs, 2006, p 113).

We start our analysis from the question of how the initiators of the GTLRC developed a 'frame' (in the sense of Snow and Benford, 1988) to construct meaning for participants and steer strategy and action (Vicari, 2010). The GTLRC as a social movement focused on a constructive critique of government policy that outlined practical and achievable reforms that can still be seen as part of a more general programme of emancipation. This showed how effectively Gypsy and Traveller communities could mobilise in transformative action, overcoming the internecine disputes between organisations of the early 1990s that provoked stereotyping comments like:

> The very notion of Gypsydom is antipathetic to the creation of a coherent programme of action or campaign for recognition and respect for Gypsies in the modern world. (Hawes and Perez, 1996, p 174)

The progress and development of the GTLRC as a social movement illustrates that, for a time at least, Gramscian 'organic intellectuals' can work with outsiders who have undergone 'conscientisation' to develop their own capacity for action. Such respect for people's potential must be fostered if social movements are not just to be based on those with existing cultural capital but to include groups marginalised in society (Acton and Ryder, 2013).

Origins and composition

The foundation of the GTLRC in 2002 was the result of a series of events. The growing shortage of sites, the increasing number of evictions and the tragic death of the Irish Traveller teenage boy Johnny Delaney, who was kicked to death that year by a racist gang (Richardson and Ryder, 2012), all highlighted the continued and growing exclusion of Gypsies and Travellers. From 1996 Luke Clements and Rachel Morris of the Traveller Law Research Unit (TLRU) at Cardiff University Law School coordinated a series of working groups on Gypsy and Traveller issues that fed into the Traveller Law Reform Conference in 1999 (Morris and Clements, 1999). From 1999 the TLRU was funded by the Joseph Rowntree Charitable Trust to undertake research concerning the costs borne by public bodies in dealing with unlawful Gypsy and Traveller encampments. This led to the formulation of a draft parliamentary Bill, the Traveller Law Reform Bill, which sought to return a duty on local authorities to provide and facilitate sites (Morris and Clements, 2002). An important dimension of this work was to include the diverse range of Gypsy and Traveller leaders and activists in drafting and framing the Bill. Not only did this give many of the newer activists a useful introduction to the nuances of policy development but it also created better working relationships and a greater semblance of unity than had existed hitherto. The Traveller Law Reform Bill was finalised in 2002 and Clements and Morris felt that they had completed their task through facilitating the drafting of the Bill. It was now up to the community itself to take it forward. The community was thus rightfully 'left holding the baby'. The challenge was how to nurture this gift and proceed to run a national campaign and lobbying strategy. This was the key impetus in the formation of the GTLRC.

During the first five years of the New Labour administration there appeared little sympathy towards Gypsies and Travellers. The first major public intervention on this topic by Labour was made when Home Secretary Jack Straw vilified Travellers for their perceived anti-social behaviour in contrast to the traditional Romanies of bygone days (Richardson and Ryder, 2012). It is telling that the first legislative act in this policy area by the Labour government appeared in its Anti-Social Behaviour Act 2002, which accorded local authorities greater eviction powers if Travellers on unauthorised encampments could be directed to lawful sites. However, from 2002 there were signs of a change in direction. McAdam (1996) has argued that protest and social movement formation is most likely to occur when political systems are opening up and when there is a balanced mixture of political opportunities and political constraints. It would be fair to say that one key factor in encouraging the Gypsy and Traveller groups to form a coalition was the fact that the Labour government appeared finally to acknowledge that the policy it had inherited (Circular 1/94 – see Chapter Five) was not working and that there was a need to develop alternative strategies (Richardson and Ryder, 2012). Hence a series of consultations started that energised Gypsy and Traveller organisations and made them accept the logic of working more closely together.

The GTLRC was established in 2002 as an umbrella group to promote the Traveller Law Reform Bill. It was a coalition of national non-governmental organisations (NGOs) (Irish Traveller Movement in Britain (ITMB); Friends, Families and Travellers (FFT); Gypsy Council (GC)), smaller localised groups and traditional Gypsy and Traveller charismatic leaders. It has been noted that within social movements a high percentage of those who are active are from 'mid to high' social positions (Della Porta and Diani, 1999). This may have been true of the 'outsider' non-Gypsy and Traveller workers in the national NGOs listed above but was certainly not the case with the community members who were involved in the GTLRC. At the time none of the ethnic Gypsy and Traveller members had a university-level education; at best these members had received some secondary school education. However, within the Gypsy and Traveller community these activists had unique facets that made them different from many in their communities. Most of them were already experienced activists, at least at a local level, and were involved in informal or constituted local groups and in some cases were even employed within such. Another important point was that a majority of these activists were women who had to challenge more traditional gender role expectations within their communities (Ryder, 2013; see also Chapter Nine). Despite the range and diversity of actors within the GTLRC, attempts to form a non-hierarchical organisation, channels of deliberation and collective frames (visions) helped to create a sense of unity.

Organisational features

The GTLRC could be considered as a new social movement primarily defined by anti-racism, human rights and ethnic interests, but more generally representing, like other groups within this term, marginal social actors who could be deemed a new radical constituency.

A key concern within the GTLRC was to achieve community empowerment and avoid hierarchical structures within what became a broad umbrella coalition. Like other new social movements (Chesters and Welsh, 2011), the GTLRC had a high degree of informality and spontaneity, and a low degree of horizontal and vertical differentiation. Fuchs (2006) argues that a flat organisational structure suits protest-focused social movements because the concept of self-organisation is closely related to the ideas of self-determination, self-management and minimal centralised authority. The GTLRC strove through its self-organisation and grassroots activity to remain close to its ideals, and its success and failure were very much linked to organisational matters.

During its first year the GTLRC was an informal, volunteer-led grouping with virtually no funding. During this start-up period Father Joe Browne of the ITMB and Andrew Ryder of the LCTR[1] were invited to coordinate the campaign. The campaign grew apace and it was evident that a full-time worker would be needed to service the GTLRC. Funding was secured from Comic Relief, which proved to be flexible and understanding, having a tradition of supporting excluded and underfunded groups.

The different groups mediated a framework for how the coalition should operate, in which the GTLRC was to be project-managed by the Travellers' Aid Trust (TAT), a small charity (see Chapter Eight). The full-time worker was hosted and supervised by three lead agencies on a rotating annual basis, namely the ITMB, the GC and FFT. These lead agencies were the most-established national groups that were also on the Charities Register and had paid staff. Each of these three groups was identified with one of the three principal UK Gypsy and Traveller groups, namely Irish Travellers, Gypsies and New Travellers. The Coalition was composed of members from all three groupings and this rotation helped to overcome tensions and fears about one group dominating the campaign agenda. Although the GTLRC worker was hosted by established NGOs, the committee directed broad campaign decisions, and between meetings long-standing elders like the late Len Smith provided useful guidance when immediate decisions were needed, fulfilling the traditional role of elders as points of advice and guidance.

Skills development was another important dimension of the GTLRC. Support was given to the lead GTLRC activists to introduce them to parliamentary processes. Engagement platforms were created, giving activists a lead role in lobbying activities through addressing parliamentary meetings, select committees and conferences, being interviewed by the media and holding meetings with ministers, civil servants and other stakeholders. Sometimes this support was guided, but it was also delivered through more interactive and traditional Traveller modes of learning through involvement, observation and discussion, which in reality is the main training ground for many engaged in community development (Gilchrist and Taylor, 2011).

Deliberative processes

In framing the platform of the GTLRC, the Gypsy and Traveller voice was given prominence in formulating strategy development through informal deliberative and communal decision making without challenging or ranking the various presidents, chairmen, vice-presidents, and secretaries of its affiliated groups. Thus the GTLRC had no officers of its own and campaign decisions were collectively reached by a committee, of which the great majority came from the Gypsy and Traveller community. Meetings of the GTLRC could be extremely long and even rambling, as attempts were made to avoid herding the committee into a rigid agenda. Committee members were encouraged to link their personal experiences of evictions, homelessness and being forced to settle with the objectives of the campaign. Hence there was a fusion of the personal and political, which was a marked feature of the GTLRC. If campaigns and organisations are not rooted in the experiences of communities there is the danger of the 'political' becoming sterile and moribund (Chambers, 2003). Dialogue based on shared experiences proved to be bonding and contributed to perceptions of solidarity within the GTLRC, an important ingredient for transformative change (Ledwith and Springett, 2010).

Links to the grassroots were maintained through civic engagement tools (Campbell et al, 2005), which present a culturally appropriate and comfortable first step into a new world of advocacy (King and Cruickshank, 2012). One such example was 'search conferences'. These were one-day events focusing on key community concerns, involving Gypsy and Traveller community members outside the sphere of activism and through deliberation linking their concerns to policy and strategy. The GTLRC held seven of these conferences, which generally attracted in excess of 200 attendees, often the majority being Gypsies and Travellers. The organisers ensured that the community was prominent as speakers and presenters, but at the core of the conferences were workshops that maximised the potential for community discussion. It was also ensured that the conferences identified key concerns and aspirations and that these were built into the campaign.

Key forums where relationships were established, reaffirmed and renewed included the long meetings of the coordinating committee and the search conferences. In between these an important link was a large e-mail discussion group (Trav-Net) to which most GTLRC members belonged, including the community members. This chatroom was an important source of information and a tool for mobilising responses to local incidents such as evictions or political attacks, reflecting the increasingly recognised value of information technology in social movement mobilisation. Cottle (2008) is correct to underscore the value of the internet as an alternative platform to mainstream and traditional media, thus allowing for the disruption of vertical, top-down mass media depictions. Horizontal communicative networks among GTLRC members (for example, e-mail) enabled them to build collective responses to media and political attacks, formulated through chatrooms and websites, to convey the realities of their lives. By assisting in building awareness and developing counter-hegemonic action, electronic communication also built up forms of social and emotional capital and promoted activist skills, and hence forms of cultural capital.

Collective frames

We will analyse the statements and strategies devised by the GTLRC, and in particular the Gypsy activist Len Smith, to gain insights into collective action frames within the GTLRC, using the method advocated by Gillan (2008), who suggests that the frames of belief structures utilised by movement actors can be made clear through the ideas found in activists' language, actions, published speeches, press releases and e-mails.

The late Len Smith was a key member of the GTLRC, playing a pivotal role in fulfilling what Zald (1996) describes as the need for a social movement to portray injustice and define pathways to change. Len Smith was highly instrumental in shaping the aims of the GTLRC. As Joe Jones (Chair of the GC) noted when Len died in 2007, 'Len has been the driving force behind so many of our successful campaigns, particularly with law reform. He has been an inspiration to us all' (*Southern Daily Echo*, 2007). Len had travelled in the South West, working as a wheelwright and carriage builder, but had found a nomadic lifestyle to be increasingly unsustainable. On one occasion he returned to a stopping-place and found his trailer had been set alight. The cycle of eviction and harassment led to him moving into housing in the early 1970s. Len had experienced regular education up to secondary level and prided himself on his level of literacy. In later years he published a local history on the Gypsies of the New Forest entitled *Nevi Wesh* (Smith, 2004). Len became an activist, as his literacy skills had led to him becoming an informal source of help to Gypsies and Travellers in the Southampton area who were grappling with planning cases and other disputes with the authorities. Towards the end of his life Len was incapacitated by a chronic bronchial problem and emphysema, but attended the GTLRC meetings, despite his increasing infirmity, and was a mentor to the GTLRC policy worker. In addition, his drafting of GTLRC press releases and statements and moderation of the Trav-Net e-mail list actively shaped GTLRC perspectives. Len thus played the role of a social movement (or Gramscian 'organic') intellectual in forming a collective frame. Len's age, literacy and wisdom often meant that his was the most revered and influential voice in deliberative processes. Snow and Benford (1988) define collective action frames as encompassing three core tasks: diagnostic, prognostic and motivational. Each of these core tasks was tackled by the GTLRC.

On the question of diagnosis, which involves identification of causal factors and where blame should be apportioned, a sense of injustice is often a central feature in social movement diagnosis (Gamson, 1992). The perception that the Gypsy and Traveller community had been wronged was strongly evident in Len's statements. This narrative of injustice was bolstered by a perception that central government had acted unfairly in the repeal of the Caravan Sites Act 1968, leading to a national shortage of sites. As Len noted on behalf of the Coalition, 'This situation has worsened since the Conservatives in 1994 repealed the duty on councils to provide sites. Instead, councils were asked in a government circular to help Travellers identify land to live on, but few did. Hence there is an acute shortage of sites and that is why some families have little choice but to buy land, move on to it and seek planning permission' (GTLRC, 2005b). The Labour government did not support the reintroduction of a statutory duty to provide sites, on the grounds that such a duty did not exist for the wider community. By contrast, Len argued for such a measure on the grounds of past injustice stretching back over a century.[2]

> [T]here are not thousands of families in the settled community as there are in the Traveller community living on the side of the road. Housing was not closed to the settled community but the commons and other traditional stopping places have been closed to Gypsies and Travellers by urban sprawl and development. (Smith, 2005)

In its prognosis the GTLRC defended established traditions, customs and practices namely the right to a nomadic lifestyle, and proposed policies to facilitate site provision as the solution to the problem it had diagnosed. The language of social inclusion was embraced, with the GTLRC frequently arguing that more sites would allow the Gypsy and Traveller communities to access services such as opportunities in education and to take up new roles, thus making a greater contribution to society, changes which would lead to improved social relations. In a letter to Prime Minister Tony Blair on behalf of the GTLRC, Len Smith argued: 'give our community a right to be a part of society and enable us to make the contribution we are willing and able to give' (GTLRC, 2005a). A parallel press statement asserted that 'Gypsies and Travellers have been campaigning for decades for that most basic of human rights, a place to call their home. There is a crying need for more sites, not only will this increase Gypsies and Travellers' access to services and a decent home but it will reduce the tensions between the Gypsy and Traveller and settled community by reducing the incidence of unauthorised encampments. Reform presents a 'win –win' opportunity for the settled and Gypsy and Traveller community' (GTLRC, 2004).

The GTLRC's calls for empowerment created what Benford and Snow (2000) describe as the motivational dimension of a social movement collective frame. Motivational framing provides a rationale for engaging in ameliorative collective action. The 'call to arms' for GTLRC participants was that they believed they were being given a real say in their destiny, through articulating the need for external change that might lead to the sites they wanted and or needed being established, and also nurturing change and innovation within their communities, in particular in areas such as gender and relations with wider society. Some cultural reorientation was envisaged in the GTLRC prognosis for Gypsy and Traveller communities, where more 'bridging' forms of social capital to strengthen dialogue with the settled community might be embraced, in contrast to bonding forms of social capital reflecting traditional and culturally bounded conceptions of Gypsy and Traveller identity. In this sense we can employ the term 'frame transformation' (Vijay and Kulkarni, 2012), where old values and beliefs are replaced with new ones. The GTLRC also incorporated shifting cultural attitudes towards equality issues. It had wide-ranging commitments to equality, with a negotiated mission statement opposing all forms of discrimination, including gender and sexual orientation. As well as stipulating that a majority of the committee should come from the Gypsy and Traveller community, it was resolved that there would be a gender balance.[3] A further reflection of the need for reorientation was a call for greater empowerment (Gamson, 1992), which mirrored the understanding that one factor responsible for Gypsies' and Travellers' plight was their exclusion from decision-making processes. Hence, an important call from the GTLRC was for the government to create a Gypsy and Traveller Social Inclusion Task Force that would extend and formalise the consultative role activists were playing in policy making.

Part of the collective frame for the GTLRC was that hostility between Gypsies and Travellers and wider communities was caused by the level of misunderstanding between them, which needed to be bridged through dialogue and more accurate media representation. This stance led to the GTLRC taking an active interest in conflict resolution. The logic was that if the GTLRC could liaise between local Gypsies and Travellers and members of the wider community and mediate a consensus on the provision of authorised sites, then wider support for a national policy framework could be achieved. For example, in the wake of an unauthorised encampment, the village of Firle Bonfire Society paraded a model of a caravan containing images of a Traveller family through the village. At the head of the procession was the local Liberal Democrat councillor. Finally, the model was torched as part of the village bonfire celebrations (BBC, 2003). Unfortunately for them, among the crowd of villagers was a settled Traveller, Patricia Knight, with her own children. She made a complaint to the police. The Liberal Democrat MP for Lewes, Norman Baker, argued that the action had been prompted by legitimate anger about an unauthorised encampment and that criminal elements were posing as Travellers (Baker, 2003).

Commenting on the GTLRC response, Len Smith stated: 'Fortunately, in this case, the Traveller Law Reform Coalition were able to take the moral high ground, and, instead of being vindictive, sought, successfully, to draw out the possible positives from the event. Meetings with local authority leaders, and with local MP Norman Baker brought positive results in reconciliation, and his signing of our Early Day Motion in parliament, calling for more Traveller sites' (Crawley, 2004, p 60). The success in Firle spurred the GTLRC to engage in further conflict resolution work.

Tensions between the wider society and Gypsies and Travellers were deemed by GTLRC members to be inflamed by intensely negative media coverage, which began to appear from 2003 onward in the tabloids. During the build-up of negative reporting the *Sun* newspaper had remained relatively silent, leaving the running to the *Daily Mail* and *Daily Express*. This was to change on 9 March 2005 when *The Sun* launched its campaign against unauthorised developments and encampments and the Traveller accommodation policies drafted under the aegis of Deputy Prime Minister John Prescott (Richardson and O'Neill, 2012). Over the course of three days, *The Sun* devoted 13 pages – including two whole front pages – to the subject. The first headline was 'Stamp on the Camps', with the subheading 'Sun declares war on Gypsy free for all' and picturing a Traveller camp with the headline 'Meet your neighbours ... thanks to John Prescott'. The *Daily Mail* carried six pages and a full-length leading article, while the *Daily Express* weighed in with three pages (Greenslade, 2005). The *Sun* editorial declared:

> The rule of law is flouted daily by people who don't pay taxes, give nothing to society and yet expect to be treated as untouchables. These people are far removed from the traditional Romany people with their admirable moral code. The villain of the piece is the Human Rights Act, which our judges have limply interpreted to mean that these wandering tribes have a right to family life and respect for their homes which outweighs any harm they might do to the environment or rural communities. (*The Sun*, 2005)

This encapsulates many of the themes of the reporting at the time: Travellers were immoral and anti-social, so a distinction should be drawn between these modern-day Travellers and those 'romantic' and 'respectable' Romanies of yesterday. The Conservative Party seemed to mirror the stereotypes of the tabloid campaign in the run-up to the

2005 general election. The adoption of this strategy was attributed to the advice of controversial Australian election strategist Lynton Crosby, who advised Conservative Party leader Michael Howard to recycle 'dog whistle issues', that is, populist themes with a strong tabloid appeal (White, 2005).

Alongside a statement entitled 'Fair Play', which appeared as a page-length advert in a number of newspapers as well as on billboards across the country, Howard pledged that if the Conservatives were successful in the forthcoming election campaign they would introduce a seven-point charter they had devised on Gypsies and Travellers that would criminalise unauthorised encampments and allow for swift eviction, with fines and even imprisonment for transgressors. No reference was made to increasing site provision and addressing the national shortage. The GTLRC organised a counter-campaign entitled 'Stamp out the Prejudice', which was launched on Roma Nation Day in April 2005 in the House of Commons (BBC,). At the event Gypsies and Travellers launched their own 7-Point Charter, as a rebuttal to Howard's, which called for more site provision and also the creation of a Taskforce to create consensus and agreement on this issue among a range of stakeholders. It was accompanied by a statement that parodied the style of Howard's 'fair play' statement but contained a serious message (GTLRC, 2005c).

The statement reflects a form of identity project that GTLRC members like Len Smith in particular were keen to project, namely, that in contrast to the stereotypes in the media and political discourse Gypsies and Travellers were responsible and had a legitimate case for inclusion and policy reform, which was also in the interests of the wider community. Such a moderate statement of its case was not to belie the radical and fundamental nature of the change in societal and governmental attitudes that the GTLRC sought.

The GTLRC's 7-Point Charter made its motivations evident: a desire to protect traditions while simultaneously advocating reorientation and a strategic plan that rested on rationality, fairness and pragmatism. A desire to demonstrate rationality meant that the GTLRC resisted calls by some to become more actively involved in protests at forced evictions. In opposing such action Len Smith stated: 'Unlike the mob politics of the pro-hunting lobby, we have conducted our campaign in a responsible and balanced way. We have made strenuous efforts to see both sides of the argument, even, for instance, joining forces with the Cottenham Residents Association,[4] to call for a return to a Statutory Duty. They could see that recognising our rights in this matter, and adding their voice to ours, would benefit all' (Smith,

Table 7.1: Fair play

Conservative Fair Play statement	Gypsy and Traveller Law Reform Coalition
I believe in fair play. The same rules should apply to everyone. I don't believe in special rules for special interest groups. We are all British. We are one nation.	*We Believe in Fair Play Too* We live in a modern Britain. We are proud to be part of a diverse and multicultural nation. We are proud to be Gypsies and Travellers.
Too many people today seem to think they don't have to play by the rules – and they're using so-called human rights to get away with doing the wrong thing.	Too many councils, politicians and newspapers seem to think they don't have to play by the rules. Gypsies and Travellers are being discriminated against. Fair play means being honest and telling the truth, it means giving the weak and vulnerable a helping hand not 'stamping on' them.
If you want to build a new home you have to get planning permission first. But if you are a Traveller you can bend planning law – building where you like thanks to the Human Rights Act. It's not fair that there's one rule for Travellers and another for everyone else This is one of the reasons why the Conservative Party is reviewing the Human Rights Act. And if it can't be improved we will scrap it Fairness matters – Britain needs a Government that stops people using human rights as an excuse for bending the rules Michael Howard	90% of planning applications by Gypsies and Travellers fail as opposed to 20% from the settled community. In the past councils have failed to follow planning guidance and help Gypsies and Travellers find land they can buy. It's not fair that so many Gypsies and Travellers are homeless. It's not fair that many official sites are next to rubbish dumps and sewer works. It's not fair that our children can't stay in one place long enough to get a decent education. It's not fair that our community has a life expectancy 10 years less than average. But it's not fair either that some people in the settled community are inconvenienced by unauthorised encampments. We don't want knee-jerk reactions. We want solutions that are fair for everyone. We need more choice, more legal sites, more dialogue and more understanding.

2004). Towards the end of the life of the GTLRC, Andrew Ryder and a number of GTLRC members advocated greater use of non-violent direct action to raise the profile of the campaign, but again this was not countenanced, as it was feared this would undermine the reputation ('symbolic power') that the GTLRC had built up through responsible campaigning, countering the stereotypes of the media and demonstrating that, as Caldeira (2008) suggests, framing can be altered by pressures exerted by counter-movements. Although the GTLRC was depicted by more radical elements as tame because it would not support the construction of barricades to resist evictions, it did support Gypsies and Travellers who lived on unauthorised encampments by creating public understanding of their circumstances.

End of the cycle

Lobbying started to pay dividends. A Conservative MP, David Atkinson, twice introduced the Traveller Law Reform Bill as a private member's bill and the Labour MP Kevin MacNamara established an All-Party Parliamentary Group for Gypsies and Travellers with support from the GTLRC. The Labour government started to include Gypsy and Traveller campaigners in consultations and these became a regular forum within communities and local government. This forum provided opportunities for dialogue with civil servants and ministers, but at times the meetings could lapse into informational sessions where Gypsy and Traveller attenders would be told what the department hoped to do, rather than being given a chance to shape policy. The GTLRC's objectives for participation were more ambitious, with proposals for a Taskforce of Gypsies and Travellers to guide government and oversee a civil service unit comparable to the Home Office 'rough sleepers' unit', which would drive through site-delivery plans (Crawley, 2004). This demand was partially met by the creation of a Taskforce to review progress, and the Housing Act 2004 and Planning Circular 1/2006 required councils to assess need and identify land for sites. Significant recognition came in 2004, when the GTLRC won the Liberty Human Rights Award, 'for exceptional achievement uniting communities and campaigning for human rights for Gypsies and Travellers'.

The protest cycle corresponds with what Tarrow (1998) describes as the life span of a social movement. The end is often characterised by exhaustion and polarisation, and this happened to the GTLRC, which disbanded in 2006. It had developed at a rapid pace and the tempo of work had increased steadily because of the scale of its ambition and the intensive negative tabloid campaigns over an 18-month period, which reduced the time and focus on community development as the GTLRC seemed to be continually responding to campaigns of negativity. There were also growing tensions between established NGOs and charismatic and traditional leaders and the smaller localised groups. The small groups resented the control over the project by the lead agencies that hosted the policy worker (Andrew Ryder, the sole employee of the GTLRC). These lead agencies were also perceived as more non-Gypsy led. In turn, the groups with regular constitutions felt that the informal groups formed around charismatic leaders should adopt formal structures. Mediation was unable to resolve these conflicts. Possibly the key factor for the GTLRC breaking up was the achievement of its central objective: policy change and the Labour government's pledge of more sites, which was finalised in 2006, just before the GTLRC dissolved. The rationale for an umbrella campaign therefore seemed less intense.

As the GTLRC became an increasingly established umbrella organisation at the centre of a broad campaign it had adapted formally to incorporate a worker, a larger budget and to manage a political profile that made it part of decision-making forums at a governmental level. This may have alienated some of the GTLRC members who felt more comfortable with the fluidity and informality in the early stages of the campaign. Indeed, as the GTLRC moved towards more formal line management of its worker some of the community elders may have felt that their opinion now mattered less and that they were being isolated. Some of the activists also thought the campaign was being seduced and manipulated by power elites in the Westminster village. As noted, some campaigners wanted to harness the GTLRC more closely to resistance to forced evictions from unauthorised developments.

The GTLRC seemed to be being pulled in different directions, and finding compromises was becoming ever harder to achieve. The Coalition had been formed quickly in order to respond to a critical moment in policy formulation, but its organisational development had also kept a similar pace and left some behind and/or caused tensions. In the early stages of the campaign lateral relationships had existed in a loose collective framework but the desire for the group to develop and expand had warranted some form of delegation. Once the Coalition was funded and employing a worker there was need for further formalisation and management based on legal rationality, legitimacy and bureaucracy. Greiner (1972), an organisational theorist, argued that organisations are like humans in the sense that they have a life cycle where, in the first stages, they develop and become more complex. Often the passing of one stage is marked by a crisis that threatens the organisation's survival – an observation that has been applied to social movements (Jolly, 2011). The Coalition had lurched and developed from one crisis to another, but in the end it had been unable to surmount its last organisational crisis and challenge. This did not mean the end of the process or a failure of what the GTLRC sought to achieve. In the wake of the GTLRC new groups emerged from the debris and allowed their organisations to be driven by an agenda of organisational development and group democracy (see Chapter Nine). Of note was that some of the activists who had initially adopted more informal approaches when they had first become involved in the GTLRC now themselves fused informal and formal approaches to activism and NGO organisation as the GTLRC had sought to do.

The case study of the GTLRC demonstrates that activists with limited cultural capital can take part in and direct transformative change campaigns. The lay knowledge and direct experience of injustice of GTLRC activists were harnessed, through collective deliberation and engagement in policy formation [to wider abstract theories and critical awareness (conscientisation), enabling these oppressed people to link their predicament to wider societal features. The leadership of Len Smith and other GTLRC activists demonstrates that building better ideas and strategies in social movements, learning new skills as you campaign, is not the preserve of the well-educated intelligentsia but can be shared in a broad collaborative enterprise encompassing not only the highly educated but also the marginalised.

Notes

[1] The dormant LCTR was briefly revived by Ryder, Acton and the trade unionist Rodney Bickerstaffe and played a role in establishing the GTLRC.

[2] In 1960 access to what was termed common land was denied to Gypsies and Travellers by the Caravan Sites and Control of Development Act 1960. Post-war urban development also greatly reduced the number of traditional stopping-places.

[3] In fact, as noted earlier, there were probably more female activists involved in the GTLRC, reflecting similiar trends in other social movements. The key thing was that older and established leaders like Len Smith supported and promoted a strong female input into the campaign.

[4] In Cottenham, Irish Traveller residents of the Smithy Fen unauthorised development and the GTLRC, with local Traveller leader and elder Patrick McCarthy, entered into discussions with local non-Traveller residents through the Cottenham Residents' Association. Acute tensions were being inflamed by lurid and sensationalist media reports, primarily in the tabloid press. A long series of negotiations led to a joint statement between the GTLRC and the Residents' Association that noted 'the shortage of Traveller sites has had a negative impact on the social inclusion of Gypsies and Travellers, has caused inconvenience for the settled community and led to a deterioration in community relations', but that the root cause of the problem was government policy and the shortage of sites (Kirby, 2004).

References

Acton, T.A. and Ryder, A. (2013) *Roma Civil Society: Deliberative Democracy for Change in Europe*, University of Birmingham: Third Sector Research Centre Working Paper.

Baker, N. (2003) 'Press Release: MP to meet Minister to discuss travellers' issues', normanbaker.org, www.normanbaker.org.uk/pr/2003/072_travellers.htm.

BBC (2003) 'Gypsy effigies burnt on bonfire', BBC News, 28 October, http://news.bbc.co.uk/2/hi/uk_news/england/southern_counties/3222321.stm.

BBC (2005) 'Howard rejects gypsy racist claim', BBC News, 7 April, http://news.bbc.co.uk/2/hi/uk_news/politics/vote_2005/frontpage/4422531.stm.

Benford, R.D. and Snow, D.A. (2000) 'Framing processes and social movements: an overview and assessment', *Annual Review of Sociology*, vol 26, pp 611–39.

Caldeira, R. (2008) 'My land, your social transformation: conflicts within the landless people movement', *Journal of Rural Studies*, vol 24, pp 129–37.

Campbell, D., Wunungmurra, P. and Nyomba, H. (2005) 'Starting where the people are: lessons on community development from a remote Aboriginal Australian setting', *Community Development Journal*, vol 42, no 2, pp 151–66.

Chambers, E. (2003) *Roots for Radicals: Organising for Power, Action, and Justice*, New York, NY: Continuum.

Chesters, G. and Welsh, I. (2011) *Social Movements: The Key Concepts*, London and New York: Routledge.

Cottle, S. (2008) 'Reporting demonstrations: the changing media politics of dissent', *Media, Culture and Society*, vol 30, no 6, pp 853–72.

Crawley, H. (2004) *Moving Forward: The Provision of Accommodation for Travellers and Gypsies*, London: IPPR.

Crossley, N. (2002) *Making Sense of Social Movements*, Buckingham: Open University Press.

Della Porta, D. and Diani, M. (1999) *Social Movements: An Introduction*, Oxford: Blackwell.

Fuchs, C. (2006) 'The self-organization of social movements', *Systemic Practice and Action Research*, vol 19, no 1, pp 101–37.

Gamson, W. (1992) *Talking Politics*, New York, NY: Cambridge University Press.

Gilchrist, A. and Taylor, M. (2011) *The Short Guide to Community Development*, Bristol: Policy Press.

Gillan, K. (2008) 'Understanding meaning in movements: a Hermeneutic approach to frames and ideologies', *Social Movement Studies: Journal of Social, Cultural and Political Protest*, vol 7, no 3, pp 247–63.

Greenslade, R. (2005) 'Stirring Up Tensions', *Guardian*, 14 March.

Greiner, L.E. (1972) 'Evolution and revolution as organisations grow', *Harvard Business Review*, vol 50, pp 37–46.

GTLRC (2004) 'More sites for Travellers can tackle community tensions', Press release, 4 May.

GTLRC (2005a) Letter to Prime Minister Tony Blair, 11 November.

GTLRC (2005b) 'Response to Tory/Michael Howard adverts on Travellers', Press release, 20 March.

GTLRC (2005c) 'Stamp out the prejudice', Press release, 8 April.

Hawes, D. and Perez, B. (1996) *The Gypsy and the State: The Ethnic Cleansing of British Society*, Bristol: Policy Press.

Hudson, M. (1987) '99 Members!', *Labour Campaign for Travellers' Rights Newsletter*, no 1, p 7.

Jolly, J. (2011) 'Consenting voices? Activist life stories and complex dissent', *Life Writing*, vol 8, no 4, pp 363–74.

King, C. and Cruickshank, M. (2012) 'Building capacity to engage: community engagement or government engagement', *Community Development Journal*, vol 47, no 1, pp 5–28.

Kirby, T. (2004) 'The village where Gypsies and locals learnt to live together', *The Independent*, 10 November.

Ledwith, M. and Springett, J. (2010) *Participatory Practice: Community Based Action for Transformative Change*, Bristol: Policy Press.

McAdam, D. (1996) 'Political opportunities: conceptual origins, current problems, future directions', in D. McAdam, J. McCarthy, and M.N. Zald (eds), *Comparative Perspectives on Social Movements*, Cambridge: Cambridge University Press, pp 23–40.

Morris, R. and Clements, L. (1999) *Gaining Ground: Law Reform for Gypsies and Travellers*, St Albans: University of Hertfordshire Press.

Morris, R. and Clements, L. (2002) *At What Cost? The Economics of Gypsy and Traveller Encampments*, Bristol: Policy Press.

Richardson, J. and O'Neill, R. (2012) '"Stamp on the Camps": the social construction of Gypsies and Travellers in the media and political debate', in J. Richardson and A. Ryder (eds) *Gypsies and Travellers: Accommodation, Empowerment and Inclusion in British Society*, Bristol: Policy Press, pp 169–86.

Richardson, J. and Ryder, A. (2012) *Gypsies and Travellers: Accommodation, Empowerment and Inclusion in British Society*, Bristol: Policy Press Book.

Ryder, A. (2013) 'Snakes and ladders: Inclusive community development and Gypsies and Travellers', *Community Development Journal*, vol 49, no 1, pp 21–36.

Smith, L. (2004) Unpublished acceptance speech at the Liberty Human Rights Awards, London, 11 December, see www.liberty-human-rights.org.uk/previous-award-winners.

Smith, L. (2005) Letter to the Editor, *Tribune*, May.

Snow, D.A. and Benford, R.D. (1988) 'Ideology, frame resonance, and participant mobilization', *International Social Movement Research*, vol 1, pp 197–217.

Southern Daily Echo (2007) 'Author and champion of gypsy rights dies', Obituary, 17 December.

Sun (2005) Editorial, 9 March.

Tarrow, S. (1998) *Power in Movement: Social Movements and Contentious Politics*, Cambridge: Cambridge University Press.

Vicari, S. (2010) 'Measuring collective action frames: a linguistic approach to frame analysis', *POETICS*, vol 38, pp 504–25.

Vijay, D. and Kulkarni, M. (2012) 'Frame changes in social movements: a case study', *Public Management Review*, vol 14, no 6, pp 747–70.

White, M. (2005) 'Howard denies tabloid politics', *Guardian*, 22 March.

Zald, M. (1996) 'Culture, ideology and strategic framing', in D. McAdam, J. McCarthy and M.N. Zald (eds) *Comparative Perspectives on Social Movements*, Cambridge: Cambridge University Press, pp 23–40.

EIGHT

Below the radar: Gypsy and Traveller self-help communities and the role of the Travellers Aid Trust

Susan Alexander and Margaret Greenfields

Introduction

"Who do they think they are teaching? We were a Big Society long before the government thought of it."

The quotation that opens this chapter is drawn from an interview undertaken by one of the authors with a Gypsy woman participating in a community development programme. The scathing nature of her response to a question about the impact of 'Big Society' initiatives on inclusion opportunities for members of her community is perhaps unsurprising, when we consider the duration of self-help initiatives and that strength of networks within travelling populations over many centuries (Smith and Greenfields, 2013). Despite the centuries-old vibrant culture of self-help among nomadic communities, identified by Okely (1983), and Acton's (1974) characterisation of Romanies' adaptive techniques and patterns of resilience to poverty and exclusion, in terms of popular discourse, Gypsies and Travellers are cast by service providers as either 'hard to reach' or 'victims' (Cemlyn et al, 2009), and more likely still are perceived by the general public as the undeserving beneficiaries of welfare payments and state 'special treatment' (Powell, 2010; Quarmby, 2013). In this chapter we set out to explore the strengths of Gypsy/Traveller community organisations in challenging exclusion, and the role of agencies – particularly the Travellers Aid Trust (TAT) – in capacity building among community members to assist them in developing evidence-based, culturally appropriate programmes, while providing practical support to small 'under the radar' groups entering the fiscal fray and ever-changing world of non-governmental organisations (NGOs) in austerity Britain.

McCabe et al (2010), in their review of the literature pertaining to small, ill-funded voluntary sector agencies and community groups (often organised from within the Black and Minority Ethnic (BME) sector), propose that the term 'below, or under, the radar' has become a shorthand term often applied to loosely constituted community groups undertaking informal or semi-formal activities in the third sector. The Office of the Third Sector guidance paper (2008, p 2), in an early use of the term, noted that the phrase is 'ungainly, but is the best available terminology for those organisations which are not included in the main national registers ... [and] which are not large enough to register with the Charity Commission or Companies House and are perhaps associated more closely with community building and participation than with service delivery'. While in the years of the last Labour administration (1997–2010) there was a dramatic increase in the growth of Gypsy and Traveller-led community groups (Ryder and Greenfields, 2010), many such organisations clearly fell under the heading of 'below the radar' agencies. One organisation that occupied a somewhat different position, however, perhaps both because of the date when it was constituted and the history of the original Trustees, was the Travellers Aid Trust (TAT).[1] TAT is the only independent grant maker dedicated specifically to supporting Gypsies and Travellers in the UK and, through its various incarnations over time and its early 'professionalisation' within a burgeoning sector, has been uniquely placed to gain invaluable insights into and expertise on the practicalities and challenges of Gypsy and Traveller community development. This knowledge is increasingly utilised by grant makers, agencies and government offices that in recent years have requested TAT to provide advice, broker grants and administer funding to small Gypsy/Traveller-led community groups.

Given the dispersed nature of Gypsy and Traveller populations and the challenges faced by those seeking to organise on a community basis when facing multiple domains of exclusion, not least literacy problems (Cemlyn et al, 2009), small, localised groups have an invaluable role to play, acting as an interface between the wider Gypsy and Traveller community, decision makers and service providers while playing an important role in 'ethnogenic processes', forging a collective identity for constituent members and seeking recognition and tangible forms of political/fiscal support to assist in these activities (Boxt and Raab, 2000). Moreover, culturally accessible community groups can provide leverage in mediating and negotiating intercultural dialogue, resisting acculturation and facilitating social inclusion.

Since 2000 there has been an exponential increase in the number of Gypsy and Traveller third sector groups in the UK, although the sharp decline in other BME agencies (and the simultaneous rise in need for their services) following major financial cuts must lead to concerns over the viability of the sector (Greenfields, 2011). Even taking account of the increase in Gypsy/Traveller agencies in recent years, the overall number of third sector agencies run by and for these communities remains relatively small in comparison to those operated by other ethnic minority groups. The Traveller Economic Inclusion project noted that in 2009 there were only 21 Gypsy and Traveller groups on the list of registered charities, a tiny figure when compared to the numbers in existence for other ethnic minorities (Ryder and Greenfields, 2010). The factors contributing to these low levels of formal community development are outlined in the remainder of this chapter, as are the means by which some of these obstacles can potentially be overcome.

Origins and principles

On 21 January 1988 a group of Travellers, civil liberty campaigners and solicitors came together after a series of meetings hosted by the National Council for Civil Liberties (as Liberty was then named) and formally set up the Travellers Aid Trust as a registered charity. TAT was established in an attempt to challenge hegemonic constructions of the identities of travelling people and provide legal and practical support in a climate of political hostility, directed in particular at New Travellers, when enforcement action was relatively widely used to impound living vehicles and social services departments were intervening and removing children from parents who had themselves become homeless following evictions and the seizure/destruction of their homes (see Chapter Five). While the Trustees at that time would not have explicitly theorised the model used, in essence the organisation both then and now advocates inclusive community development approaches, consciously attempting to draw on organic (in the Gramscian sense) reflexive understanding of community needs, supporting projects that centre directly on community concerns, and seeking to avoid paternalistic engagement by giving the community voice and a central role in determining direction and strategy. TAT in its present formulation also provides a dedicated space for Gypsy/Traveller third sector groups (including many 'below the radar') to develop a way forward in determining the direction and political engagement of the Traveller Law Reform Project and the All-Party Political Group on Gypsy, Traveller and Roma issues.

Craig et al (2011) and Henderson and Vercseg (2010) insist that in order to achieve inclusive community development among localised groups, the acquiring of transformative new skill-sets has to build on existing knowledge and technical expertise if such community groups are to challenge the domestication and disconnection that Bunyan (2010) says are imposed by managerialism and donor-dominated community organisation (Acton and Ryder, 2013). A number of these principles will be made explicit in the remainder of this chapter.

Until the early 1990s TAT's main work consisted in running a free legal and welfare advice line for New Travellers during 'travelling seasons' – when many festival goers were travelling across the UK, using various people's homes as a base for activities – and utilising volunteer advisors, phone lines being operated primarily via donations. By the early 1990s, despite the hostile political climate that led to the formulation of the Criminal Justice and Public Order Act 1994 (CJPOA), the activities of the charity had begun to dwindle as a result of large numbers of New Travellers and some community volunteers moving abroad, work commitments constraining the ability of Trustees to be available throughout much of the summer period and a number of long-term supporters passing away. The charity then became dormant for the next few years, although individual Trustees remained engaged in a range of political and welfare/legal activities that linked new Travellers with needs to wider nomadic populations and recognised the common experience of exclusion of all travelling people.

The different phases of the Travellers' Aid Trust

In 1998, the remaining Trustees of TAT wrote to Friends, Families and Travellers (FFT) an existing group that was administratively well supported and financially sound, asking if it would consider taking over the charity, given its more active role in the delivery of front-line services and it ability to draw down funding to support activities. FFT had been set up as a support group for New Travellers, following the implementation of the CJPOA 1994 (see Chapter Five). The FFT's directors decided that they did not have the capacity to take over TAT and did not see any clear benefit in the proposal as it then stood. TAT limped on, largely inactive other than at one or two large festivals each year, with the TAT Trustees subsisting as a small sub-set of the existing Festival Welfare Services (FWS).

During a period of intense change in the voluntary sector (in the early 1990s), the funding environment also began to change, as fewer and fewer trusts and foundations or government agencies were prepared to award grants to voluntary organisations that were not registered charities with professionally qualified staff. Despite this shift in emphasis, many funders would still allow grants to be 'brokered' or paid through registered charities to smaller, unregistered organisations, a situation that created a new and emergent role for TAT. Don Aitken (Chair and founder Trustee of TAT) subsequently approached Susan Alexander, then National Coordinator of FFT, at the Glastonbury festival, where the remaining TAT/FWS Trustees were working, and proposed that FFT consider making use of TAT to enable it to remain functioning as a mechanism that could support FFT to draw down funding.

Following some consideration, the Director and Board of FFT decided to formally approach TAT to negotiate taking it over, with the objective of using it primarily to broker grants for FFT itself and for other community groups that were beginning to emerge. The takeover was finally carried out in 2001, with a new Board of Trustees that included Margaret Greenfields, one of the original founder trustees of TAT. Susan Alexander eventually moved over to TAT charity from FFT and became the Trust Administrator.

Shortly after the re-activation of TAT, FFT was gifted a modest endowment and, in consultation with TAT and other interested parties, transferred this money to the Trust so that it could be best used for the benefit of all Gypsy, Traveller and Roma (GTR) groups as detailed in the Trust's Deed. With this asset in place, in 2003 TAT was able to begin its activities as an independent grant maker. Between then and 2013, the Trust awarded over half a million pounds in grants to individuals, families and groups (maintaining an emphasis on directly making grants to individual applicants to meet needs such as replacement of trailers that had been burnt out, provision of school uniforms for children and other activities such as supporting Traveller prisoners and elderly people). Half of the original endowment was awarded to FFT in the form of core grants and the remaining sum was utilised over a period of years both to deliver 'small grants' to a wide range of Gypsy/Traveller/ Roma and New Traveller applicants and for wider schemes such as fire safety or solar panel delivery to nomadic applicants (see annual reports on TAT website[2]).

Almost as soon as the Trust became active as an independent grant maker, TAT was approached by Comic Relief, which enquired if the Trust would be willing to administer a grant that Comic Relief was considering awarding to the recently formed Gypsy and Traveller Law Reform Coalition (GTLRC). The Coalition had emerged out of a series of national conferences arranged by Cardiff University's Traveller Law Reform Unit and brought together a wide range of stakeholders with the aim of promoting what ultimately became the Traveller Law Reform Bill (see Chapter Seven).

Having seven years' experience as National Coordinator of FFT (which included front-line case-work as well as policy development and project delivery), the Trust Administrator had an intimate knowledge of the various communities involved, had worked closely with most organisations and agencies in the field and was well known and trusted by all parties. As the former primary fund raiser for FFT, and with many years' experience of servicing grants, Susan Alexander brought her understanding of the difficulties faced by Gypsy and Traveller organisations in securing funding and from the outset this helped to inform the Trust's approach to grant making, supported by the experience and knowledge of the Trustees.

Not only was the Trust happy to support the Gypsy and Traveller law reform movement as a whole, but it soon became clear that the many smaller community-led organisations that began to emerge as a result of the GTLRC also needed support. The Trust did this by providing small grants toward the costs of core project and by giving one-to-one assistance with drawing up constitutions and policy documents, basic book-keeping and the presentation of accounts.

In addition, TAT actively sought to secure further funding for the law reform movement and, in partnership with Comic Relief, set up the Special Bursary Fund and the DIY Fund grants programme. The Special Bursary Fund reimbursed expenses for travel to political/ policy meetings and conferences and met the cost of training days on developments in law and national policy. This facility was hugely significant, as it enabled individual GTR activists working at the grassroots level to participate in debates and discussion directly affecting their communities as well as to access training relevant to their project and outreach work. The DIY Fund provided core funding to groups for the express purpose of building capacity and sustainability, with one-to-one support and advice provided by the Trust Administrator. Additional funding for the GTLRC was secured from the Joseph Rowntree Charitable Trust and the Allen Lane Foundation. All grants were applied for, administered and serviced by the Trust on behalf of the community. As a result of the endowment bequest that reactivated TAT, the Trust was able to contribute funding to both the Special Bursary Fund and the DIY Fund, as well as support all administrative and management costs for the GTLRC.

Through its support to smaller groups so as to facilitate and improve their participation in the law reform process, the difficulties they faced in relation to their long-term sustainability and development became increasingly evident to the Trust. Many complained that they felt they were being discriminated against by funders and marginalised by the larger, well-established non-Gypsy and Traveller-led voluntary sector groups working with their communities. Accordingly, it was suggested that the reason why 'below the radar' groups struggled to secure funding was because grant makers did not trust them, felt insecure as to their ability to administer grants and deliver services and did not understand the extreme hardship and discrimination they faced as communities. It became clear that only a handful of grant makers were supporting the Gypsy and Traveller communities and many of the smaller groups faced considerable difficulty in securing any funding at all, such funding mainly being accessed through the auspices of TAT, while larger, more politically astute Gypsy/Traveller-led groups were able to draw down substantial sums, concentrating grant monies in certain regions or locations. Accordingly, TAT was pivotal in assisting 'below the radar' groups to expand, build capacity and attract independent funding as they delivered programmes suitable for service users in their own localities and 'owned' by their members.

The importance and challenges of community development for Gypsies and Travellers

TAT has long recognised that for grant makers, supporting GTR communities can at times be challenging. Factors such as illiteracy, lack of familiarity with formal procedures, cultural attitudes or practices, internal politics and marginalisation can present barriers both to the community as applicants (Cemlyn et al, 2009) and to the grant maker as funder. The strength of prejudice and hatred that the general public and some sectors of the media openly express towards these communities can also impact on grant-making practices, particularly in relation to grant makers who rely on broadcast appeals and public donations. Thus one example of the media attacking donors is reflected in *The Sun* newspaper's headline 'Comic Relief's cash aid for gipsies [sic, non-capitalised] is a sick joke' (*Sun*, 2005). Such media and public hostility often results in donor organisations seeking to be discreet, as opposed to overtly supporting GTR communities, for fear of alienating other sectors of the community. That said, there are a number of grant makers who have a long track record of supporting GTR groups, although only a handful openly state in publicity materials that these groups fall within their funding criteria.

In addition to these challenges, the GTR communities are relatively dispersed and rarely found in the same concentrations in towns and cities as other BME groups, and are less visibily 'different' (Smith and Greenfields, 2013). When combined with lower degrees of integration into mainstream society and high rates of social exclusion and disadvantage in comparison to most other ethnic minorities, they thus remain largely 'voiceless' in terms of access to power, authority and self-presentation (Greenfields and Ryder, 2012).

Given that GTR communities face similar challenges to other communities across multiple domains (including poor health, domestic violence, low educational attainment, rural isolation, drug and alcohol abuse, unemployment, poverty and homelessness), and despite the fact that mainstream grant programmes are available to assist other populations experiencing these problems, TAT has repeatedly identified that GTR groups are not effectively accessing many of the grants available to redress such harms.

A key theme recognised by many commentators (Cemlyn et al, 2009) is that, historically, many adult GTR people have very poor or limited literacy skills. Inevitably this makes understanding grant-making criteria and filling in forms, let alone identifying which grant maker to approach, extremely difficult. Although many run extremely successful businesses, formal book-keeping is not common and many transactions are done verbally or in cash over a handshake (Ryder and Greenfields, 2010). Similarly, many also have limited or no information technology (IT) skills and only intermittent access to the internet (creating problems in accessing and completing online application forms), although this is changing as younger generations and more activists are becoming IT literate. Not only are barriers to access rife, but very few service providers, whether statutory or voluntary, are adequately resourced, informed about and geared up to help GTR groups to apply for funding, and there is a widespread lack of training on GTR culture and the issues that the community face, adding further obstacles to effective engagement.

As a result of the largely informal and relatively new 'below the radar' sector and 'self-help' approach favoured by Gypsies and Travellers in their everyday economic and social life (Ryder and Greenfields, 2010), very few GTR community-led groups are able to carry out proper monitoring and evaluation, even if they were to obtain grant funding. In part this is due to a failure to understand the relevance and importance of this exercise, along with a lack of experience in how to carry it out effectively. TAT has been repeatedly informed that, for GTR groups, the indicator of its success is how positively its work affects the community and that, with their limited resources, this is the groups' primary concern, particularly when service users are often in a state of crisis and experiencing evictions or chronic ill-health. Many community groups find the requirements entailed in reporting back to grant makers or the expectation that they will prepare a glossy annual report a distraction from the hard and important work they are doing, replying to requests for audited accounts with the call to 'come and see for yourself if you want to know how the money is spent'. Given the fierce pride of most Gypsies and Travellers, we are aware that offence can be (and has been) mistakenly taken when accounts are requested or questioned by funders, not because of any attempt to misappropriate funds, but due to lack of familiarity with the requirements of servicing a grant. Rather than risk any questioning of their integrity, some groups will send in every single original receipt and invoice to account for their expenditure, or have been known to return funding if they believe that their honesty is being questioned.

There are also recurrent issues over privacy, with communities that have experienced centuries of monitoring and control (Richardson and Ryder, 2012) being concerned that a request for data on the work they are doing equates to a demand for detailed personal information about the individuals they are helping. Historical experiences mean that GTR people are inherently wary of data collected on them, and activists are reluctant to gather potentially 'dangerous' information from their own community for the benefit of an 'outsider'.

Perhaps of greatest significance, however, is the fact that most GTR people face difficulties in their own personal circumstances. This is usually centred on a lack of secure accommodation (such as threat of eviction for sited or roadside families or racism experienced by house-dwellers), which impacts directly on access to adequate healthcare, education and employment. Those that are working to help their own communities frequently either face these issues themselves or are trying to help individuals and families in crisis, with little or no support. Accordingly, despite an urgent need of funding, dealing with application forms and the required accompanying documentation becomes a secondary priority for such grassroots organisations.

Internal competition and structural challenges

There are a number of common themes among the barriers to organisational development that are faced by GTR communities. While these issues are not unique to these populations, overlapping with the hurdles experienced by many grassroots community groups (and indeed there are some exceptions, with a number of very professional, successful and effective GTR-led projects), most organisations with which we have contact report at least one or more of these issues, which act as an obstacle to securing funding and ensuring sustainability.

Firstly, many of the groups have very similar aims and appear to overlap in their objectives (even if working on a localised basis). Grant makers thus raise concerns over the possibility of duplication of work. Secondly, many groups are not technically 'fit for purpose', with insufficient capacity in relation to staffing, resources and management. Thirdly, there can be a lack of transparency and 'democracy', with many groups being led by strong individuals and/or being family run. In addition to this, the level of skills on management committees is generally weak, with membership often being tokenistic. Despite the above points, many groups still manage to achieve very positive outcomes for their communities, but these outcomes are often 'soft' and indistinct, failing to meet the reporting criteria imposed by funding bodies. When challenged over these 'organisational failings' – particularly in relation to record-keeping of how income is utilised – as noted above, a cycle of misunderstandings and break-down of relationships between funders and applicants can occur.

Community development and donor relationships

It is evident from the above discussion that more work needs to be done to strengthen 'formal' capacity within many groups and to build upon existing inspirational, grassroots-level activities. However, capacity building is frequently more complex than simply providing training. Supporting GTR groups often requires a more proactive, hands-on approach and can be time intensive, a situation that may cause difficulties, in particular for bigger grant makers that receive large numbers of applications across a broad spectrum of applicants. Indeed, regardless of the size of the grant maker, dedicating resources to a small and select number of beneficiaries may not only be impossible or impractical, but can also be seen as unfair to other applicant groups and flying in the face of increased 'mainstreaming' of services/funding.

A further challenge is that some of the requirements set by grant makers can go against the grain of GTR cultures. The kind of accountability, the level of monitoring or data collection required and the types of organisational structure commonly found in mainstream agencies often do not blend well with modes of working that sit comfortably within traditional networks and community practices and that offer different forms of accountability congruent with membership of closed, close-knit communities. It has also been suggested by a number of external professionals and agencies that GTR communities may often 'tell you what you want to hear', rather than what funders want or need. While there may be some justification in this claim, such 'assertive positivity' is not meant as a deception but is a mechanism for self-preservation that has emerged from years of persecution, and works as a way of 'dealing with outsiders' and avoiding undue interference. Breaking through such barriers and reaching 'the truth' can be very difficult – particularly if it requires community members to acknowledge that they are finding it difficult to meet certain requirements, or if a lack of literacy or numeracy skills is a hurdle to meeting bureaucratic demands. Such openness requires that a relationship of trust exist between grant makers and the communities concerned. Accordingly, it is not a case simply of 'imparting' skills to GTR activists, but one of finding a way to engage communities in the grant distribution process without compromising those elements of their culture that make Gypsies and Travellers who they are.

Grant makers have taken a range of approaches to dealing with these issues, and in relation to GTR groups this has included funding broad capacity-development projects, and providing basic core costs while groups develop and improve internal structures and access to funding to some of the larger, more established groups to enable them to support emerging local agencies; and paying consultants to work with local communities to help them identify needs and ways of delivering services. Although a significant amount of work has been done with GTR communities since the start of the 21st century by a number of grant makers (particularly around policy development, law reform and capacity building), overall the main advances have been achieved with the handful of well-established national agencies, while many smaller local or regional groups continue to struggle with the above skills.

Building solid national networks

In order to identify ways of strengthening community skills and exploring issues related to funding difficulties, the Trust approached the Wates Foundation and obtained financial support to hold a two-day seminar in September 2008 that brought members of the GTR communities together with grant makers. Prior to the event, the Trust commissioned a telephone survey with community groups to help identify their experiences and perceptions of applying for funding and carried out an online survey with grant makers to assess their level of knowledge of the community and develop a profile of grant-making practices.

The research showed that grant makers were keen to support the community but received very few applications, and identified that Gypsy and Traveller groups automatically assumed that they would be unsuccessful in approaching funders if criteria did not explicitly state that Gypsies and Travellers were eligible for grants. Analysis of data also suggested that many applications would have been rejected by grant makers at the initial assessment stage as not meeting basic requirements. While TAT would have identified that the application was from a community group with low literacy skills, poor or minimal monitoring and very informal structures, and consequently would have sought to address these issues by contacting the group and supporting an amended application, larger grant makers tended to simply discard forms as incomplete, unclear and lacking sufficient information or required documentation. It rapidly became clear that where this occurred there was no negative intent, merely that bigger funders were overwhelmed with applications and applied a strictly even-handed approach that was not necessarily equitable when all of the above factors were taken into account, compounding the difficulties experienced by community groups in obtaining grant income. As noted above, lack of 'fitness for purpose' (in the sense of minimal staffing and administrative resources and poorly trained management committees) was also repeatedly identified as a reason for failure to access grants.

In response, the DIY Fund had been set up specifically to support new and emerging community-led groups, with the Trust providing input into helping groups to become formally constituted and providing training in core administrative skills and record-keeping requirements and information on the expectations of grant funders. Unfortunately, as with so many short-term schemes, the core funding jointly provided by TAT and Comic Relief supported only three years of programmes and hence could not develop many projects, or prove totally effective in succession planning, leaving a number of projects still struggling to survive. One of the most significant factors in developing sustainability is the unwillingness of most grant makers to provide core funding for community groups, opting instead to fund project working. In turn, while project funding may be useful, many GTR groups were not prepared to compromise their core activity of reactively supporting their communities in times of crisis by (in their view) wasting time fabricating project proposals to meet the restrictive criteria of funders in their struggle to bring in income – a situation exacerbated by the history of the majority of the groups of sustaining services through the efforts of committed, determined individuals working on a voluntary basis to challenge the inequalities and discrimination experienced by their communities.

Subsequently TAT set up a Gypsy and Traveller Issue Based Network (IBN) through the Association of Charitable Foundations (ACF), as well as designing free, downloadable factsheets for funders on working with GTR groups. The Trust also produced a booklet entitled *A Grant Maker's Guide to Supporting Gypsies and Travellers* and ran workshops at the ACF annual conference to highlight the hurdles that faced communities in obtaining funding. Finally, building upon TAT's previous experience it reached the conclusion that there was a need for truly bespoke support with careful diagnosis and time to enable knowledge and trust to be developed, so TAT worked with the Tudor Trust to commission the Institute of Voluntary Action Research to provide bespoke one-to-one capacity building and developmental support for eight community groups in 2011–12.

Financial squeezes and the Big Society

The terrain of funding and capacity building among 'below the radar' GTR groups is complex, not least in the light of the on-going fiscal austerities that are impacting significantly on Gypsy and Traveller services, a theme consistently reiterated in the report *A Big or Divided Society?* (Ryder et al, 2011) funded by the Joseph Rowntree Charitable Trust and organised by TAT through a two-day Panel Review into how Coalition government policies impact on the lives and well-being of Gypsies and Travellers. The panel, which mirrored the format of parliamentary select committees and was held at the House of Lords under the auspices of the veteran campaigner Lord Avebury, pilot of the Caravan Sites Act 1968, consisted of a series of sessions that heard evidence from a range of politicians from across the main political parties as well as academics, legal practitioners, health and education specialists working with the communities, local government, other service providers, the police and, of course, Gypsies and Travellers themselves. It was noteworthy that the government submission to the Panel Review suggested that GTR communities are perceived as deliberately turning their backs on opportunities to engage with wider communities, and failed to recognise the structural barriers outlined above,

> Community tensions can often be based on irrational feelings of unfamiliarity and mistrust, but there is no reason for Gypsies, Roma and Travellers to stand back from the

> Big Society ethos of social participation and contribution, they are members of society like anyone else. By working alongside their neighbours on issues of common interest there is an opportunity for breaking down artificial barriers for the benefit of everyone. (Ryder et al, 2011, p 39)

In contrast, mirroring the title of this chapter, Gloria Buckley MBE (in her submission to the hearings) stated:

> 'I don't know what "Big Society" is. If, as has been suggested, it is local communities, neighbourhoods and families looking after each other, then Gypsies and Travellers have always been members of a Big Society; it has been the only one we could rely on.' (Ryder et al, 2011, p 75)

Overall, the review found that, despite the emphasis on community solidarity and action, the Big Society agenda was counterproductive of GTR inclusion, given the way in which barriers to equality of access were completely ignored and the disproportionate impact on vulnerable families of the severe cuts to Traveller Education Services and specialist health outreach delivery.

Indeed a strong fear was expressed at the Panel Review that the existing but vulnerable GTR third sector would be seriously threatened by national and local authority cutbacks. As the Roma Support Group noted in its submission to the Panel Review, there was a contradiction between Big Society rhetoric and the reality of austerity politics and cuts:

> How does this agree with the government's rhetoric to engage our sector in opportunities to build vibrant and resilient civil society? Many small–medium size community groups, which deliver vital and life-saving work for the most marginalised members of our society, will go under well before opportunities ever emerge. (Ryder et al, 2011, p 75)

The future

In this brief history of TAT and the development of explicitly 'Traveller-proofed' engagement with 'below the radar' community groups and funders, it has been noted that, despite the efforts of a handful of sensitive grant makers, much work still remains to be done to ensure a level playing field in terms of equality of access. On the one hand, these communities are fighting against a government-driven agenda that implicitly erodes their culture and appears to overtly force assimilation with the mainstream. On the other hand, they face a hostile, misinformed public, misguided by a demonising media that creates a climate of fear and suspicion in relation to specialist services for these populations. Small community groups must fight for resources in a climate of austerity and severe cuts to services, which in turn puts greater pressure on trusts and foundations, creating a vicious cycle of financial exclusion for grassroots organisations and increasing a sense of hopelessness and frustration among groups that are continually rejected for funding.

We have sought to demonstrate that supporting GTR communities requires considerable commitment in terms of time and resources as well as in terms of fighting the prejudice, discrimination and institutional racism that they face on a daily basis. The issues affecting them are complex, with a range of differing and often conflicting agendas and motivations. There are no easy fixes, and success depends entirely on devoting enough time and energy to understanding the issues in their entirety. To effectively support these communities, the voluntary and charitable sector must think outside the box, be prepared to compromise and take risks and, most importantly, establish a relationship of mutual respect and trust with the Gypsies, Travellers and Roma with whom it seeks to work.

At the time of writing, the long-term future of TAT is unclear. For the moment we continue to exist, brokering grants and open to other suggestions for assisting funders to work for the benefit of Gypsies, Travellers and Roma. It was always the intention of the Trustees to 'spend out' the original asset, and as of June 2013, all the Trust's own grants programmes ceased. However, a partnership with the Esmée Fairbairn Foundation has been established and in late 2012 funding was secured for the Trust to deliver a two-year programme of grants to the community on behalf of the Foundation. These grants focus on developing the skills of young people, improving literacy and numeracy and working with Travellers in prison/offenders. The Trust also successfully secured funding for a two-day residential event (Alexander, 2013) to bring groups together to discuss the future of the law reform movement and ways of seeking to influence policy and parliamentary decision making. Following this event the Trust was given a clear mandate to seek further funding to facilitate further conferences, meetings and activities to take this work forward. While funding was secured in July 2013 to work on supporting law reform/ parliamentary issues for a further 18 months, no funding currently exists for the Trust to continue after June 2015, unless another shift in its fortunes occurs.

Notes

[1] Not to be confused with the other TAT – the Travellers Advice Team, which runs a national helpline and newsletter from the Community Law Partnership in Birmingham.

[2] http://travellersaidtrust.org/.

References

Acton, T. (1974) *Gypsy Politics and Social Change*, London: Routledge.

Acton, T. and Ryder, A. (2013) *Roma Civil Society: Deliberative Democracy for Change in Europe*, Birmingham: Third Sector Research Centre Working Paper, University of Birmingham, www.tsrc.ac.uk/LinkClick.aspx?fileticket=6h%2bX5ZLX6%2fs%3d&tabid=500.

Alexander, S. (2013) 'Report on the Gypsy, Traveller and Roma Communities' residential event. Trafford Hall, 4–5 February', http://travellersaidtrust.org/wp-content/uploads/2012/03/GTR-Residential-Report.pdf.

Boxt, M. and Raab, M. (2000) 'Puvunga and point conception: A comparative study of Southern California Indian traditionalism', *Journal of California and Great Basin Anthropology*, vol 22, no 1, pp 43–67.

Bunyan, P. (2010) 'Broad based organising in the UK: reasserting the centrality of political activity in community development', *Community Development Journal*, vol 45, no 1, pp 111–27.

Cemlyn, S., Greenfields, M., Burnett, S., Matthews, Z. and Whitwell, C. (2009) *Inequalities Experienced by Gypsy and Traveller Communities: A Review*, London: Equalities and Human Rights Commission.

Craig, G., Mayo, M., Popple, K., Shaw, M. and Taylor, M. (eds) (2011) *The Community Development Reader: History, Themes and Issues*, Bristol: Policy Press.

Greenfields, M. (2011) 'Community/Third Sector Employment opportunities and the impact of the Big Society on opportunities for minority women', unpublished conference paper, Social Policy Association conference, University of Lincoln, July.

Greenfields, M. and Ryder, A. (2012) 'Research with and for Gypsies, Roma and Travellers: combining policy, practice and community in action research', in J. Richardson and A. Ryder (eds) *Gypsies and Travellers: accommodation, empowerment and inclusion in British society*, Bristol: Policy Press, pp 151–67.

Henderson, P. and Vercseg, I. (2010) *Community Development and Civil Society: Making Connections in the European Context*, Bristol: Policy Press.

McCabe, A., Phillimore, J. and Maybin, L. (2010) *'Below the Radar' Activities and Organisations in the Third Sector: A Summary Review of the Literature*, Birmingham: Third Sector Research Centre Working Paper.

Office of the Third Sector (2008) 'Draft Guidance: National Survey of Third Sector Organisations "Under the Radar" Pilot', www.ncvo-vol.org.uk/sites/default/files/UploadedFiles/Research_Events/Phillimore_et_al.pdf.

Okely, J. (1983) *The Traveller-Gypsies*, Cambridge: Cambridge University Press.

Powell, R. (2010) 'Gypsy-Travellers and welfare professional discourse: on individualisation and social integration', *Antipode*, vol 43, no 2, pp 471–93.

Quarmby, K. (2013) *No Place to Call Home: Gypsies, Travellers and the Road Beyond Dale Farm*, London: Oneworld Publications.

Richardson, J. and Ryder, A. (2012) *Gypsies and Travellers: Accommodation, Empowerment and Inclusion in British Society*, Bristol: Policy Press.

Ryder, A. and Greenfields, M. (2010) *Roads to Success: Routes to Economic and Social Inclusion for Gypsies and Travellers*, London: Irish Traveller Movement in Britain.

Ryder, A., Acton, T., Alexander, S., Cemlyn, S., Cleemput, P., Greenfields, M., Richardson, J. and Smith, D. (2011) *A Big or Divided Society? Final Recommendations and Report of the Panel Review into the Impact of the Localism Bill and Coalition Government Policy on Gypsies and Travellers*, Kidwelly: Travellers' Aid Trust Report.

Smith, D. and Greenfields, M. (2013) *Gypsies and Travellers in Housing: The Decline of Nomadism*, Bristol: Policy Press.

Sun (2005) 'Comic Relief's cash aid for Gypsies is a sick joke', 6 March.

NINE

Gender and community activism: the role of women in the work of the National Federation of Gypsy Liaison Groups

Sarah Cemlyn, Maggie Smith-Bendell, Siobhan Spencer and Sally Woodbury

"Very strong women – wherever you look there has been a strong woman."

Introduction

This chapter outlines the work of key women activists within the National Federation of Gypsy Liaison Groups (NFGLG) who are working to support their communities locally and nationally to gain stable places to live and to promote improved understanding and relationships between the settled and Gypsy/Traveller communities. A major aspect of their work involves advocating for planning permission for families, as well as educating officials and the public about Gypsies' and Travellers' culture, lives and needs, and commemorating Gypsy history.

Through reflections on their experiences, underpinned by feminist community work theory and insights from other theory and research, the chapter explores the gender dimensions of activism for Gypsy and Traveller women, the deep roots in their communities that generate both strengths and barriers and the theoretical developments their practice suggests. It reflects a partnership between activism and research in being co-written by Gypsy activists and a non-Gypsy researcher who had the privilege of joining these discussions. The authors also acknowledge the inspiring contribution of other women, some of whose work is reflected in other chapters or referred to below.

After outlining a feminist perspective on community development and the experience of gender within Gypsy and Traveller communities, the chapter considers the development of Gypsy and Traveller women's activism, before focusing on the experience of NFGLG activists. It concludes by examining some of the main differences from and parallels with 'mainstream' feminist community action, reflecting minority group experiences.

Women and community development

Gypsy and Traveller women, like many other women who are active on behalf of their communities, may not identify as 'feminist'. Media portrayals have not assisted understanding of this term. However, feminist writers, including activists, practitioners and academics (for example Mayo, 1977; Curno et al, 1982; Ledwith 2005; Dominelli 2006) have focused on the activities of women in communities that had otherwise remained obscured because men often took the prominent roles while women undertook vital activity behind the scenes. They have brought women's wide-ranging activism to light in order to celebrate it and analyse its relationship to women's lives and the principles that inform its specific contributions to community development (and have in turn informed community development more broadly). These include working collaboratively, supportively and not in hierarchical ways, paying attention to individual experience and emotional issues and building from these personal experiences to political analysis and action.

As with other concepts of 'community' and 'culture', feminism is not a unitary theory (Orme, 2003). Standpoint feminism, which built on Marxian theory, asserts that the experiences of oppressed people and their engagement in struggle provide an alternative, less distorted basis for knowledge than does dominant or hegemonic thinking (see Harding, 2004). This analysis was in turn critiqued as a white-dominated approach by Black and disabled feminists (for example, Hill Collins 1990; Sandoval, 1991; Begum et al, 1994). Thus there is no single 'standpoint' or 'feminism'; the diversity of women's experiences needs to be understood within an analysis of structural power relationships and diverse cultures (Ledwith, 2005).

Similarly, within feminist community development theory there are also internal critiques. Emeluju (2011) argues that the literature presents 'women' and 'community development' as 'essentialised' (that is, uniform and unchanging), and so provides an inadequate basis for theorising political activism. Nevertheless, despite intersectional oppression and multifaceted identities, Takkar (2011) argues, in relation to South Asian women, that collective identity can be mobilised for political activism without compromising other aspects of identity, in a kind of strategic essentialism that Brubaker (2004, p 10) claims is 'central to the *practice* of politicised ethnicity'.

Women in Gypsy and Traveller communities

Gender roles in Gypsy and Traveller communities are strongly differentiated, with clear responsibilities for either sex (Spencer, 2003). Women have a central role in managing the home and caring for children and elders and, by extension, dealing with agencies like health and education. There can be strong cultural pride in this role. It also means that women are at the forefront in coping with the physical and emotional impact of social exclusion and racism on their families, which for caravan-dwelling families without a secure site means many hardships, and for many house-dwelling families means isolation, stress and additional exposure to racism (Cemlyn et al, 2009). This combination has led some women to involvement in a range of community activities.

At the same time family expectations can limit their opportunities to work more widely in community activism. When communities are under pressure, experiencing discrimination and lack of access to services, there can be a tendency to adhere more firmly to cultural traditions. Women becoming involved in community activism may face additional difficulties because of moving beyond culturally ascribed gender roles.

Gypsy and Traveller women's previous involvement in community activism

There has been a wide range of work by Gypsy and Traveller women's groups and by mixed groups with women in leading roles since the 1990s. Some of this activism built on the women's cultural role, their keen sense of community and strong bonding social capital to promote the interests of their communities and understanding of their culture in the wider society. The marginalisation, exclusion and demonisation to which the communities are subject, based on racism, 'othering' and projection of stereotypes (Richardson and Ryder, 2012), constitute cultural 'misrecognition', alongside the 'maldistribution' arising from lack of services and resources (Young, 1990; Fraser, 1995, 2005). To counter this, community groups themselves mobilised positive cultural images, undertook educational work with public services and produced cultural materials (Southwark Traveller Women's Group, 1992; Cemlyn, 1997) so as to increase awareness, counteract stereotypes and enhance cultural 'recognition'. Some joined campaigns with others, for example the National Traveller Women's Forum in Ireland. Groups like the UK Association of Gypsy Women have undertaken dedicated work to support community members in difficulties and to campaign for sites.

In the last decade more women-led groups have been formed (for example One Voice) that have extended work in health and education by training health advocates and promoting improved services. Many women are now entering employment with voluntary sector groups (see Chapter Nine), gaining training and further and higher education, often using this to increase their contribution to community activism. Individuals have assumed political positions, including the late Sylvia Dunn, who stood in a parliamentary election against Michael Howard in 2005, and, more recently, the work of Candy Sheridan as a local councillor.

The National Federation of Gypsy Liaison Groups

Following the disbandment of the Gypsy and Traveller Law Reform Coalition, and building on the work of the Derbyshire Gypsy Liaison Group (DGLG), the National Federation of Gypsy Liaison Groups[1] was formed in 2005 as a separate national organisation chaired by Peter Mercer (see Chapter Two). With his support it plays a key role in providing a forum for the development of local and regional groups. Its wide-ranging work includes policy and good practice work on accommodation, education, health, criminal justice, culture, heritage, Holocaust memorial and representation at the European Roma and Travellers Forum to monitor progress (or lack of the same) on national Roma integration strategies (NFGLG, 2012). Some of these aspects feature more prominently than others in this chapter.

The experience of women activists

Often at the heart of this organisational network are women activists. Three of the authors of this chapter, Maggie Smith-Bendell,[2] Siobhan Spencer[3] and Sally Woodbury,[4] reflected on their experience in this work and their hopes for the future through interviews with Sarah Cemlyn. A further interview with a younger activist, Tammy Holland working with Maggie Smith-Bendell, also informs aspects of the discussion.

Their experiences are explored through several themes, with Sarah providing linking discussion. There are varieties of emphasis between the three activists, but many parallels. To aid analysis, comparisons are made with theoretical ideas outlined above or with other research.

Trajectory of current activists

Although routes into activism are often complex (Perkins, 2012) and other more specific reasons were described, there is a common thread for some of the women. For Maggie and Sally the activist pathway started with the experience of seeking planning permission for their own family site, which exposed them to the prejudice and dishonesty of local authority officials and the hostility of neighbours. This 'tortured' experience raised awareness of the depths of discrimination they and their communities faced, including lack of cultural capital, but also empowered them to take on further challenges in supporting others. Critical reflection leading to conscientisation (Freire, 1972) is implicit in this process.

> "It was all quite sad because me and my husband went for planning here and we ended up with a very, very prejudiced planning officer who took a personal issue to make sure I did not get planning and did not have any rights of any description and during that 12 months of fighting for planning it made me realise that I was in a very good position of fighting for planning … and it made me realise that a huge number of Romani Gypsies out there were not in that position, they wouldn't be able to understand filling out forms and understand things said to them on planning issues … We have always been brought up to have a fear of anyone in authority and it was overcoming that fear that put me on the road I went on … It was a hard-fought battle." (Maggie)

> I found a piece of land … and then I got planning and I also then saw the objections and the nastiness that local people could bring to you … I experienced the most racism when I bought my land and I applied for planning permission." (Sally)

A younger activist, Tammy, was similarly referred to as having "sleepless nights asking why am I being treated like this … she had such opposition from the local village it will stay with her forever … she has gone through that dark tunnel of being abused in a racial way, it has taught [her] the reality of what is going on ... and it will help her with the planning ... she can give information and help" (Maggie).

Gallagher (1977) and Curno et al (1992) refer to the rapid mobilisation of women in desperate situations to seek collective redress for social injustices. These Gypsy activists used their own negative experience not as an immediate focus but as a foundation from which to take action on behalf of others.

For Siobhan there was a longer family and personal history of fighting for social justice, including doing "letters from being little because people would call around", a variable pattern also found in other social movements (Spence and Stephenson, 2007). A particular influence was her grandfather, and her mother had worked for Gypsies in Derbyshire. One story her grandfather told stayed with her: how, in a lean time after the Second World War he nonetheless refused to participate in the eviction of a young family in difficulty when he found that that was the work he had been offered.

> "He was appalled as he did not realise he was going to be involved in an eviction. The man who was being evicted ... had not handled things well on coming out [of the army] ... my grandfather felt sorry for him ... the man in charge of the eviction was pointing at things to go and he pointed at the baby's cot and ... my grandfather said no you won't and ... it ended up with him getting into his van and driving home. ... It was a tight time for everybody. ... he had ethics about what he would and wouldn't do. ... In the village people were not evicted ..., grandfather would get involved with the parish council and stop people being evicted." (Siobhan)

Her continuing broader and international involvement with social justice led back to a focus on the needs of her own communities.

> "It was doing work with other people that made me reflect on my own. We used to raise money for Indian people in America – it makes you reflect there are a lot of similarities to what are happening to people over there and to our people." (Siobhan)

For all the women there was an emphasis on the importance of Gypsies themselves undertaking this work to support their communities, and of encouraging new volunteers. This implicitly mobilises an essentialised identity, but one primarily based on historical and intense contemporary experience of discrimination and the lack of a wider understanding of the way of life.

> "I think all these people on the local authority sites or those being pushed on the road..need someone from their own culture who will listen to them. ... I am challenging about one site ... I am obliged to do it because of what happened to my people through history ... They relate to me better as a Gypsy working for them rather than to a legal expert." (Maggie)

> "A lot of Travellers get upset with non-Travellers doing work for Travellers." (Sally)

Continuing routes into activism involved meeting other activists, development of wider regional and national organisations, notably the DGLG and the Romany Gypsy Advisory Group in the South West, and subsequently the NFGLG. Building power from local networks to organisations to broader federations is a significant strand of community development (Gilchrist, 2009). As well as advocacy and cultural activities, the NFGLG provides a mutual support network.

Motivation

The women powerfully expressed a deep commitment to and passion for helping others and sustaining their communities, inspiring them to continue to advocate for others to gain a secure place to live, through which the lives of families can develop and flourish, and a strong belief that achieving somewhere secure to live will have a beneficial effect on all aspects of life for the younger generation growing up. With little or no financial reward, this represents investment of emotional capital (Nowotny 1981), 'defined in terms of the social and cultural resources generated primarily by women through affective relationships within the private sphere of the family' (Gillies, 2006, p 284). Because of close community ties, some families that are supported with planning applications are already known as relatives or acquaintances, with frequent word-of-mouth referral, so affective relationships and obligations span a wider concept of the family. Though frequently neglected within community work (Hoggett and Miller, 2000), the emotional dimension has always existed within women's domain. Women's emotional labour has been highlighted in other fields of women's activism, for example women in the 1984–85 miners' strike (Spence and Stephenson, 2007).

> "The main thing is that it did not take long for me to realise that very few of my race of people [Gypsies] have anywhere to live and they do not have access to healthcare or education or even access to water or a toilet and I had all those things and that is what made me do what I did to get the children of the generation I was fighting for to have those things ... I think [the younger generation will be more aware of their rights] because when you do the planning you educate that particular family ..." (Maggie)

> "Whereas the majority of Travellers are not educated and don't know where to start ... You have to be passionate about it." (Sally)

Activism can also be informed by an understanding of inequalities and hardship experienced by all, regardless of background, reaching out to non-Gypsies and Travellers.

> "People have similar issues and concerns and there is that danger that Gypsy people become inward-looking at times – they work together but only on their issues but sometimes it makes you stronger if you say this is a similar issue to such and such ... It does make a difference [when you make links with other groups] because they see where you are coming from." (Siobhan)

What is also needed is for settled community groups to demonstrate a similar commitment to shared understanding and mutual support, rather than stoking up antagonism. There are hopeful signs when such connections are made, for example the work of Siobhan Spencer as a parish councillor supporting affordable housing for local people instead of holiday homes, which led to the parish council resisting efforts to stir up hostility to a proposed site – "all these small things can add up".

Strategies and relationships

The women's work also means building collaborative links with other communities, with agencies and practitioners such as lawyers, health workers and educationalists, with non-Gypsy activists, voluntary organisations, churches and politicians and officials at local and national level, for example Pride not Prejudice conferences led by DGLG, which promote understanding and partnership between police and Gypsies and Travellers (Coxhead, 2007).

Strong informal networks reinforce and are reinforced by the activists' work, and are also the foundation for bridging social capital (Ryder, 2012), facilitating links with mainstream communities. Every planning appeal involves an educative element to increase understanding and awareness of the values and needs of the communities. Activists also undertake direct educational work with politicians, councillors and service providers that can facilitate more favourable policies and planning processes. Gypsies are faced with re-experiencing racism during these activities, as in Sally's training work with councils about the need for sites, but are prepared for this, through the 'long tunnel' they have previously been through, to promote both redistribution of resources and recognition of difference.

> "I would sit with [the councillors delivering the training] and they would give the background, history and policy of it and people would start to ask them what they thought about Gypsies as councillors – and I was sat in front of them and they would say all sorts. I did manage to control my facial expressions but the good thing was they did not know what a Gypsy was as one was sitting right in front of them." (Sally)

Contacts outside the community still have to be treated cautiously, though some stand out.

> "You have officers in councils who are trying to do the right thing and you have higher people above them ... It looks like the council are doing the right thing but they are not." (Sally)

> "Penny Dane[5] – she was mustard, really good." (Maggie)

Combined with this is a commitment to dialogue, to promote the conditions for avoiding conflict.

> "With our group we use the word 'liaison' a lot — we are not a united Gypsy front with pick-axe handles, it's better to talk to people and come to some agreement." (Siobhan)

A strongly political element manifests in campaigning, lobbying and negotiating at local, regional and national levels working directly with politicians, ministers and the All-Party Parliamentary Group.

Achievements and rewards

The women did not dwell on achievements but gave glimpses of the astounding level of work, with astronomical planning caseloads, the great majority of which are successful, providing further insight into non-material rewards.

> "I have cases written down and I have a shedful of files — it was getting to be 400 … It was taking over my life." (Maggie)

> "I meet people that I did planning for 15 years ago and … they tell me about how well their children can read and write and that was the chance I gave them…. the reward is bigger than money — you meet those families again and again and you can see the difference and the confidence in the parents and children." (Maggie)

> "It will be in the 100s [helped with planning] — if you take the Big Lottery project, over five years encampments fell from 50 to 9 … because we got sites passed." (Siobhan)

Success generates hope among families, willingness and confidence to fight for what is needed and further work for activists. In parallel, training to change attitudes lays the conditions for more favourable consideration of applications, though not all work is acknowledged.

> "As …we did more of these [talks] and I helped Gypsies in planning cases in [those] areas where I had given talks — the councillors would talk in favour of the applications — that

was the most rewarding thing as you would see the success of it." (Sally)

Reflection and learning from experience

Reflection on practice and in practice (praxis) (Gramsci, 1971; Freire, 1972) is integral to community development (Ledwith, 2005). The women's sharp analysis of their communities' problems and needs reflects Gramsci's notion of 'organic intellectuals'. Despite previous educational disadvantage, they also learnt rapidly from experience, leapfrogging over early educational gaps to build up a high level of skills and knowledge, using conscious and focused on-the-job learning through listening, learning from each other, reflecting on experiences good and bad, adapting their approach, supporting people in previously unfamiliar situations such as prison, finding their way round bureaucracy and, in Siobhan's case, enhancing this with a degree in law "to support my work so I could do what I do better".

> "When I first started doing planning I tried to do it without the retrospective[6] ... and 99% of the time I would get turned away [by the authority] and years later I would recognise that land and by that time the land had been used for other things other than Gypsies ... We could have used it if I had had the knowledge to put in an application and not taking their word on it. I learnt very quickly within a year not to take notice and put in an application and not give up and I have learnt that when you look at a piece of land you need to tick boxes [re planning criteria]." (Maggie)

> "Originally I wasn't going to take the job at FFT but I got educated and made friends with New Travellers." (Sally)

Learning was shared, and also passed on to families to promote a better chance of success with planning applications.

> "So after we had a few failures, I started educating people and said before you pay for the land give me a ring ... and I will have a look at it. It took a while but we got there." (Maggie)

"I learnt from Maggie..Maggie had worked with the police and in government so all the hard work had been done." (Sally)

"You feel you are there so they can tick a box [re Gypsy representation] ... but I have learnt now ... I will tell them about their councillors and how they are prejudiced." (Sally)

"[Activism has] made me more brazen and not frightened to speak for what I believe in. I used to want to say things to people but was holding back in case I offended them with my views and now it's built me up to such a strong person." (Maggie)

"[Activism] has changed me, with everything that has happened in my life..I reflect a bit more. I used to be very fiery and say that's not right!..I just reflect more now." (Siobhan)

Barriers and difficulties

There are difficulties for the women and their families. Their advocacy is underpinned by their ethnic identity and community roots. However, the community foundation can be a double-edged sword. The expectation on women to put their families first creates potential barriers to activism. The co-authors of this chapter have jointly noted that being married to non-Traveller men has given them more freedom to undertake these wider roles outside the family. Indeed Maggie recorded in her first autobiographic book (Smith-Bendell, 2009) how she decided at a young age to marry outside the community because she did not want to be controlled and valued her freedom of action. The personal relationship with community is strategically managed.

"I think the main point is that had I not married a gorgio I would not have been allowed to do what I have done – I would have had to be at home doing housework, cooking and cleaning but because I married T. I was allowed to be my own woman and he encouraged me ... we are all Gypsy Traveller activists and we married gorgio." (Maggie)

"We [Gypsy women featured in this chapter] have all said this..we have departed from traditional roles because we married Gorgi men." (Siobhan)

"It's a lot easier for me because I am not married to a Gypsy. If my husband was a Traveller it would be harder to be an activist." (Sally)

The younger activist equally acknowledged that it makes a difference for her, being married to a non-Gypsy, but spoke for all the women in stating that

"If you're a Traveller you're a Traveller, whoever you are married to." (Tammy)

At the same time non-Gypsy partners have engaged with the Gypsy way of life without losing their own identity, and provided support for the activism of their wives. 'Having the back-up of my husband' was identified as one crucial factor.

Occasionally in some families a woman gains freedom for activism through being married to a co-activist:

"For example X and Y, she can go anywhere and X is a little bit more forward thinking ... some might say, oh you can't do that! You can't go there on your own!" (Siobhan)

"If a woman is married to a Romany man it's not going to happen unless it's a husband and wife thing." (Maggie)

A further liberating factor is age. It is easier for older women than younger women to be activists, and continued difficulties are foreseen for younger women because of their families' desire to protect them from perceived dangers. Indeed this dynamic may be increasing rather than diminishing, making it an uphill struggle to involve younger women.

"Well, my age helps also, that gives me a certain status in the community." (Maggie)

"I think it's changing but only for older women not so much younger women – there is a lot of fear out there – evil comes into your life place very quickly off the TV and internet and people say it's happened here and it's happening there and people think it's happening all over the place. I think in some respects some may have got stricter – they were getting more relaxed – because of what they perceive is happening in the world." (Siobhan)

Strategic decisions and actions facilitate activism, while remaining embedded in their families. They all actively continued their domestic roles, but sought more and added an activist dimension.

"My traditional role still continues being a mum and a housewife." (Sally)

"You get your cleaning done and then your mind starts racing." (Tammy)

Because of the success of their work for their communities, the women occupy a special – sometimes iconic – status, which seems to put them outside the usual cultural expectations of women's lower public profile.

"They admire me … People say 'It's all right for you because you are married to a Gorgio." (Sally)

"I think the community has put me on a pedestal and made me bigger than what I truly am." (Maggie)

However, as often for women activists, pressures and frustrations arise for the family also, for example when the women are phoned constantly at home.

"My husband got so annoyed with it he changed [the phone number]." (Sally)

"I think we need to thank our families and husbands, they have to put up with a lot … it's very hard, you think about your families and that but sometimes it's hard for things not to crash." (Siobhan)

Because of the high level of demand for their services, and with so few people doing the work, there can be a high level of stress, frustration and risk of burnout, as well as meeting hostility when they challenge officials, for example about site conditions. Funding and other difficulties have resulted in reduced numbers of groups, compounding the pressure.

> "There are not many of us working for Gypsies and everyone comes to us for help … and you just end up saying yes to everybody … and burning yourself out … You have to take time out and a lot of people who do this type of work do suffer and have breakdowns … I wish there was more people to do it." (Sally)

> "Although there are fewer groups and people doing the work, there is still lots of work to do, I could take three cases a week easily." (Maggie)

> "Sometimes you have to give yourself a stiff talking to – you can't save the whole world but you can only do a few things and not let things slide at home … There might be a case where 80 things come in. Do you make a hash of all of them or do you say I can do 10 of those and you can make a success of that?" (Siobhan)

The uphill struggle of achieving positive policies and practice can be negated by changes of government and local authority policy and politicians.

> "It's getting harder what with all the law changes – you think you have got on top of the problem and then the government change all the laws again and policies, and then you get elections where bad councillors come in and you need to start all over again." (Sally)

There are problems of funding for small groups. Depending on personal circumstances, this can cause significant additional pressure for activists. All have worked as volunteers for lengthy periods of time, even if paid posts later become available.

> "When we were voluntary it got hard and it's better now – we have been able to get extra people in – some paid, some voluntary." (Siobhan)

> "I worked three or four years for voluntary and you learn if you go anywhere you should ask for travel and child care

as I thought no one would offer it ... so learnt the hard way." (Sally)

Women's strengths as activists

The women brought their existing skills, knowledge and qualities to the work, including empathy, compassion, solidarity, assertiveness, determination and articulate advocacy, while teaching themselves on the job. This section reviews the gender dimensions of capacities employed and the impact on relationships within communities.

> "I suppose I was a very strong-willed person, I had an aim and I would go for it." (Maggie)

> "I am quite an open person ... I put my face on TV..I've always been very blunt, I've always said to people I'm not that sort of literacy person, during the years I picked it up and taught myself." (Sally)

> "There was this whole thing about social housing and I took this up locally as it was difficult for young people to get a home." (Siobhan)

They have overcome obstacles to gain a very high level of respect and authority within their communities, which can mean taking a firm line with women and with men, a line that sometimes may not be popular.

> "Sometimes things come in and you have to say well people can help themselves, ... you can give advice but sometimes the advice is not taken and you think well it's your fault, if you had taken the advice you wouldn't be in this situation. You are going to have to go to such and such a body because it's become legal now." (Siobhan)

> "When I go out I bully the men, not the women – when I say bully them I mean I say to them 'look if you don't do this we will get nowhere'. They need pushing 'this is what you do, this is what you don't do'." (Maggie)

> "I think sticking to what you believe and having integrity – like DGLG has always said we do not support big sites and they can be a problem to manage – it's difficult, people

say I've got a 20-pitch site will you support me in getting another 15 and we say well we think it's not a good thing." (Siobhan)

Given the centrality of social circumstances to many planning appeals, and women's family responsibilities, an activist's gender can be significant. Qualities that make a positive difference to organisational development were also noted, including juggling different responsibilities.

"It's like when you do planning you have to take into account personal circumstances and I have been in Brian Cox's office [solicitor] and women would tell me and I would tell Brian because they would not want to say it to a man, so there are many barriers." (Maggie)

"Women are very good at multi-tasking, they can think and do more than one thing at once – men don't seem to be able to do that so much."[2] (Siobhan)

It was felt that while some key activists have been men, regrettably there were currently very few involved. Sally's experience was that men could more easily get argumentative, which might hinder rather than help get results. Cemlyn et al (2009, p 232), referring to the increasing involvement of young Gypsy and Traveller women in advocacy and community projects, speculate that the 'feminisation of political activism' may deter men from coming forward.

The women reflected on the influence of women's perspective on the development of the NFGLG and other organisations, and noted the on-going mutual support and strength of women activists.

"… there is Siobhan Spencer and also Bridie Jones and me and Muzzelly McCready. There's not a lot of Gypsy women activists but I think the way we met at meetings and gave each other advice and I think that is one of the reasons that the women stuck at it. Siobhan has been doing it longer than me and she has been the main one we ring up." (Maggie)

"Very strong women – wherever you look there has been a strong woman – take Janie Codona and Shirley Barrett in One Voice.[7] You've got the two sisters in the UK Association of Gypsy Women[8] … Kay Beard and Rachel Francis Ingham." (Siobhan)

The future

Despite these role models, many obstacles are encountered in encouraging more women to be involved. Once they had achieved their own site they mainly, and understandably, resumed their lives.

> "Once they got what they needed they didn't go any more [to meetings]." (Sally)

> "We tried but they revert back to the Romani way of life and don't speak and are not heard ... I think we have a long way to go." (Maggie)

However, there were rallying calls about how more women might be encouraged into activity, in all areas of women's activism, and the support that would be offered.

> "I think we need to persuade new people we will support them and bring them on, no matter what part of the country they come from ...We are all getting aged now and we have got to encourage the young to come out of the woodwork and be proud to be a Romany or Traveller ... if one of them reads the book it would be good to encourage them." (Maggie)

Conclusion

The NFGLG has changed the lives of many Gypsy/Traveller families who can now flourish with a stable and secure home; enhanced, wider understanding and respect; and a fairer share of resources for the communities. The inspiring contribution of women prompts discussion of the ways in which their activism demonstrates, questions or develops the feminist principles outlined earlier.

Some differences from these perspectives have emerged, based on the specific situation of Gypsies and Travellers. Their historic shared persecution results in an awareness of the reasons for hardship that may be less available to other oppressed populations without a clear group identity. However, what is needed is the second stage of conscientisation, the hope and empowerment that oppression and discrimination can be overcome, which we have seen generated here.

Second, these activists are often working as sole community representatives, in planning appeals or training, and rather than being immediate, group support is by phone or e-mail, which differs from many women's or community groups. They are out on a limb, 'put on a pedestal'. Arguably, therefore, a hierarchy of sorts develops, though this is not sought, indeed they long for more people to join the work. Questions arise as to whether they enter a somewhat different category of 'Gypsy women'.

Their gender is a complex attribute: they have to overcome cultural barriers, in which marriage and age play a part; but their gender is crucial in dealing with women who themselves have a significant role in fighting for their families, and the passionate way they express their feelings for those they support is arguably gender related. But they develop authority over men, while having difficulties in encouraging other women to join them because of gender roles.

There are also parallels with other women's activism. Some pathways to activism, from a standing start, do reflect those identified for other multiply oppressed women. Learning through activism, reflection and continuing education mirror strong strands in wider community development.

The women draw knowledge and strength from their strong base in family and community. They combine analysis, emotion and values in a powerful, integrated strategy. Above all, personal and political dimensions are strongly linked, grounded in their own painful experiences of fighting for planning permission or witnessing oppression as a source of strategy, empathy and resilience to assist others.

However, the minority experience requires an extension of mainstream feminist analysis: strong personal and political dimensions are mediated through community because individual identity is closely tied to Gypsy and Traveller community identity. Gypsy women's activism extends feminist community development principles by building minority perspectives into the personal–political dimension (Cemlyn, 1997) and making a particular contribution to this way of working, through powerful integration of personal, family, community and political issues.

Notes

[1] For further information see www.nationalgypsytravellerfederation.org/.

[2] Maggie Smith-Bendell has supported countless Gypsy families to gain planning permission on appeal throughout the country, and taken up the cudgel on behalf of families experiencing harassment and poor conditions on local authority sites. With her brother Robert she established the Romani Gypsy Council in Somerset, and later with Sally Woodbury the South West

Romani Gypsy Advisory Group. She was previously involved in the Gypsy and Traveller Law Reform Coalition (see Chapter Six) and is a core member of the NFGLG. For a fuller account of her life and work, see her 2009 book, *Our Forgotten Years*, and its 2013 sequel, *After All These Years*.

[3] Siobhan Spencer is a long-term Gypsy activist who became the leading Gypsy member of the previously non-Gypsy-led DGLG. She has undertaken countless planning appeals, built the DGLG to provide a range of other support services, and worked locally and nationally with many agencies and services such as the police in community-led training and conferences. She was previously involved in the Gypsy and Traveller Law Reform Coalition (see Chapter Six). Through fostering links between the DGLG and other activists, the NFGLG developed as the umbrella support group for many local Gypsy and Traveller groups after 2005. Siobhan recently completed a law degree to further enhance her activism.

[4] Sally Woodbury became involved with Maggie Smith-Bendell, undertaking planning appeals, liaising with councils and establishing the South West Romani Gypsy Advisory Group. Subsequently Sally has joined work sponsored nationally by the Local Government Association to raise awareness and educate councillors and officials about Gypsy and Traveller culture and the realities of their lives. She has also undertaken Holocaust memorial work, visiting Auschwitz and making a DVD for schools

[5] Penny Dane worked at Devon Race Equality Council.

[6] Developing a site first and then submitting a planning application.

[7] An NGO based in the East of England.

[8] An NGO based in the North of England.

References

Begum, N., Hill, N. and Stevens, A. (eds) (1994) *Reflections: Views of Black Disabled People on their Lives and Community Care*, London: CCETSW.

Brubaker, R. (2004) *Ethnicity Without Groups*, Cambridge, MA: Harvard University Press.

Cemlyn, S. (1997) 'Groupwork as a tool in the celebration, resourcing and development of Gypsy and Traveller culture', in T. Mistry and A. Brown (eds) *Race and Groupwork*, London: Whiting and Birch, pp 110–37.

Cemlyn, S., Greenfields, M., Burnett, S., Matthews, Z. and Whitwell, C. (2009) *Inequalities Experienced by Gypsy and Traveller Communities: A Review*, London: Equality and Human Rights Commission.

Coxhead, J. (2007) *The Last Bastion of Racism*, Stoke on Trent: Trentham Books.

Curno, A., Lamming, A., Leach, L., Stiles, J., Ward, V. and Ziff, T. (1982) *Women in Collective Action*, London: Association of Community Workers.

Dominelli, L. (2006) *Women and Community Action*, Bristol: Policy Press.

Emeluju, A. (2011) 'Re-theorizing feminist community development: towards a radical democratic citizenship', *Community Development Journal*, vol 46, no 3, pp 378–90.

Fraser, N. (1995) 'From Redistribution to Recognition? Dilemmas of Justice in a "Post-Socialist" Age', *New Left Review*, vol 212, pp 68–93.

Fraser, N. (2005) 'Reframing justice in a globalizing world', *New Left Review*, vol 36, pp 69–88.

Freire, P. (1972) *Pedagogy of the Oppressed*, Harmondsworth: Penguin.

Gallagher, A. (1977) 'Women and community work' in M. Mayo (ed) *Women in the Community*, London: Routledge and Kegan Paul, pp 121–41.

Gilchrist, A. (2009) *The Well-Connected Community. A Networking Approach to Community Development*, Bristol: Policy Press.

Gillies, V. (2006) 'Working class mothers and school life: exploring the role of emotional capital', *Gender and Education*, vol 18, no 3, pp 281–93.

Gramsci, A. (1971) *Selections from Prison Notebooks*, London: Lawrence and Wishart.

Harding, S. (ed) (2004) *The Feminist Standpoint Theory Reader. Intellectual and Political Controversies*, London: Routledge.

Hill Collins, P. (1990) *Black Feminist Thought*, London: Unwin Hyman.

Hoggett, P. and Miller, C. (2000) 'Working with emotions in community organizations', *Community Development Journal*, vol 35, no 4, pp 352–64.

Ledwith, M. (2005) *Community Development: A Critical Approach*, Bristol: Policy Press.

Mayo, M. (1977) *Women in the Community*, London: Routledge and Kegan Paul.

NFGLG (National Federation of Gypsy Liaison Groups) (2012) *Annual Review 2011–2012,* http://nationalgypsytravellerfederation.org/nfglg-documents-and-reports/NFGLG%20Annual%20Report%20 2011-2012(1).pdf.

Nowotny, H. (1981) 'Women in public life in Austria', in C. Fuchs Epstein and R. Laub Coser (eds) *Access to Power: Cross-National Studies of Women and Elites*, London: George Allen and Unwin, pp 147–56.

Orme, J. (2003) '"It's Feminist because I say so!" Feminism, social work and critical practice in the UK', *Qualitative Social Work*, vol 2, no 2, pp 131–53.

Perkins, T. (2012) 'Women's pathways into activism: rethinking the women's environmental justice narrative in California's San Joaquin Valley', *Organization Environment*, vol 25, pp 76–94.

Ryder, A. (2012) *The Real Big Society: Gypsy Traveller Tenants and Residents' Associations and the Role of Social Capital and Empowerment in Reversing Exclusion*, University of Birmingham: Third Sector Research Centre Working Paper.

Richardson, J. and Ryder, A. (2012) *Gypsies and Travellers: Accommodation, Empowerment and Inclusion in British Society*, Bristol: Policy Press.

Sandoval, C. (1991) 'US third world feminism: the theory and method of oppositional consciousness in the postmodern world', *Genders*, vol 10, pp 1–24.

Smith-Bendell, M. (2009) *Our Forgotten Years: A Gypsy Woman's Life on the Road*, Hatfield: University of Hertfordshire Press.

Spence, J. and Stephenson, C. (2007) 'Female Involvement in the Miners' Strike 1984–1985: Trajectories of Activism', *Sociological Research Online*, vol 12, no 1, www.socresonline.org.uk/12/1/spence.html.

Southwark Traveller Women's Group (1992) *Moving Stories: Traveller Women Write*, London: Traveller Education Team.

Spencer, S. (2003) *A Better Road: An Information Booklet for Health Care and Other Professionals*, Matlock: Derbyshire Gypsy Liaison Group.

Takkar, S. (2011) 'The construction of political agency: South Asian women and political activism', *Community Development Journal*, vol 46, no 3, pp 341–50.

Young, I.M. (1990) *Justice and the Politics of Difference*, Princeton, NJ: Princeton University Press.

TEN

The Roma in Europe: the debate over the possibilities for empowerment to seek social justice

Thomas Acton, Iulius Rostas and Andrew Ryder

In this chapter the authors examine whether the powerful who make policy can actually share that power with those within Roma communities who are seeking social advancement and justice, and what kind of changes within government, Roma civil society and communities and the academic establishment would be necessary. This requires a strong theory of how inequality works. There are many dimensions of inequality, like ethnicity, class, age, ability and disability, and gender, which make us see other people as different from ourselves. Older theories of inequality used to concentrate on single dimensions, but after the impact of feminist standpoint theory, as discussed in the previous two chapters, contemporary sociologists have tended to merge the older conceptual clusters that emerged in the second half of the 20th century, such as 'race relations', '(multi-)cultural studies', women's studies, disability studies, Black studies (and Romani studies), diasporic studies, hybridity, poverty and the revival of class into a powerful tool of 'intersectional analysis' that can combine reflection, research, deliberation, activism and civil society as core components in the achievement of social justice. This intellectual development has been mirrored politically by the emergence of general anti-discrimination laws at national and European level, replacing separate laws against racism, sexism, disablism and ageism.

Some anti-racists (including the late Charles Smith) have been concerned that this development might undermine the specific struggle about racism, and some Roma activists continue to draw on a critical race theory (Hylton, 2012), which emphasises the importance of action against inequality that is constantly aware of the anti-racist dimension of all the struggles. The debate around the Roma and empowerment has been given impetus by a growing number of Roma scholars and activists who are critical of the structures and practices that have marginalised them in academia and the non-governmental organisations (NGOs) sector. Could this critique establish a dialogue with power to bring about transformative change?

Chapter One pointed out that such a dialogue was envisaged a quarter of a century ago by Habermas (1984, p 95), and renewed in his recent (2010) journalism, to suggest that a more deliberative democracy can deliver a renewed civil society through communicative action and new social movements, creating consensus and mutual understanding to sustain more egalitarian economic and social models. Deliberative democracy involves citizens and their representatives actively debating problems and solutions in an environment that is conducive to reflection and a mutual willingness to understand the values, perspectives and interests of others.

Chapter One also noted difficulties with this approach, highlighted by Kellner (2000) and Somin (2010), namely the way in which the bourgeois sphere can exclude marginalised people, which has led some critics to dismiss Habermas's approach as just another ineffectual part of liberal academic tradition (Kóczé, 2012). Nonetheless, Caterino and Hansen (2009, p 90) suggest that it has a reflective awareness that might transcend liberal inaction:

> A critical theory of democracy should not only illuminate the unavoidable connection of the economic to the political, of the structures of capitalism as a system of social power to formal political institutions, a connection neoliberal discourse strives to sever, deny, or cover over. It must also retrieve the normative core of democracy and its links with solidarity among agents bound together in a common situation shaped by and through processes of mutual recognition and mutual understanding. This retrieval involves the ways in which radically reformed social institutions both make possible and arise from the transformative, developmental possibilities that individuals must be assumed to possess if the aspirations associated with alternatives to neoliberal politics are to be plausible.

While there may be flaws in Habermas's thesis about the hegemonic discourse of power elites in the 20*th* century being corrupted by the 'refeudalisation' of the inclusive bourgeois public sphere, still it envisages a 'radical democracy' where the people are sovereign. Thus there may be a danger of professional and more affluent members of society monopolising transformative mobilisations in the name of the people (Acton and Ryder, 2013). But the fact that most people lack the cultural capital to wield power now does not mean they will never develop it. The earliest studies of Roma political mobilisation in the West (Acton, 1974; Liégeois, 1976) show how Romani activists, many of them autodidacts (self-taught community leaders), have exemplified the assertion of Gramsci (1971) that everyone can be an 'organic intellectual', an expert on their own localised situation and, from this starting point, be capable of developing valid and meaningful positions. This notion is a central theme in this chapter.

Neoliberal governments of the New Right have tried to outsource many of the jobs of government, without losing power over the people. Foucauldian analysis, making rather a crude pun on the French word 'mentalité', coined the term 'gouvernamentalité' for the process of social control through the common mindset of the new dispersed, corporate ruling class. Although the joke is rather lost in the translation, political scientists have used the word 'governmentality' in their analysis of how the delegated decision-making processes do not take note of hard-won historic experience on the limits of power and necessary preconditions of efficient administration. To use the term of the New Right, 'pulling back the state' has been accompanied by a series of governmental strategies and technologies aimed at shaping institutions and subjects in particular ways, and proliferated in regimes of enterprise, accounting and commodification (Dean, 1999).

Devolved centres of power in corporations, and even philanthropy, have adopted bureaucratic processes stifling funding streams for community organisations, creating projects with limited goals to achieve service efficiency or give the impression of consultation, but which create hierarchical regulation of community projects and representation with limited manoeuvrability or appetite for more transformative action (Van Baar, 2005). Deliberative democracy, by contrast, 'demands' a fusion of 'top down' and 'bottom up' approaches where at the grassroots aspirations and agency can be articulated and nurtured through transfer of resources and an enabling political environment that initiates partnership, dialogue and intervention to further social justice.

'Canaries in the mine shaft'

Roma communities have been among the most prominent victims of both poverty and xenophobia in Europe. Filcak and Skobla (2012) recycle the cliché that Roma are the 'canary in the mine shaft', the harbinger of future crisis. Roma have experienced acute forms of marginalisation in Central and Eastern Europe during the transition period to a market economy. Since the early 1990s this minority has often suffered the most as a consequence of the economic, social and political failings of prevailing power elites and systems. Since the sixteenth century their fate in Europe has alternated between marginalisation, violent persecution and attempts to change and assimilate them. Today the policies to address Roma marginalisation are couched, in particular by the European Union (EU), in the language of social inclusion. However, the term 'social inclusion' has proved to be rather elastic, with associated strategies ranging from structural change to a need for individual reform (Levitas, 1998). Making the Roma meaningfully involved in decision-making processes that might shape their destiny has rarely been at the fore of policy makers' actions. In fact the Roma are often viewed by welfare and community development projects as a minority in need of assimilatory, modernising policy agendas, often designed by outsiders and based on normative assumptions (Powell, 2010), just like the settlement policies of the Habsburgs and the proletarianisation policies of the Soviets (Liégeois, 2007). A central question that this chapter seeks to answer is: how can we ensure in new and on-going policy cycles that history does not repeat itself and lead to social inclusion discourses merely reformulating previously discredited policies?

Hennink et al (2012) have devised a tool of measurement that can be used as a benchmark as to whether empowerment and development is inclusive and emancipatory (Table 10.1).

It is important to note that there are interlinkages between the different mechanisms, and efforts to support empowerment through just one mechanism may have limited effects. Thus the challenge is to develop empowerment initiatives using all the mechanisms through effective multi-sector partnerships and initiatives. In our discussion we will first assess the effectiveness of governmental power on the Roma question, then on Roma civil society and communities and finally on the educational and academic establishment.

Table 10.1: Mechanisms of empowerment

Mechanism	Definition
Knowledge	Access to education, training and information from formal or other sources such as through dialogue, experience and conscientisation
Agency	Capacity to act independently and make choices – comprised of three components:
(a) self-identity	(a) self-confidence and self-efficacy to set and achieve goals
(b) decision making	(b) ability to make informed decisions that are recognised and respected
(c) effecting change	(c) belief in own ability to take action to effect change based on own goals
Opportunity structure	Existence of an enabling environment of social, political, institutional and community support to foster individual and community development
Capacity building	Harnessing community capacity to provide or advocate for services or self-governance, and to seek accountability from government service-provision agencies
Resources	Access to physical and financial resources, or skills for seeking resources, to develop communities
Sustainability	Ability of communities to develop and support initiatives towards long-term sustainability

Source: Hennink et al (2012, p 206)

A new beginning?

The European Union Open Method of Coordination (EUOMC) provides a framework for national policy development and coordination for EU members. The rationale is that EU members will examine their policies critically, thus leading to the exchange of good practice, and that peer pressure will spur on some to 'do better' (Meyer, 2010). The EU Framework for National Roma Integration Strategies (hereafter referred to as the Roma Framework) is based on the EUOMC and involves member states devising National Roma Integration Strategies (NRIS). This can be described as a deliberative framework, and the European Commission (EC) has stressed in the Roma Framework the importance of on-going dialogue and partnerships between governments and Roma groups.

At the launch of the Roma Framework the Vice President of the EC, Viviane Reding, described the framework as 'beyond all expectations' and declared that '[t]his is a beginning of a new future' (EU Presidency, 2011). As Acton and Ryder (2013) note, 'To a student of history, this is not as auspicious as it sounds...."New Futures" for the Roma have been multiplying themselves since the time of the Hapsburgs. These visions have all floundered, either being based on assimilationist templates, or lacking resources and political commitment, in a recurrent cycle of neglect and naive interventionism.'

In view of this history of disempowerment, calls at the centre of the Roma Framework for the Roma to be more directly involved in decision making present a radical new departure. The EC has stated that resulting strategies should 'be designed, implemented and monitored in close co-operation and continuous dialogue with Roma civil society and regional and local authorities' (European Commission, 2011, p 9).

However, to date the results of the NRIS have been disappointing. Governments are not adequately entering into dialogue and partnership with Roma communities and/or are devising weak and limited strategies and programmes (OSF, 2012). Political intransigence towards the Roma has been accentuated by the current economic crisis. Governments are responding by cutting social services and expenditure (Richardson, 2010). Evidence is emerging that Roma civil society and communities are suffering from these cutbacks and the unwillingness to initiate new programmes (Rostas and Ryder, 2012). EU commissioner László Andor, at the Sixth Roma Platform in Brussels in November 2011, described such political downgrading and side-lining as creating a 'social time bomb' that could explode at any moment (Andor, 2011).

In the prevailing economic crisis Europe appears to be at a 'crossroads' and a new debate has been sparked as to the direction of the EU, and ideals upon which it should be predicated. The Centre Right parties of Europe seem to have been more successful than progressive political forces in capturing the public's imagination, a development that has led to the very existence of the EU being called into question, and the Roma being increasingly portrayed as a danger and menace that springs from open borders and union.

In contrast to austerity politics and the ascendancy of neoliberalism, Craig et al (2008) argue that supra-collective (international) action could counter 'social dumping' and create a system governed by principles of social justice based on equality but that also understands and values human rights. These ideals can be articulated in the concept of 'A Social Europe', which incorporates a vision of society based on solidarity, equality, social justice, internationalism and the view that economic wealth should be fairly distributed, without excluding or discriminating against groups or individuals (Ségol, 2012).

It would thus be in the spirit of such principles that the EU would more effectively use the budget of €50 billion per year in structural funds to resolve economic and social problems for Roma communities (OSRI, 2011), but only if the EC were robust in intervening against those member states that are reluctant to devise Roma integration strategies or that contravene European equality conventions, especially the Race Directive. Making the receipt of European funding conditional on achieving Roma Framework goals is something which has been indicated in a number of statements by Viviane Reding, the EU commissioner for justice, fundamental rights and citizenship (Rostas and Ryder, 2012). However, such political action cannot be dependent on the EU alone, for there would be a danger of 'Europeanising' the Roma question, leading to national states abdicating their responsibilities to Roma and arguing that the issue was one primarily for the attention of the EU (Vermeersch, 2012). The ideals and action set out also need to be mirrored in the strategies of national governments. These changes would imply, though, a shift from neoliberal ideals to forms of governance centred on Keynesian notions of intervention and assistance and a revival in the concept of 'social contract', where centres of power take on the role of champions and defenders of the weak and seek to readdress imbalances. By adopting such roles, centres of power will become 'enablers', providing the resources that, according to Hennink et al (2012), are one prerequisite for empowerment.

Defining civil society

Civil society has been defined by Diamond (1999, p 221) as 'the realm of organized social life that is open, voluntary, self-generating, at least partially self-supporting, autonomous from the state, and bound by a legal order or set of shared rules'. The concept of civil society generally assumes that individuals act collectively in the public sphere and that this is different from the private sphere – the space of the individual and family life – or the economic sphere (Smolar, p 2002).

The concept of civil society has undergone adjustments over time. The founding fathers of liberalism regarded civil society as a complement to the state. Alexis de Toqueville (1832) was one of the first to theorise civil society, conceiving it as a counter to selfish individualism and also a constraint on the potential excesses of the state. For the anti-communist dissidents of Central and Eastern Europe the achievement of a civil society was the road to re-establishing sovereignty and liberty, free from the menace of the totalitarian state. Influenced by this vein of thought, and by donors and philanthropists imbued with the idealism of American civil rights, there was hope in the region that civil society could make great advances for Roma communities.

The creation of client organisations of Roma college-leavers primed to act out the dreams of the donors has, so far from advancing a Roma civil society, attracted criticism from actual Roma public intellectuals that those organisations fail to generate public trust and to build those skills and norms necessary for the democratic process (Kóczé, 2012). The formal membership of these organisations means they have a very limited capacity to create mass organisations and have tended to be hierarchical and possess vertical patron–client relationship with their 'users' (Rostas, 2009). Trehan's (2001) complaints about 'NGO-isation' are endorsed by Stubbs (2007): 'the transformation of social movements into organizations and the increasing dominance of "modern" NGOs which emphasize "issue-specific interventions" and pragmatic strategies with a strong employment focus, rather than the establishment of a new democratic counter-culture'. Lack of transparency has been compounded by Roma NGOs having very limited autonomy, being accountable mostly to their donors rather than to their communities/ constituencies. Some of the most powerful donors have imposed liberal/ neoliberal agendas, leading to a focus on civil rights and the neglect of wider economic and social issues (Sigona and Trehan, 2010).

Some Romani organisations have become overly bureaucratic and professionalised, showing a high degree of institutionalisation. NGOs have become a specific sector that offers employment and career opportunities for a new generation of Roma (Bíró, et al, 2013). But this process tends to limit the dynamics and flexibility of civil society and has led key activists like Gheorghe to conclude that Roma civil society is becoming increasingly estranged from Roma communities, many of which remain oblivious to what is being done in their name.

Roma politics has often run counter to grassroots organisation. The self-proclaimed Roma civil society often seems to focus on working at a strategic level and, although increasingly involving an educated Roma elite, lacks legitimacy and a popular mandate (Bíró, et al, 2013). More nationalistic forms of Roma politics have again directed energy at power elites at a national and European level so as to build support for nation-building projects. Again, popular support for and identification with this agenda from Roma communities is limited in the extreme (cf Gay Y Blasco, 2002), and these forms of nationalism have been accused of divisiveness and alienating wider support and alliance construction (Kapralski, 2012).

Appeals have been made for Roma activism to embrace more bridging and linking dimensions (partnerships/coalitions), where activists work with and through external agencies like political parties, trade unions and churches and other agents of change where they can become known and form wider alliances. Identity and recognition thus form part of the campaign agenda, but without dominating and fostering a politics of 'otherness' and isolation (Kovats, 2013). To date such participation and representation in wider decision-making forums has been difficult to achieve, yet there is the hope that one day a vibrant Roma NGO sector might prepare activists and communities for such roles by promoting and facilitating participation and civic education (Rostas, 2009).

Despite these aspirations for the Roma movement, it remains a fact that for many Roma communities, family and community networks based on bonding social capital and trust have proved to be more reliable sources of support than have formal organisations (Rostas and Ryder, 2012). Informal groups and institutions belong also to civil society, and are difficult to categorise. For example, mutual help groups are part of civil society but are not taken into account when using the term 'Roma civil society', not to mention those institutions the Roma have developed over centuries and that have ensured their survival as a distinct ethnic group. Nevertheless these institutions are not part of the state (although some originated in the functioning of previous state institutions); for example, the institution of the traditional tribunals – such as the Vlach Romani Kris – as an alternative conflict-resolution instrument within sections of the Roma community.

It is important to differentiate between what are often referred to as 'Roma civil society' and the broader Roma movement. In the discourse of the Eurocrats 'Roma civil society' has come to refer to those organisations seeking to act as representatives of the Roma in dialogue with governments and funders. It includes support organisations that share the goals of Roma organisations but do not declare themselves as Roma organisations. Sometimes these organisations are more influential and effective in promoting a certain kind of public discourse about Roma than are organisations that claim to belong to the Roma. An example is the European Roma Rights Center, which does not declare itself to be a Roma organisation but which is very influential in promoting a human rights discourse in describing the current situation of Roma in Europe. Peter Vermeersch, however, defines the Roma movement as 'all activities in the context of defence and cultivation of a common Roma identity' (Vermeersch, 2006, pp 9–10), but clearly, 'Roma civil society' and the broader social movement for the Roma both vary in how their position towards Romani identity is constructed, and are interested in issues like welfare, poverty and anti-racism in general, not just identity politics. A narrow and artificial 'Roma civil society', hierarchical and donor-driven and focused on identity, may have contributed to the disempowerment of the Roma and failure to construct a vibrant Roma movement that mobilises those at the grassroots. But could these dry bones yet be brought to life and serve as a useful tool in the achievement of empowerment and social justice for Roma communities?

Reviving civil society

We argue that forms of deliberation centred upon inclusive community development could mobilise the marginalised and legitimate the proposed agenda of a 'Social Europe' and revival in support for the social contract, but this needs to be sustained through popular support, including that of the marginalised and Roma, and mobilised, as this book has argued happened in the UK with Gypsy, Traveller and Roma organisations, through Freire's (1972) methods of critical pedagogy. We agree with Darder (2002) that inclusive community development is inherently 'deliberative' and can provide space for reflection, critique and action between different social factions. The effectiveness of the involvement of Roma, Gypsy and Traveller communities, as the proverbial 'canaries in the mine shaft', is a crucial test of the viability of the construction of 'Social Europe'. However, present low levels of formal Roma community organisation and participation present an impediment to this goal, which needs to be overcome.

If centres of power adopt bolder action and policy frameworks, as we have advocated, there is a need to ensure that Roma communities have agency in this process, thus avoiding the danger of their being perceived as 'passive victims'. Indeed Hennink et al (2012) identify 'agency' as articulated through self-identity, decision making and effecting change as central components in mechanisms of empowerment. Sections of civil society have enthusiastically asserted, since the advent of transition society in the former communist bloc, that they could perform such a role. Despite the proposals by the EC and, indeed, civil society itself for NGOs to be afforded key roles in new partnerships and decision-making processes we need to recognise the weaknesses that exist at present in civil society. Internally, Roma activists have to build institutions that are democratic and have the capacity to mobilise the communities; this may necessitate greater self-funding, or donor funding that is more flexible and sympathetic to localised NGOs and activism. 'New social movements' focusing on race and ethnicity tend to favour flat and non-hierarchical forms of organisation (Fuchs, 2006), but this key trait has been missing in Roma civil society.

Despite the causes for concern outlined above there are some positive signs of a willingness to reflect and reform on the part of Roma civil society. 'Empowerment' has become a key 'buzzword' for Roma activists, leading to important debates. Reflecting this mood, the Open Society Foundation, one of the most influential donors, has developed a new strategy with empowerment at its centre that may give some impetus to much-needed internal reform. At the margins evangelical Christians have demonstrated that communities can be mobilised, organised and re-orientated. Evangelism has brought forward a new, younger Roma generation as pastors, which has in some cases displaced an older generation of leaders (Gay Y Blasco, 1999). As Russinov has noted, in some cases the potency of such religious movements within Roma communities is that they alone have been present at the local level and have been the only ones offering actual support and direction (Rostas, 2012). This is a salutary lesson that many externally sponsored NGOs in Roma civil society have yet to learn. Yet we should be cautious in our praise of these religious movements. Male domination of the leadership, and in some cases excessive emphasis on the spiritual to the neglect of the material, has been counter-productive to these movements developing a greater challenge to the status quo. In contrast, a number of community activists, from Loulou Demeter in the 1970s to Lars Demetri and the late Florin Cioba in the 21st century, are pastors who draw political strength from the Pentecostal movement and forward a progressive agenda (Acton and Ryder, 2013).

Strategies to revitalise Roma civil society and to mobilise the grassroots can be set out. Trained and experienced community organisers could form what Freire (1972) described as outsider catalysts. A starting point might be to define the problems a community faces through 'community profiles' that detail exclusion and suggest means by which it can be overcome. These can provide useful baselines for monitoring or evaluation and demonstrate where services are not being delivered equitably. This creates what critical race theory describes as a 'counter-story', a means to challenge dominant discourses (Dixson and Rousseau, 2005). However, such surveys should assist the process of community development by also charting the cultural and social resources that exist within marginalised communities (Hawtin and Percy-Smith, 2007). Such an approach is typical of critical race theory, which seeks to promote participatory practice, the voices and narrative of minority ethnic groups, voices that are generally undervalued and marginalised (Ladson–Billings, 1998; Power, 2007; Ledwith and Springett, 2010).

Through these processes of critical pedagogy local actors are engaged in transformative action at the local level as skills, knowledge and awareness increase. An associational approach emphasises radical decentralisation of the state and can include tools like citizens' juries and participatory budgeting, which can democratise local agencies and lead to the creation of neighbourhood control and consensus, where the state is accountable to civil society rather than vice versa (Gough et al, 2006). Indeed, as Gramsci (1971) noted, participation, construction and organisation are important facets of the development of 'organic intellectuals'. Local mobilisation will not be sufficient of itself to deliver transformative change. Those who subscribe to a 'communitarian' discourse suggest that strong forms of social capital centred on families and communities can create social cohesion and increase social inclusion (Etzioni, 1993). However, such coping mechanisms cannot overcome the exclusion caused by an unequal distribution of resources. At best, social capital through self-help networks can only mitigate the negative effect of exclusion for marginalised people but in itself does not pose a major challenge to cycles of poverty and exclusion (Smith, 2005). This emphasises the importance of localised Roma activists being able to draw connections between the local situation and wider developments at the national, European and global levels. Being able to conceptualise the need for structural change and the necessity of national and transnational activism, but also to recognise the limits that the absence of such change places on progress at the local level, may thus avoid activists becoming frustrated by the limitations of securing only local change. Going beyond critical race theory, activism needs to be premised on an agenda of intersectionality, where questions of class, race, gender, age and sexuality are seen as intersectional dimensions in the prevailing social order (Hylton, 2012). Such debates and awareness serve to identify and challenge not only external oppressions but also those that are internal and wedded to conservatism and narrow interpretations of tradition.

Localised activism can thus attempt to school and train activists and so give them agency, self-confidence, skills and knowledge in accordance with the criteria identified by Hennink et al (2012). The process of critical pedagogy can be a long and intensive one involving not just upskilling but trust formation (Rostas, 2009). Indeed this is where the self-proclaimed civil society organisations have often failed in their work with Roma, through an inability to inspire and galvanise at the grassroots.

Education and scholarship

Education has long been a much-heralded tool to 'civilise' and assimilate the Roma (Liégeois, 2007). Yet, while knowledge and education remain important tools in transformative change, activism is in itself an experience that develops skills, increases awareness and confidence and can facilitate and equip those with limited education to take up prominent positions in transformative change. Such processes can be greatly assisted through educational achievement and success, providing the requisite cultural capital for the Roma to organise, frame and articulate their counter-narrative.

At present, though, the opportunities for such achievement are limited in many countries by the segregation of Roma children in the education system, despite the growing body of legal statutes and policy directives aimed at creating integrated education and that has been formally reaffirmed at the European Court of Human Rights (Rostas, 2012). However, the impacts of these measures are not visible at the local level and in many cases there is no clear mapping of direct or affirmative policy to address this situation. The formation and maintenance of separate schools is linked to the cultural, economic and political powers of a privileged majority who are able to legitimise the power and control of the status quo and who remain unchallenged through liberal 'colour blind' equality laws that stress equal opportunities but do little to challenge power differentials (Dixson and Rousseau, 2005).

School desegregation and the promotion of inclusive education contend that education is a basic human right and the foundation for a more just society (Ainscow and Sandill, 2010). Such objectives are thus an important priority for Roma communities. Such change, as Hennink et al (2012) note, creates access to formal knowlege where institutions like schools and universities enable and facilitate the development of cultural capital. However, it should also be noted that such is the distrust of some sections of the Roma community towards formal education that there is an element of self exclusion that restricts participation and achievement (Rostas, 2012). Participation, dialogue and flexible curricula are means by which such forms of resistance can be overcome and can contribute to inclusive forms of community development. Indeed schools may be one of the first and most important institutions within which local dialogue and activism are initiated between sections of the wider and Roma communities as well as centres of power, and this may be a stepping-stone to wider involvement (Ryder et al, 2014).

Fear and mistrust also exist between sections of the Roma community and academia, which limits the ability of activists to use research as a tool to increase understanding and bring about change. Ledwith and Springett (2010, p 199), argue: 'Emancipatory action research must not be seen as an optional extra, but an integral component of any approach to participatory practice offering an evolving dynamic between theory, policy and practice in an engagement with the ever changing political context of our lives.' The root of the disconnection stems from the fact that academics have been criticised by community members and fellow researchers (Marti et al, 2010) for failing to engage properly with the realities of Roma communities, instead using abstracted conceptualisations of them as building blocks for theories and notions that hold little meaning or relevance for the communities themselves. It has been charged that an academic elite has often monopolised 'expert opinion' on this group and, in their role as 'expert advisors' of decision makers and centres of power, act as substitutes for an absence of genuine community involvement, while failing to question this state of affairs (Acton and Ryder, 2013). In some cases such practices are maintained through notions of scientific enquiry derived from classical social anthropology in the colonial era. Conservative observers such as Barany (2002) contend that too great a level of familiarity with the research subjects can lead to 'going native' and producing biased and unsound research, undisciplined by proper peer review. Against such classical positivist approaches, advocates of participatory forms of research assert that transparent forms of research and channels of communication with the researched, in opposition to hierarchies of knowledge that treat academic experts as all-knowing authorities who should not be challenged, produce research that stands up more broadly, bridges discourses and reduces the unchallenged prevalence of stereotypes (Greenfields and Ryder, 2012). It is important to note that the EC in a communication document for the Roma Framework emphasises the importance of applying the Principles of the Roma Platform, namely community involvement and the need for robust evidence to assess progress within the Framework. In addition the communication document calls upon the Fundamental Rights Agency (FRA) to review progress. The FRA has placed participatory research at the centre of its methodology for this review (EC, 2011; FRA, 2013). It remains to be seen to what degree such research is genuinely promoted and practised within the Roma Framework.

In recognition of the important role that the research community can play on the Roma issue, the European Academic Network on Romani Studies (EANRS) was established in June 2011 by the EC and Council of Europe. It was envisaged that this body might foster a more consensual approach, bringing together the most respected scholars, both non-Roma and Roma, Gypsies and Travellers (RGT). An academic elite that had dominated scholarship in this field often felt disconcerted or even resentful towards the challenge from the first generations of RGT scholars, often self-taught autodidacts or latecomers to formal education. They established a 'first-past-the-post' system for the scientific committee of the EANRS. The franchise was restricted to PhD holders and denied doctoral students a say in the election (it is here that most academics of RGT heritage are presently located) and subsequently failed to elect any RGT scholars to the Scientific Committee. After a debate over whether this was a structural problem or whether it meant Roma just were not ready yet, Thomas Acton resigned in protest (Acton and Ryder, 2013).[1] The Scientific Committee has since changed its policy, to co-opt a scholar of RGT heritage who was among the runners-up and elect two junior (pre-PhD) researchers, who just happen to be of RGT heritage. It is evident, though, that within the academic community, as in centres of power and Roma civil society and communities, debates and struggles are taking place between those who seek to promote more emancipatory and transformative strategies and those wedded to the status quo.

Conclusion

The EC has noted the intransigence of member states on the Roma question and the dangers and challenges that inertia and xenophobia hold for Europe, and has sought to shape new policy agendas among member states through the Roma Framework. Yet this initiative is in part dependent on the determination of centres of power at the European, national and local levels and new policy approaches that depart from austerity politics to embrace social justice and openness to a more autonomous Roma civil society. As this chapter has argued, in the realisation of a 'Social Europe' policies and resources need to materialise that provide agency, confidence and capacity building and create an enabling environment of social, political, institutional and community action to bring about transformative change. Such measures can avoid the current danger of 'dialogue' descending into 'verbalism', namely empty rhetoric and disillusionment.

Note

[1] Following Acton's departure there were further resignations from the Scientific Committee: Eniko Vincze (May 2013) and Jean Pierre Liégeois

(April 2014). In April 2014 the Council of Europe mooted a proposal supported by George Soros to establish a European Roma Institute (ERI), which would have a board of Romani experts who would nominate non-Roma to sit with them on the governing body. This prompted a statement from the scientific committee which was interpreted as hostile to ERI and which proclaimed that research and academic inquiry into Roma should be centred within universities. The statement was denounced by some EANRS members as elitist, in particular by those who support research alliances with communities and 'standpoint theory'. Some of these academics and activists have called for early elections within EANRS to mediate a new consensus. At the time of writing it remains to be seen what the outcome of this dispute will be.

References

Acton, T.A. (1974) *Gypsy Politics and Social Change*, London: Routledge and Kegan Paul.

Acton, A. and Ryder, A. (2013) *Roma Civil Society: Deliberative Democracy for Change in Europe*, Birmingham: Third Sector Research Centre Working Paper, University of Birmingham.

Ainscow, M. and Sandill, A. (2010) 'Developing inclusive education systems: the role of organisational cultures and leadership', *International Journal of Inclusive Education*, vol 14, no 4, pp 401–16.

Andor, L. (2011) 'Getting member states to draw up their Roma integration strategies – opening of Roma platform', Sixth meeting of the European Roma Platform Brussels, 17 November, European Commission, http://europa.eu/rapid/press-release_SPEECH-11-771_en.htm?locale=en

Barany, Z. (2002) *The East European Gypsies: Regime Change, Marginality and Ethnopolitics*, Cambridge: Cambridge University Press.

Bíró, A., Gheorghe, N. and Kovats, M. (eds) (2013) *From Victimhood to Citizenship*, Budapest: Kossuth Publishing.

Caterino, B. and Hansen, P. (2009) 'Macpherson, Habermas, and the demands of democratic theory', *Studies in Political Economy*, vol 83, spring, pp 85–110.

Craig, G., Burchardt, T. and Gordon, D. (2008) *Social Justice and Public Policy: Seeking Fairness in Diverse Societies*, Bristol: Policy Press.

Darder, A. (2002) *Reinventing Paulo Friere. A Pedagogy of Love*, Boulder, CO: Westview Press.

Dean, M. (1999) *Govermentality. Power and Rule in Modern Society*, London: Sage.

de Toqueville, A. (1832) *On Democracy in America*, Chicago, IL: University of Chicago Press.

Diamond, L. (1999) *Developing Democracy towards Consolidation*, Baltimore, MD and London: Johns Hopkins University Press.

Dixson, A.D. and Rousseau, C.K. (2005) 'And we are still not saved: critical race theory in education ten years later', *Race Ethnicity and Education*, vol 8, no 1, pp 7–27.

Etzioni, A. (1993) *The Spirit of Community*, New York: Crown.

EC (European Commission) (2011) Communication from the Commission to the European Parliament, The Council, The European Economic and Social Committee and the Committee of the Regions, An EU Framework for National Roma Integration Strategies up to 2020, Brussels, 5.4.2011, COM(2011) 173 final, http://eur-lex. europa.eu/legal-content/EN/TXT/PDF/?uri=CELEX:52011DC 0173&from=en.

EU Presidency (2011) 'Roma integration: the Presidency takes action', Press release, 8 April, Brussels: European Union.

Filcak, R. and Skobla, D. (2012) 'Social solidarity, human rights and Roma: unequal access to basic resources', in M. Ellison (ed) *Reinventing social solidarity across Europe*, Bristol: Policy Press, pp 227–50.

Freire, P. (1972) *Pedagogy of the Oppressed*, Harmondsworth: Penguin.

FRA (Fundamental Rights Agency) (2013) Annex A.1 – Technical specifications open call for tenders F-SE-13-T06 Provision of services for participatory action research on local Roma integration plans, http://fra.europa.eu/sites/default/files/annex_a1_technical_ specifications_f-se-13-t06.pdf.

Fuchs, C. (2006) 'The self-organization of social movements', *Systemic Practice and Action Research*, vol 19, no 1, pp, 101–37.

Gay Y Blasco, P. (1999) *Gypsies in Madrid. Sex, Gender and the Performance of Identity*, Oxford: Berg.

Gay Y Blasco, P. (2002) 'Gypsy/Roma Diasporas: Introducing a Comparative Perspective', *Social Anthropology, the Journal of the European Association of Social Anthropologists*, vol 10, no 2, pp 173–88.

Gough, J., Eisenschitz, A. and McCulloch, A. (2006) *Spaces of Social Exclusion*, New York: Routlege.

Gramsci, A. (1971) *Selections from the Prison Notebooks*, London: Lawrence and Wishart.

Greenfields, M. and Ryder, A. (2012) 'Research with and for Gypsies, Roma and Travellers: combining policy, practice and community in action research', in J. Richardson and A. Ryder (eds) *Gypsies and Travellers: Accommodation, Empowerment and Inclusion in British Society*, Bristol: Policy Press, pp 151–67.

Habermas, J. (1984) *The Theory of Communicative Action*, trans. T. McCarthy, Boston, MA: Beacon Press.

Habermas, J. (2010) 'Germany and the Euro-crisis'. *The Nation*, 9 June.

Hawtin, M. and Percy-Smith, J. (2007) *Community Profiling: A Practical Guide*, Buckingham: Open University Press.

Hennink, M., Kiiti, N., Pillinger, M. and Jayakaran, R. (2012) 'Defining empowerment: perspectives from international development organisations', *Development in Practice*, vol 22, no 2, pp 202–15.

Hylton, K. (2012) 'Talk the talk, walk the walk: defining critical race theory', *Race, Ethnicity and Education*, vol 15, no 1, pp 23–41.

Kapralski, S. (2012) 'Symbols and rituals in the mobilisation of the Romani national ideal', *Studies in Ethnicity and Nationalism*, vol 12, no 1, pp 64–81.

Kellner, D. (2000) 'Habermas, the public sphere, and democracy: a critical intervention', in L. Hahn (ed) *Perspectives on Habermas*, Chicago, IL: Open Court Press, pp 259–88.

Kóczé, A. (2012) *Bridging the Gap: Involving Civil Society Organisations*, Bratislava: United Nations Development Project.

Kovats, M. (2013) 'Integration and the politicisation of Roma identity', in W. Guy (ed) *From Victimhood to Citizenship: The Path of Roma Integration*, Budapest: Kossuth Kiadó.

Ladson-Billings, G. (1998) 'Just what is critical race theory and what is it doing in a nice field like education?', *International Journal of Qualitative Studies in Education*, vol 11, no 1, pp 7–24.

Ledwith, M. and Springett, J. (2010) *Participatory Practice: Community Based Action for Transformative Change*, Bristol: Policy Press.

Levitas, R. (1998) *The Inclusive Society? Social Exclusion and New Labour*, London: Palgrave Macmillan Limited.

Liégeois, J.-P. (1976) *Mutation Tsigane: La RévolutionBohémienne*, Bruxelles: Presses Universitaires de France/ÉditionsComplexe, Collection 'L'humanitécomplexe'.

Liégeois, J.-P. (2007) *Roma in Europe*, Strasbourg: Council of Europe.

Marti, S.M., Munte, A., Contreras, A. and Prieto-Flores, O. (2010) 'Immigrant and native Romani women in Spain: building alliances and developing shared strategies', *Journal of Ethnic and Migration Studies*, vol 38, no 8, pp 1233–49.

Meyer, H. (2010) 'The Open Method of Coordination (OMC) – a governance mechanism for the G20?', *Social Europe* journal website, www.social-europe.eu/2010/12/the-open-method-of-coordination-omc-a-governance-mechanism-for-the-g20/.

OSF (Open Society Foundation) (2012) *Review of EU Framework National Roma Integration Strategies*, Budapest: OSF.

Open Society Roma Initiatives (OSRI) (2011) *Beyond Rhetoric: Roma Integration Roadmap for* 2020, Budapest, Open Society Institute, www.opensocietyfoundations.org/sites/default/files/beyond-rhetoric-2011-0616.pdf.

Powell, R. (2010) 'Gypsy-Travellers and welfare professional discourse: on individualization and social integration', *Antipode*, vol 43, no 2, pp 471–93.

Power, J.M. (2007) 'The relevance of critical race theory to educational theory and practice', *Journal of Philosophy of Education*, vol 41, no 1, pp 151–66.

Richardson, J. (ed) (2010) *From Recession to Renewal: the impact of the financial crisis on public services and local government*, Bristol: Policy Press

Rostas, I. (2009) 'The Romani movement in Romania: institutionalization and (de)mobilization in England', in C. Trehan and N. Sigona (eds) *Contemporary Romani Politics: Recognition, Mobilisation and Participation*, London: Palgrave Macmillan.

Rostas, I. (2012) (ed) *Ten Years After: A History of Roma School Desegregation in Central and Eastern Europe*, Budapest: Central European University and Roma Education Fund.

Rostas, I. and Ryder, A. (2012) 'EU framework for national Roma integration strategies: insights into empowerment and inclusive policy development', in J. Richardson and A. Ryder (eds) *Gypsies and Travellers: Accommodation, Empowerment and Inclusion in British Society*, Bristol: Policy Press, pp 187–206.

Ryder, A., Rostas, I. and Taba, M. (2014) 'Nothing about us without us: the role of inclusive community development in school desegregation for Roma communities', *Journal for Race Ethnicity and Education*, www.tandfonline.com/doi/ref/10.1080/13613324.2014.885426#. U3m9JNKSxWI

Ségol, B. (2012) *Whither Europe? Looking ahead to the future of Social Europe*. Stockholm: Speech delivered by the General Secretary of the European Trade Union Confederation at 25–28 May meeting, www.etuc.org/a/9893.

Sigona, N. and Trehan, N. (2010) (eds) *Contemporary Romani Politics: Recognition, Mobilisation and Participation*, London: Palgrave Macmillan.

Smith, D.M. (2005) *On the Margins of Inclusion: Changing Labour Markets and Social Exclusion in London*, Bristol: Policy Press.

Smolar, A. (2002) 'Civil society after communism', in L. Diamond and M. Plattner (eds) *Democracy after Communism*, Baltimore, MD and London: Johns Hopkins University Press,

Somin, I. (2010) 'Deliberative democracy and political ignorance', *Critical Review*, vol 22, nos 2–3, pp 253–79.

Stubbs, P. (2007) 'Aspects of community development in contemporary Croatia: globalisation, neo-liberalisation and NGO-isation', in L. Dominelli (ed) *Revitalising Communities in a Globalising World*, Aldershot: Ashgate, pp 161–74.

Trehan, N. (2001) 'In the Name of the Roma', in W. Guy (ed) *Between Past and Future: The Roma of Central and Eastern Europe*, Hatfield: University of Hertfordshire Press.

Van Baar, H. (2005) *Scaling the Romany Grassroots: Europeanization and Transnational Networking. Conference paper. Re-activism: Re-drawing the Boundaries of Activism*, Budapest: CEU.

Vermeersch, P. (2006) *The Romani Movement: Minority Politics and Ethnic Mobilization in Contemporary Central Europe*, New York and Oxford: Berghahn Books.

Vermeersch, P. (2012) 'Special issue: the Roma in the new EU: policies, frames and everyday experiences', *Journal of Ethnic and Migration Studies*, vol 38, no 8, pp 1195–212.

ELEVEN

Roma communities in the UK: 'opening doors', taking new directions

Sylvia Ingmire and Natalie Stables[1]

Roma migrant communities in the UK, as elsewhere (Pantea, 2012a), are a highly heterogeneous group reflecting the differing regions of Europe as well as intra-group variations in local tradition. Variation also stems from the differing situations that these Roma are faced with in the UK, which have triggered a range of coping strategies, some traditional, some innovative. The Roma migrants often become an issue of local politics, with sections of the local populace opposing their presence, as Nacu (2011) has noted in Paris. Community cohesion is endangered as some actors and agencies promote coercive agendas while others, influenced by discourses of inclusion, may fluctuate between ideals of social justice and empowerment and more subtle forms of control through policies of assimilation or integration. This chapter examines the work of the Roma Support Group (RSG), a non-governmental organisation (NGO), and the Salford Ethnic Minority Traveller Achievement Service (EMTAS), part of a local authority, which have developed pioneering work supporting Roma communities, helping them to build advocacy skills and more broadly facilitating skills development and innovation.

As noted in Chapter One, there has been a rise in the number of Roma in the UK since the accession of East European countries to the European Union. Roma who have settled in the UK are primarily A8 and A2 migrants.[2] Research by European Dialogue, conducted by Fremlova and Ureche (2009), found that a desire to find employment, which is often impossible to access in their home countries, has been the strongest motivating factor for migrant Roma (cited by 59% of their sample), while a further 37% reported moving to the UK to seek a better life for their children or to escape discrimination at home.[3] Inadequate ethnic monitoring of Roma in the UK means that no clear evidence exists on the size of the community. Fremlova and Ureche (2009) noted estimates by interviewees that there was a

Roma migrant population of 100,000 to 1,000,000 in the UK, most of whom have arrived since the collapse of the communist bloc in Central/Eastern Europe. A more recent study (Brown et al, 2013) estimated a Roma population of approximately 200,000.[4] The media have shown a readiness to sensationalise statistics so as to play on fears of Roma migration with sensationalist and exaggerated claims (Clark and Campbell, 2000). The *Daily Express* front page on 20 January 2004 claimed that 1.6 million Roma 'were ready to flood' into the UK to 'leech on us' (Hill, 2004). As noted, however, in Chapter One, the reality is that for a significant number of Roma in the UK it is they who have been exploited. The Roma constitute a pool of cheap and flexible labour, often working in poor conditions. This economic marginalisation is in part due to employment restrictions placed on Bulgarian and Romanian workers, leading to some working within the informal economy for below the minimum wage. Economic exclusion in turn leads to poor access to services and poor accommodation (Ryder and Greenfields, 2010).

Collective action and community mobilisation among Roma communities have been limited. Fremlova and Ureche noted in their survey of 104 local authorities the numbers and forms of advocacy that existed (see box).

Roma advocacy and support in the UK

The figures here derive from the Fremlova and Ureche (2009) European Dialogue report and the numbers cited are for local authorities that stated they did or did not have certain forms of Roma organisation and/or advocacy and support groups. The total sample was 104 local authorities.

5 Roma community organisations
43 No Roma community organisations
6 Roma community leaders
42 No Roma community leaders
11 Roma support groups
37 No Roma support groups
27 Wider support groups
21 No wider support groups

Brown et al (2013, p 38) note that responding authorities in their survey were asked whether there were any projects or initiatives coordinated by NGOs that focused on migrant Roma in their local area. Just under half of the authorities that answered this question were aware of such initiatives, and were all located in major urban centres. A similar number did have regular dialogue with such groups. In only five instances were such initiatives thought to be led by Roma populations themselves.

The low figures for advocacy and support structures are attributable to a number of factors. First of all, in terms of advocacy some families, facing acute pressures to survive and forced to work long and hard hours in precarious work conditions, may not have the wherewithal to organise collectively as a pressure group. Instead, some are reliant upon intense social networks that seek solutions based on tradition and extended family and kin self-help. In some cases networks reflect the traditions and power hierarchies from their place of origin; in other cases these networks have adapted culturally or are looser (Pantea, 2012b). Different intense traditional networks may discourage or encourage Roma to seek betterment through more formal types of collectivity, by working with or establishing support and advocacy groups. Anecdotal evidence suggests that some Roma have sought to avoid drawing attention to their ethnicity in the UK and have been hesitant to form community groups. In considering the problem of Roma being exploited by unscrupulous landlords and employers, Fremlova and Ureche (2009, p 89) note:

> The difficulty in tackling this issue lies in the fact that the situation of the majority of Central and Eastern European Roma tends to be much better in England if compared to their standard of living in their respective countries of origin. Even when they are being blatantly exploited here by landlords or employment agencies, their circumstances are better in relative terms. This results in Roma having very low expectations and also very high levels of tolerance of both exploitation and discrimination. The victims often do not take action as they fear losing their 'better life'.

Such perceptions may reduce the impetus to form community groups or engage in advocacy. It should also be noted that some Romani communities, disempowered in their countries of origin, may not have the concept or insights on to how to mobilise. Furthermore, some of the Roma, in particular those with low levels of education, literacy and language skills, will be hindered in such activity. Moreover, some Roma are isolated in the wider communities in which they are located, with local authorities in some cases making little effort to recognise and reach out to Roma communities.

Despite these obstacles to empowerment, some sections of the Roma community are recognising the value of advocacy. Some are taking up roles as community spokespersons and mediators and/ or developing new skills and competencies; others see the value of forming community groups or working within support groups or other agencies promoting their community's culture through events like Gypsy, Roma, Traveller History Month (GRTHM).[5] These strategies can help to shape the growing attention Roma migration has received from politicians and activists. Journalists' and academics' insights into the strategies they adopt remain sparse (Grill, 2012). Through the work of the Roma Support Group and Salford EMTAS this chapter seeks to explore these new directions in advocacy and accessing education.

The Roma Support Group

Seventeen years have passed since a little Roma boy took Sylvia Ingmire's hand and led her to a group of Roma women from the Czech Republic who were sitting on the floor of a crowded lobby of the Refugee Council in Vauxhall. The place was teeming with people from all over the world and it remains a mystery to her to this day why he had chosen her out of all those hundreds of people. How could he have known that she had come to the Refugee Council that day to volunteer her help? How could he have known that she was tired of waiting to speak to someone about volunteering and that she had decided not to try again, especially since she had so many other things to do in her life? As she will never know the answers, all she knows is that from that moment, with her hand held by a little 10-year-old Roma boy, her journey with his mother, aunts, siblings, cousins and his people had begun. Those 17 years have been a steep learning curve for her, filled with many hardships, challenges and perhaps even more joy and satisfaction. Have those years changed her? No, but they certainly have brought her closer to an understanding of the meaning of her life.

Over the years, the RSG has evolved to become one of the leading Roma-led charity organisations in the UK. Since its founding, it has assisted and empowered thousands of Roma refugee and migrant families in London through a wide range of front-line advocacy programmes, developing and implementing models of best practice. As the situation of the Roma community in the UK changed, due to the accession of new European Union (EU) member states, so have the RSG's services needed to be flexible to adapt to the continually evolving needs and aspirations of Roma refugees and migrants. The initial emphasis on supporting Roma asylum seekers in detention centres, combating illegal deportations, compiling and disseminating information on anti-Roma persecution in East European countries, offering advice and practical support to destitute asylum seekers, has been replaced by matters related to accessing mainstream services (for example health, welfare, housing, education), employability, and projects enhancing the social inclusion and integration of Roma.[6]

Salford Ethnic Minority and Traveller Achievement Service

In 2005–06 Salford EMTAS started to identify young people in schools who were of Roma origin, and reports began to come in from the neighbourhood management teams in certain areas of the city that there were large numbers of children playing out in the streets who were not attending school. This development happened quite suddenly as more and more Roma families began to move into the area. The vast majority of these families were Czech or Slovakian. Based on its previous experience of working with the UK Gypsy and Traveller communities, EMTAS understood the need to 'get out there' and begin assertive outreach in order to begin to develop positive relations with these young people and their parents. Developing a strategy to meet the needs of the new arrivals was essential and a holistic partnership approach needed to be adopted. Salford EMTAS initially liaised closely with the education welfare team to speak to the families about their statutory responsibilities in relation to schooling and the importance of getting the children into school as soon as possible. This was important from a safeguarding point of view, and also in regard to community cohesion. Non-Roma neighbours were not always understanding of the situation and didn't perhaps realise that many of the Roma families might have been unaware of their statutory obligations, or indeed of how to contact the authorities to get their children into school. Based on their prior experiences in their countries of origin, perhaps they felt that no one cared if their children attended school or not. There is no doubt that these early days provided a steep learning curve for professionals, officers and community members alike. Although the EMTAS could identify several cultural similarities with the English Gypsies, the situation of many of these families was much more complicated and challenging in many respects. First and foremost, English was not their first language, family relationships and dynamics were not apparently obvious, as several families were living in a single household, and there was high mobility, with movement from street to street. As Pavlina Fakova, a Czech Romani, notes:

"When we first arrived in the UK we had to live with friends or other family members until we could find a house for ourselves. We didn't choose to live together, we had no choice."

Many families were having tenancy issues, struggling to find permanent work and were denied access to benefits, due to the Worker's Registration Scheme. They also had issues around health and accessing appropriate medical care. Added to this, there were tensions within the community around environmental waste (the bins provided to households were not sufficient for the multi-occupancy of the Roma). There was a general lack of knowledge of who these 'people' were and why they had migrated to the UK.

Empowering Roma

In the work of the RSG, empowering the community has been a key focus. From the outset, the role that Roma played in the organisation was proactive. Rather than being 'powerless', Roma asylum seekers from the Czech Republic and Slovakia actively participated in every stage of establishing the organisation, from writing the constitution to recruiting and mobilising the first volunteers, finding the first operational venue (a church hall in West London) and launching the RSG with its governing document at a meeting attended by over 80 Roma people at the Holy Cross Church in Kings Cross in 1998.

Retrospectively, the establishment of the RSG was an exercise in community empowerment. Fifteen years of the RSG's work have illustrated the ways in which the organisation has stayed close to its community ethos, implementing services based on community empowerment and trust. A holistic approach is the cornerstone of the RSG's work. This whole-person approach to the provision of advice and advocacy looks beyond the immediate issues and their triggers, and seeks to address underlying causes by working collaboratively both within the organisation and with external agencies to address multiple and complex needs.

Many Roma community members perceive the RSG as supporting processes of community development and empowerment. One of the Polish Roma participants in the RSG Action Research stated:

"We made the organisation and we are making it as we go along. We entrust you with the information, which we would not entrust to anybody else, so you can open the doors for us. And when one door is open, we will give you more information to open another door ... So the process has started and there is no stopping it ... for as long as the organisation exists." [Man, aged 58] (Ingmire, 2010, p 28)

Reflecting best practice in inclusive community development, there is an increasing engagement of Roma service users in the management of the organisation. A majority of the RSG's Management Committee are Roma[7] migrants, whose insight and determination help to shape strategy. In addition to this Roma are employed as staff and contribute their time as volunteers. Education support, music/dance classes, football and karate sessions are run by Roma professionals, who become role models for children and young people.

Furthermore, the RSG continually consults with the Roma community through evaluation/focus/steering-group meetings and informal one-to-one interviews. These consultations involve community members in the delivery of activities and help to generate a sense of community ownership of projects and services. They also facilitate a better understanding of the needs, concerns and aspirations of the community, their barriers and the most effective and culturally sensitive ways of overcoming them.

Since 2005, Salford EMTAS has tried to be as proactive as possible in promoting the empowerment of Roma community members. It has encouraged community members to deliver awareness-raising sessions in schools or take part in delivering training to a wide variety of organisations. Salford has a Voice of the Child agenda, which must also include and capture the voice of the most vulnerable and marginalised children and young people, including GRT children. In Salford the Roma community (particularly Roma youth) has always had an active part in helping to organise community events. In 2012 a young Roma student had a work placement with EMTAS as part of his work experience; he not only worked in the office but went on placement to some local primary schools with high numbers of Roma children, which was really successful. There are plans to continue to support Roma students in this way.

Over the last year, the service has taken on a young Czech Roma as an apprentice administrative assistant. Despite his lack of formal education and qualifications, he is doing exceptionally well and it is hoped this will lead to a secure employment contract with the local authority in the future. "I never thought I would have the opportunity to work for the council, I have hardly been to school and I have moved around so much with my mum it has been difficult to stick at anything. It has totally changed my life." (Lubomir Jano, Czech Roma 18-year-old council apprentice)

Salford EMTAS has also employed a Czech Roma community member as a teaching assistant to support a blind Roma student who recently arrived in Salford.

Empowering the Roma community has to be a priority for any inclusive service, whether we are talking about children and young people or their parents and the wider community. However, enabling empowerment can be difficult. Any individual going into a new environment needs appropriate support and guidance and an understanding from colleagues as to their training needs. A significant number of Roma community members in Salford do not have any formal qualifications, as many of them received a substandard or indeed a 'special' education in their countries of origin. English is also their second or third language. Although they may have good oral skills these are not always backed up with the necessary literacy skills for the workplace. Many Roma community members have a whole host of other skills they can offer, language skills and links with the community, but there needs to be an understanding on the part of potential employers that it requires time, resources and mentors who also have time, despite the current cuts and austerity. With the right support, this does happen.

In an observation that can be applied to Roma experiences across the UK, it has been noted that the lack of understanding within the wider Roma community about that specific role that a Roma person may have in the workplace can create tensions. For example, if one has a job in the council, no matter how small, there can sometimes be an expectation on the part of other community members that that one can help them out in some way, when in fact they have no power or authority to so. Such expectations are often symptoms of these families' difficulties in navigating local bureaucracies. Located in a new cultural environment, different to those of traditional Roma work practices, a Roma employee in the service sector can sometimes become very isolated from their own community (this is particularly the case for Roma women) and need extra support and encouragement in order to continue to balance home and work life successfully. Conversely, some bureaucracies, while recognising the value of 'natural leaders', become fearful when such community members fail to act within the confines of what can become rigid managerial structures that can stifle engagement.

Cultural mobilisation

Promoting an understanding of Roma culture has been a central feature of the RSG's work. Roma need to be heard on their own terms through self-representation and cultural contribution. Romani Rad, a music and dance ensemble, was formed by RSG in 1999 and trained over 100 young Roma people, preparing them to perform in hundreds of music events across London and the UK. The instruction was delivered by Roma musicians and dancers. Since its foundation Romani Rad has put Roma music firmly on the cultural map of Britain, collaborating with well-known music professionals and agencies, for example Asian Dub Foundation, Terry Hall and the BBC. The poster prepared for Romani Rad's first concert in 1999 set out the cultural manifesto of RSG, stating:

> We note a lack of positive media coverage on Roma refugees and asylum-seekers in this country. We are actively seeking to make a cultural contribution to British multicultural society.

The cultural politics of the Roma stemmed from their virtuoso instrumental and dance skills: a music heritage that has been passed down from one generation to another in many Roma families. The RSG answered the need for the creation of a learning environment, motivating young Roma to acquire these skills, and expanded it to include non-Roma people through Roma-led music classes, concerts and festivals. By using culture as a channel for communication and intertwining it with social action, the RSG has advanced the Roma agenda while advocating for the community and expanding a network of support for Roma refugees and migrants. This model of community mobilisation has over the past ten years been followed by many other GRT [Gypsy, Roma and Traveller] organisations, especially in talent shows, which have been organised as part of Gypsy, Roma, Traveller History Month over the past three or four years' (Acton and Ingmire, 2012).

Cultural mobilisation has proved to be an effective tool of social inclusion and empowerment both for individuals and for the Roma community at large. One young member of Romani Rad stated on the day of its performance in Hyde Park to an audience of 80,000 during

Pope Benedict XVI's visit to London: "For us Roma being here is a great honour. We came to share our culture with everyone present, representing not only Roma from Eastern Europe but also all Gypsy, Traveller communities in the UK. We feel part of British society and we want to be treated as such."[8]

The RSG and Salford EMTAS have been active proponents of Gypsy, Roma, Traveller History Month (GRTHM) since its inception in 2008. GRTHM has provided Salford EMTAS with a vehicle to raise the participation and involvement of the Roma community through many events in primary and secondary schools, in community centres, Salford Arts Theatre, libraries, museums, local radio and Salford University. More generally, Salford EMTAS has also been active in supporting the Roma contribution to the Holocaust memorial event. Whether the events have had a focus on music, drama, dance or history, they have all included active participation by Roma young people and families. Working sensitively with young people and families, assuring them that their involvement is valued and appreciated, has enabled them to open up and contribute meaningfully. "The only time we have the opportunity to show off our musical talents is at the Gypsy, Roma, Traveller History Month events, we look forward to it every year" (Robert Lakatos, 18-year-old Roma musician).

Some cultural work with GRT communities could be labelled narrow 'multiculturalism', which caricatures and reifies culture (cf Sarup, 1991, p 31) with 'wagons and campfires', rather than 'samosas and sarees'. But, as Acton (2004) argues, following Van Peebles' (1995) analysis of Black cinema in the US, stereotypes have to be transcended rather than merely discarded if the audience is to know what the new representations are addressing. The cultural mobilisation by RSG and Salford EMTAS has given them and the Roma community a platform not only to be ambassadors of their community but to convey messages and appeals about inclusion and to develop a network of supporters. Both Salford EMTAS and RSG believe the cultural work of Roma has led to senior council officers and elected members gaining a greater knowledge of the Roma. All too often Traveller Education Services across the country have found themselves marginalised alongside the Roma, Gypsy and Traveller communities, with little chance of having any impact on policy decisions or strategic plans. The clear message of GRTHM to policy makers and opinion formers is that Roma are very much part of London and Salford and have a voice that needs to be heard.

Intercultural change and empowerment

As Pinnock (1999) showed for Bulgaria, state policies of inclusion often reinforce the exclusion for Roma, a truth emphasised in Britain when Prime Minister Tony Blair's Social Exclusion Unit left Gypsies/Travellers/Roma out of its remit (Ryder, 2002). The long-standing debate about whether policies of inclusion smuggle in assimilation under the guise of community development (Ryder, 2014) obviously informs the work of the RSG and Salford EMTAS. Both organisations assert that the change their work brings to the Roma communities is not imposed but, rather, negotiated interculturally through dialogue and partnership.

One of the main objectives of the RSG is to promote an understanding of Roma culture, history and arts within mainstream society, while challenging stereotypes and anti-Roma/Gypsy discrimination. Throughout its existence, the organisation has engaged thousands of Roma and non-Roma people in intercultural dialogue, which is aimed at facilitating integration and building cultural bridges between the Roma community and British society. The projects that carry out these aims vary as much as the forms that they are given. They include organising events (for example festivals, concerts, exhibitions, forum theatres, conferences); publishing/disseminating educational resources (for example books, DVDs, CDs, learning packs, reports); engaging Roma and non-Roma of all ages in delivering short-term and long-term cultural and art schemes (such as organising exhibitions, delivering training workshops and consultancy work). The Roma Culture Participation Project focuses on delivering workshops in schools and has mobilised Roma community members of all ages in a process of creative thinking about the best ways to introduce their culture and history to audiences of Roma and non-Roma school children and their teachers. The project has had an impact on non-Roma beneficiaries through initiating a two-way process: in learning about Roma culture, they also learn about their own.

Each group has benefited from the project in a different way. For Roma artists and story-tellers, the project is an empowering experience, helping them to learn new skills, integrate and have their expertise valued by educators. They are also empowered by the opportunity to shape intercultural dialogue between Roma and mainstream society, while leading a debate on how to embed aspects of Roma culture into compulsory education. Since its foundation, the RSG has reached out to hundreds of schools[9] in London and South East England, and has mobilised 80 Roma older and young people in planning and delivering this work.

Over a decade of work with children and young people through advocacy programmes, education support and extra-curricular activities (such as football, karate, music, dance, visual arts and drama) has produced a myriad of positive intercultural outcomes. One is guiding young Roma in navigating the tensions between community traditions and experiences in the countries from which their families emigrated and the new cultural context within which they find themselves. An important dimension of this work has been helping Roma youth to take pride in their identity and also achieve in sport and education. One 15-year-old girl who has a student work placement with RSG asserts:

> "In my opinion, there is no contradiction between going to school and living a 'Gypsy life'. I go to school to gain knowledge and living a 'Gypsy life' is my culture and tradition, which I will never throw away or lose. I am really looking forward to going to college and university because it will improve the quality of my life in so many ways. I know that college is for many people a key to success. I am positive that almost every day I will hear something interesting in the class that will expand my knowledge and make me more prepared and confident to deal with the world and people from all walks of life."

Such aspirations signify new and radical directions for sections of the Roma community, but there are occasions when community members can be pulled in different directions or experience cultural tension. Salford EMTAS encountered a situation in a Salford secondary school that highlights some of the challenges surrounding interculturalism and the changing lives of the young Roma, and how these impact on their perception of gender roles. The school approached EMTAS for assistance in dealing with difficult behaviours that were presented by a large group of Roma males in the school. Among its concerns were the attitude of the male Roma students towards females within their own community and to girls in general and also a 'lack of respect for female staff working in the school'. The school explained that tensions were running high between Roma and non-Roma pupils and there was a growing negative perception among non-Roma parents about this community. While not condoning inappropriate behaviour, which is neither part of the culture nor acceptable, this situation does highlight the tensions surrounding the role of women and girls in society today and the 'traditional' role of a woman growing up in the Roma community. EMTAS is currently organising a support package for the school, including honest and open dialogue with the Roma parents (in particular the mothers), and a course on 'Respect and Relationships' will be delivered to mixed groups of young people (girls and boys, Roma and non-Roma). The whole staff will also receive training to improve their understanding of the Roma community.

The RSG has also witnessed cases of tension caused by the competing pulls of tradition and innovation. For example, a young Polish Roma woman, Ilona Marjanska, was for several years captain of the RSG-supported football club Roma United, becoming a source of inspiration for many Roma girls. She was regarded as a rising star in women's football, went on to play for Leyton Orient Ladies and studied sport development at Southampton University. Initially there was some surprise and hesitancy among some of the more traditional members of the community that a Roma girl could play football and wear shorts. However, these doubts were overcome by the success she achieved and she became a role model for the RSG and the Roma community (Huczko, 2006). Ilona features on the 'Lets Kick Racism out of Football' website, which notes that 'Ilona arrived in the UK at the age of six, and the only English words she knew were "apple" and "dog". Ten years later, she was studying for her A-Levels and playing for two women's teams, Roma United and Leyton Orient Ladies' (www.kickitout.org/499.php). Young Roma like Ilona who are taking new directions, yet who are still proud of their ethnicity, are powerful examples of what can happen when interculturalism and innovation are sustained and facilitated through inclusive environments and support. In this quest, inclusive schools and the provision of youth and sports projects like those run by RSG have a pivotal role to play through providing space for young people to explore and experiment with their culture and that of the host society in which they are now situated.

The positive outcomes of interculturalism and the mediation of new directions are evident in the sense that many Eastern and Central European Roma families now see the neighbourhoods in which they live, such as Salford and Newham, as their home, their children are bilingual, they have mixed friends, they attend school and college and are making the most of opportunities that their parents never had. It is through education that the lives of the Roma people in the UK will continue to change. Education is the key to opening up a brighter future: it supports integration, it empowers and informs people and gives the Roma people an opportunity to contribute to their new country of choice. A particular focus for the future needs to be on early years' education and the role of women as mums or as young adults in the community and the influence they can have in moving things forward for the community. In this way future generations of Roma children, young people and adults will be more able to play an active role in a fairer and more equal society.

Strategic work

Reflecting the pioneering and innovative work of the RSG and Salford EMTAS, both play an active role in more strategic work at a regional and national level. In recognition of its expertise and successes in developing best models of practice, the RSG received a grant from the Department for Education in 2011–13 that enabled the organisation to expand its services across other regions of the UK, providing indirect support to some 30,000 Roma by working with 1,800 professionals from statutory and non-statutory agencies via the delivery of Roma Culture Awareness training for professionals, Roma Culture Workshops in schools, specialist advice, strategic Roma Forums to share good practice and facilitating Roma Families Support Schemes and supporting grassroots initiatives.

Since 2011, the RSG has been actively lobbying and influencing the Department for Communities and Local Government to include Roma refugees and migrants in the UK's National Roma Integration Strategy, which the UK as well as all other EU member states had to submit to the European Commission as part of the EU Framework for National Roma Integration Strategies. In England, a decision was taken to exclude migrant Roma from this submission, except 'where their issues overlap with those impacting on this country's ethnic Gypsies and Travellers', which means that at present there is little official recognition of the overlap areas other than in education. Sylvia Ingmire commented: "Again and again, those in power seem to hold the keys to making definitions, which aim at excluding, fragmenting, dividing and polarising." One of the most important findings that the RSG's regional work has revealed is the need for national action to safeguard and promote the welfare of vulnerable Roma children and young people. Since 2012 all training sessions and forum meetings organised by the RSG have included this agenda. Over 80% of its consultancy work relates to enhancing local authorities' understanding of the safeguarding needs of Roma children and young people in the context of their culture and community dynamics.[10]

Salford EMTAS has also networked with other colleagues and practitioners working with GRT families and has been active in organisations such as NATT+ (The National Association of Teachers of Travellers and other Professionals), a national network of teachers that provides guidance and resources. Natalie Stables coordinates the NATT+ Roma Focus Group, which seeks to disseminate good practice with Roma communities and has organised a number of NATT visits to Central and Eastern Europe to promote links and dialogue between practitioners there and in the UK.

Future dangers and hopes

As is evident from a review of the media and popular discourse, the 'immigration' issue is never far from the political agenda. The concerns from certain sections of society and media about the lifting of employment restrictions on A2 countries and the impact it will have on migration to the UK, and the rise of anti-Gypsy sentiment across Europe in general, creates uncertainty and insecurity for all Roma families. Unemployment is a major concern; years of living in poverty and new benefit changes which came into force in 2014 could make life even more difficult for many Roma migrants. As a result of tighter benefits rules, all EU migrants will have to wait three months before they can claim Jobseeker's Allowance and other out-of-work benefits. The government says they will then face a more robust residence test before any claim is approved. This will include questions about their efforts to find work and English language skills. Concerns have been expressed that these new welfare regulations could force more Roma into dangerous and exploitative work practices within the informal economy. The 'right to reside' and 'habitual residency' tests are currently being challenged by the European Commission in court (Mednick, 2014). The demise of Traveller Education Services in the UK, the austerity measures and resulting cuts to local authority budgets mean that all those supporting Roma communities will have to work a lot harder to make sure that issues around inclusion and equality for all remain high on the agenda.

There can, however, be a fight-back. Cuts made by London Councils (an association of London boroughs) to hundreds of services, including the Roma Education Support Project, were successfully challenged by Roma community members in the High Court in 2011,[11] showing that cuts usually hit front-line support for the most disadvantaged and socially excluded groups without 'due regard' paid to equality duties. Elizabeth Henry, chief executive officer of Race on the Agenda, commented:

The challenge from Roma service users and the Roma Support Group ... was an extraordinary act of courage, which other much bigger and more powerful organisations have not shown. It deserves commendations and applause as it has inspired the whole voluntary sector, as well as securing services for the most vulnerable residents of London. (Personal communication to S. Ingmire)

Despite their marginalised status, Roma refugees and migrants have begun to be active subjects in the making of their own history by using community and institutional structures to achieve empowerment. RSG and Salford EMTAS exemplify inclusive community development approaches, trying at least, through careful mediation and negotiation, to steer away from paternalism or assimilationism.

Acknowledgement

Acknowledgements and thanks to the staff, volunteers, partners and clients of RSG and Salford EMTAS and Pavlina Fakova, Frantisek Machalek, Lubomir Jano and Robert Lakatos.

Notes

[1] Sylvia Ingmire is a founding member of the Roma Support Group (RSG) and its current director. Natalie Stables is coordinator of Salford Ethnic Minority and Traveller Achievement Service (EMTAS). The chapter was drafted by asking Natalie and Sylvia to respond to a number of questions, their responses were combined and they then edited their piece with the assistance of Acton and Ryder.

[2] A8 countries include Poland, the Czech Republic, Hungary, Estonia, Lithuania, Latvia, Slovenia and Slovakia, which acceded to the EU in 2004 and A2 countries include Romania and Bulgaria, which acceded to the EU in 2007.

[3] The report by European Dialogue was commissioned by the Department for Children, Schools and Families. Qualitative and quantitative data on Roma was collected in a nationwide survey of local authorities in England. In total, 104 local authorities completed the survey; 104 A2 and A8 Roma respondents were interviewed in ten locations in England. The research report is not accessible on the Department for Education website, yet it remains the most comprehensive survey of Roma communities in the UK.

[4] The figure derives from a total of 151 questionnaires that were returned out of 406 issued to local authorities (a response rate of 37%).

[5] A month initiated by the Department for Children, Schools and Families in 2008, where schools, libraries and other services work with communities to celebrate GRT culture and history (see Acton and Ryder, 2012).

[6] For more information about the RSG's front-line work in London, see: www.romasupportgroup.org.uk (Projects).

[7] Eight out of fourteen Trustees are Roma (2012–13): three Romanian Roma and five Polish Roma.

[8] Interview with Romani Rad's artists, 18 September 2010 (RSG Press Release, 22 September 2010).

[9] In 2012 alone, the RSG delivered 11 Roma Culture Workshops and five school assemblies, reaching approximately 1,360 school children and 70 teaching staff.

[10] This problem has also been highlighted by officials from local authorities who participated in the National Roma Network led by Leeds City Council (Roma Source). The official minutes of the meeting recorded: 'The issue of Roma children being taken into care was raised again. It continues to cause issues in local authority areas and members reported that Roma families were living in fear. The issues seem to stem from the criteria that social services use to determine whether a child is at risk and it was felt that the criteria were inflexible and do not take into account the cultural difference of Roma families.' (Minutes, National Roma Network, Town Hall, Leeds, 6 February 2013)

[11] *R (on the application of Hajrula and Hamza) v London Councils* [2011] EWHC 861 (Admin) (www.edf.org.uk/blog/?p=18461), and *R (on the application of Zofia Siwak) v London Borough of Newham* [2012] EWHC 1520 (Admin) (www. edf.org.uk/blog/?p=20044).

References

Acton, T. (2004) 'Modernity, culture and Gypsies. Is there a meta-scientific method for understanding the representation of "Gypsies"? And do the Dutch really exist?', in N. Saul and S. Tebbutt (eds) *The Role of the Romanies: Images and Counter-Images of Gypsies/Romanies in European Cultures*, Liverpool: Liverpool University Press, pp 98–116.

Acton, T. and Ingmire, S. (2012) '"I niktnierzuca w niekameniami" ("And nobody throws stones at them"): Polish Roma migrants and their contribution to Roma, Gypsy, Traveller politics in the United Kingdom', paper delivered to the 2011 Gypsy Lore Society Conference, Graz, and published in *Studia Romologica*, vol 5, pp 77–96.

Acton, T. and Ryder, A. (2012) 'Recognising Gypsy/Roma/Traveller history and culture' in J. Richardson and A. Ryder (eds) *Gypsies and Travellers: Accommodation, Empowerment and Inclusion in British Society*, Bristol: Policy Press, pp 135–50.

Brown, P., Scullion, L. and Martin, P. (2013) *Migrant Roma in the UK*, Salford: University of Salford.

Clark, C. and Campbell, E. (2000) '"Gypsy Invasion": a critical analysis of newspaper reaction to Czech and Slovak Romani asylum-seekers in Britain, 1997', *Romani Studies* (continuing the *Journal of the Gypsy Lore Society*), series 5, vol 10, no 1, pp 23–47.

Fremlova, L. and Ureche, H. (2009) *Patterns of Settlement and Current Situation of New Roma Communities in England: A Report Prepared for DCSF*, London: European Dialogue.

Grill, Jan (2012) '"Going up to England": exploring mobilities among Roma from Eastern Slovakia', *Journal of Ethnic and Migration Studies*, vol 38, no 8, pp 1269–87.

Hill, P. (2004) 'The great invasion' and Editorial, *Daily Express*, 20 January, pp 1 and 3.

Huczko, S., Dir. (2006) *Be Roma or Die Tryin'*, film on DVD, London: Roma Support Group.

Ingmire, S. (2010) *Improving Engagement with the Roma Community: Action Research Report*, London: Roma Support Group, p 28.

Mednick, R. (2014) 'Europe takes UK to court over benefits', *The Telegraph*, 22 March, www.telegraph.co.uk/news/worldnews/europe/eu/10088297/Brussels-takes-Britain-to-EU-court-over-immigrant-benefits.html.

Nacu, A. (2011) 'The politics of Roma migration: framing identity struggles among Romanian and Bulgarian Roma in the Paris region', *Journal of Ethnic and Migration Studies*, vol 37, no 1, pp 135–50.

Pantea, M.-C. (2012a) 'From "making a living" to "getting ahead": Roma women's experiences of migration', *Journal of Ethnic and Migration Studies*, vol 38, no 8, pp 1251–68.

Pantea, M.-C. (2012b) 'Social ties at work: Roma migrants and the community dynamics', *Ethnic and Racial Studies*, vol 1, pp 1–19.

Pinnock, K. (1999) 'Social exclusion and resistance. A study of Gypsies and the non-governmental sector in Bulgaria 1989–1997', PhD thesis, University of Wolverhampton.

Ryder, A. (2002) 'The Gypsies and exclusion', *Social Work in Europe*, vol 9, no 3, pp 52–60.

Ryder, A. (2014) 'Snakes and ladders: inclusive community development and Gypsies and Travellers', *Community Development Journal*, vol 49, no 1, pp 21–36.

Ryder, A. and Greenfields, M. (2010) *Roads to Success: Routes to Economic and Social Inclusion for Gypsies and Travellers, a report by the Irish Traveller Movement in Britain*, London: ITMB.

Sarup, M. (1991) *Education and the Ideologies of Racism*, Stoke on Trent: Trentham Books.

Van Peebles, M. (1995) *Panthers*, New York: Thunder's Mouth.

TWELVE

Conclusion: in search of empowerment

Thomas Acton, Sarah Cemlyn
and Andrew Ryder

Inside the ghetto

How can young Roma envisage a better future and their own empowerment? We have heard from older community activists, and practitioners and researchers with long-standing community involvement, but the voice of young people has not been so apparent. A report of a visit by Andrew Ryder to a Roma settlement in a small provincial Hungarian town may give us some insights. He was accompanied by Professor Karunanithi, an academic based in India, and Katya Dunajeva, a PhD student from the University of Oregon, who had been conducting fieldwork in the community visited by the group. For nine months Katya had been giving support to young Roma people in the community centre and after-school club. Andrew Ryder describes this visit.

We were surrounded by a group of ten or so children and young people aged between 7 and 19. The dynamics of the meeting took a series of sharp turns. Tired after a long school day, at first there was frivolity on the part of the children, with some playing out extreme caricatures of the community to test our reaction. Katya felt also that this flippancy was prompted by weariness on the part of the young people at the stream of funders, decision makers, researchers and students who descend on the community and just as suddenly depart, often not to be seen again. Later Katya informed me that adults in the community often greet (non-Roma) newcomers to the ghetto by asking what the visitors can help with, whether they can provide some financial or other support. According to Katya, 'this expectation of the "outsiders" assistance often further immobilises the community and crowds out grassroots resourcefulness to tackle poverty and various disadvantages that most Roma people face today'.

Passing through the first phase, of gaiety, the young people were inquisitive about India and the UK and, through Katya acting as translator, a dialogue was initiated that eventually turned to focus on what they wanted for themselves and their community.

"I want to have a girl and a boy. I want to have a job. I want to be a server/waitress. I want to stay in the slum;¹ this is where I grew up. But I want to see some change in the slum and the change should come from Gypsies themselves creating order." (Roma girl)

"I want to have a good paying job and family, but not yet. I want to create an environment that is good and positive. For this environment one needs a good job, good house and a wife, and then I would start a family." (Roma boy)

"I want to have children, a boy and a girl. I want to be a cook and don't want to stay in the slum. I want to move to London, where my sister lives. She moved there half a year ago and she likes it there." (Roma girl)

"It's good if women are independent, but it is very important that they take care of their children so that they are not on the streets and get into trouble." (Roma boy)

"Roma women with children … should stay home at least while those children are small." (Roma boy)

"Women should not work, that's what the men are here for! Women should cook and clean." (Roma girl)

"I want to go to a university and be an architect." (Roma boy, 7th grade, recipient of one of the scholarships for young Roma)

"People should go to tanning booths so everyone is equally dark." (Roma boy, joking again)

The seeds of possible change and future tension are evident in these comments, with some indicating preferences for new directions and roles while some remain wedded to tradition. Some of the aspirations appear modest but, given the level of poverty within which they are located, they should not be seen that way. In 1997 a large number of families in this community, who were resident in social housing and experiencing some difficulties already, were moved by the local authority into circus carts (wooden caravans). This act was deeply traumatising for these families. Since 2004 the charity that works in this community has been able to move these families back into houses, increase the number of households that have running water, establish a communal bath house and organise community activities including sport, a youth club, after-school club and mothers and toddlers' club. A new community centre is being designed and will be built with the active involvement of the community. One of the community workers is himself from the community and has qualified as a social worker and leads the local Roma Self Government in the town.

The non-Roma project leader informed us: "Our basic philosophy is 'to be there' [referring to the fact that they place the charity in the ghetto and work there]. So if you want to solve the problem you really have to be there and be among those people. This is important because laws and policies many times are made from behind the desk without any contact with those people. It is important to understand them … Until now it wasn't an easy situation … we were the charity service, or we were the helpers and they were the helped. Now I strive to make it clear that we have to work together and we have to be partners." However, the project leader confided that it is sometimes difficult to work with and involve the adults, given the tensions that exist between those who were moved from the circus carts into the town and those Roma who never left – tensions that revolve around 'old' and 'new' inhabitants and competition for scarce resources and that are compounded by long-term unemployment and addictions. The tensions also exist along inter-ethnic lines: 'musician' Gypsies, or Romungre, complain about the 'dirty Olah/Vlach' and vice versa. If empowerment can be assumed to strive to create solidarity and unity among members of a given community, there is still a way to go in the ghetto. According to Katya, these tensions are passed on to the younger generation, who often talk about inter-community conflicts as an unquestioned and given part of their lives. The charity leader explained that they have to integrate various groups of Roma first before they can implement any community-based projects. Children and young people are more likely to overcome such differences and imagine collective goals, such as the above-mentioned youth centre or neighbourhood waste collector, which the young boys built for the benefit of all.

Andrew Ryder's reflection

As with so many trips such as this that I have made and experiences of working and living in Gypsy, Roma and Traveller (GRT) spaces of social and spatial exclusion primarily in the UK, but also in Central and Eastern Europe, my thoughts were consumed by the positive and negative of what I had witnessed. From this visit and the other experiences stored in my mind, the same series of questions surfaces: Will the younger generation make a breakthrough? Will effective community leadership emerge? Is the local charity/project achieving its objectives? What will happen if the funding ends? What could be achieved with more resources? Are the pulls of tradition disempowering? Will my observation achieve something for this community? Will I give something back or have I just taken? When articulating their aspirations, none of the young people whom I met in the ghetto or other locations in the past expressed a desire for empowerment. Is this a failure of GRT politics and community organisation? Is it a symptom of profound exclusion, where disempowerment and multiple exclusions make it difficult for these young people to conceptualise a greater role in decision-making processes? More broadly, would it not be likely that young people in other communities would have expressed a similar disinterest in activism? Is it not generally the case that only a small stratum of a community ever has the inclination to become activists?

This description of the visit to the ghetto reminds the reader of the difficulties facing GRT communities, which, though not always uniform, reflect multiple forms of exclusion based on ethnicity, culture, space and economy. These problems are compounded in some cases by a lack of agency and disunity, but also throw into relief the value and/or dangers caused by 'outsiders' playing the role of either catalysts and facilitators or paternalistic benefactors. The questions prompted by the visit are questions that this book has sought to consider.

Praxis and obstacles to empowerment

Hearing the Voices of Gypsy, Roma and Traveller Communities has, as promised in Chapter One, reflected a coming together of the radical community development tradition revitalised by Habermas's notion of deliberative democracy, and the practical, counter-hegemonic coalitions of feminist theorists and supporters of intersectional approaches to multi-dimensional oppression. These build on the foundational feminist insights of standpoint theory (cf Harding, 2004) in valuing oppressed perspectives as the basis for knowledge. This also meets the challenge laid down by critical race theory to engage with the persistent ethnic inequalities that have outlasted formal renunciations of 'scientific racist' discourses, by taking seriously knowledge formulated from the standpoint of those whose unequal position provides clearer insights into the nature of society than those of the occupants of privileged positions. The creation of a vibrant GRT civil society in Europe, however, has been restrained by the co-option of young educated Roma into funder-driven discourses, while the low expectations and disillusion of those they have left behind in the ghetto perpetuates the 'culture of silence' (in Freire's (1972) sense). Together with barriers created by discrimination, lack of recognition and limited funding, this compounds the difficulties facing GRT community organisation and activism and frustrates hopes.

Another aim of the book has been to facilitate reflection; but reflection on activism with highly marginalised groups like Gypsies, Roma and Travellers can be challenging. Acute unmet need and limited resources mean that activists too often succumb to exhaustion and fatigue. Servicing and meeting huge demands means that there is a danger of reflexivity being marginalised. Here lies a fundamental danger. If activists do not have space to reflect, then strategies and collective frames are not renewed and campaigns can become moribund and fracture. Conversely, we have also seen that reflection, learning and mutual support underpin the growth of activism and community development.

This book has brought to the fore personal testimony and stories from a range of actors that embody the narrators' values, and reflection on those stories can lead to forms of critical pedagogy or 'conscientisation', where connections are made between life experience and the structural nature of inequality and, just as importantly, hope for change is generated and acted on. Thus, as Ledwith and Springett (2010) suggest, through critical dialogue and reflection on action, marginalised and oppressed people can move on from a passive, naive 'magical consciousness' that naturalises the disadvantages in someone's lifeworld (in other words, assumes that injustice is a natural and localised part of the social landscape). By involving community members and activists in the writing of this book we have sought to forge a participatory process where 'praxis' can be shaped and so encourage an emerging trend in research on GRT communities, where researchers attempt to form partnerships with the community and 'give something back' in terms of skills development and input into and ownership of research outcomes (Greenfields and Ryder, 2012).

As noted in Chapter Ten, the relations between GRT communities and researchers have been soured by the work of researchers who adopt a hierarchical and positivist approach to research, sometimes called 'Gypsylorist'. While the overt racism and elitist amateurism of the old Gypsy Lore Society may be history, the idea that scholarship should provide a non-political expertise, which serves the well-meaning neoliberal authorities attempting the integration of Roma, is alive and well (Acton, 2013).

This state of affairs often alienates Roma activists from academic researchers and damages the symbiotic relationship between them. A tradition of collaborative action research began in the 1960s both in the West (Acton, 1974) and in some state socialist countries, such as the research of Istvan Kemény, Ottilia Solt, Gábor Havas and Zsolt Csalog in Hungary into the experiences of poverty by the Roma (Bíró, 2013). The exemplar of this approach may be the late Nicolae Gheorghe, a Romanian Rom scholar and activist. According to the anthropologist Sam Beck (private communication), 'He was one of the bravest public intellectuals I have known … He taught me that, at least for some of us, it is critical to be engaged with the struggles of the people we study.' Gheorghe played a pivotal role in promoting the Roma issue on the European agenda, but it is significant that in later years he expressed concerns at the distancing of Roma civil society from the grassroots (Gheorghe, 2013). The fears expressed by Gheorghe can be articulated through Freire's concept of 'horizontal violence', where campaigners become collaborators in oppression through forms of managerialism and bureaucratisation, both of which are often driven through narrow donor agendas diverting and hijacking community aspirations (Chapter Ten).

Existing forms of governmentality do not lead the powerful to take note of the views of GRT communities. Policies that invoke the language of 'social inclusion' rest upon narrow, assimilative interpretations of what it is to 'civilise' and integrate (Van Baar, 2005). Such structures lead to bureaucratic processes stifling funding streams for community organisations and creating projects with limited goals to achieve service adjustment or give the impression of consultation. This imposes hierarchy on community organisation and constrains community leaders to dance to the tunes of their funders, smothering their appetite for more transformative action. As discussed in Chapter One, this is also a wider theme in contemporary community development. Present forms of governmentality normalise neoliberal and assimilative policy agendas in the sense of Foucault (1997), and individualise and pathologise the victims rather than the agents of Roma exclusion. Hitherto governments and international agencies have been seeking 'the right negotiating partners' from the GRT community. We suggest that GRT movements can turn that process on its head and seek a new governmentality predicated on social justice and empowerment where the state is decentred and accountable to a civil society composed of what Fung (2002) has called 'deliberative publics'. These will have been built 'from the bottom up', where excluded people can develop self-help and reciprocity through forms of mutualism and participation, which will shrink and ultimately dissolve what Gough et al (2006) have called the 'spaces of social exclusion'.

Within GRT communities social capital has been a valuable defence against hostile forces, but cultural trauma engendered by centuries of marginalisation can lead to distrust of outsiders. Chapters Two and Three reveal the disunity that can be spawned through disagreements as to the degree to which the community or outsiders are perceived to be in control of community organisations. Nonetheless, effective coalitions have been built sometimes, for limited periods (as seen in Chapters Two, Seven and Nine). Solidarity has often been rooted in activists' engagement in battles that seemed impossible to win, as was the case in the early days of Friends, Families and Travellers (FFT, Chapter Five). For women activists (Chapter Nine), the pressure of helping families to get through the complexity and partisanship of the planning process has created huge demands, but mutual support has counteracted damage and promoted hope. Women's growing involvement is prominent in successful partnership and the generation of a cadre of activists, though structural and sometimes cultural barriers remain.

Social justice and identity

Limited and localised visions of justice can still present a counter-narrative to the hegemony of neoliberalism and its limited conceptions of equality and justice. The refusal of community voices to assimilate demonstrates that though individuals have to navigate through structures not of their own making they are able to create their own meaningful frameworks for action (cf Willis, 1977).

There have been times when GRT campaign activity has been consumed by a narrow form of identity politics that has reified identity and simplified change agendas into ones based on recognition, to the exclusion of redistribution. This is a trend that Thompson (2005) suggests is evident in many contemporary societies. Fraser (1995) has argued that redistribution and recognition must be united in attempts to understand and challenge social injustice, but this may require radical approaches favouring the deconstruction and destabilisation of existing identities, codes and symbolic orders, in place of liberal multicultural inclusion strategies. Becoming aware of the interplay of the family, school and political experiences that constitute the different identities with which we 'play' (Gheorghe, 1997), or 'standpoints' from which we experience our interactions with those who have power over us (Hill, 2003), can promote critical consciousness and enable us to move on from purely reactive and sometimes conservative forms of identity (Ballard and Ballard, 1977) without succumbing to someone else's 'civilising agenda'.

Collectivity and empowerment

Although the acquisition of new knowledge and know-how represents a multitude of individual journeys, to be politically effective it also has to be a collective journey. Olsen (2006) has picked up Fraser's (1995) juxtaposition of distribution and participation to argue for an 'enabling' state to guarantee genuine opportunities for participation. If Gypsy/Roma/Traveller community organisations/non-governmental organisations (NGOs) wish to be a part of such a dialogue with the state, both they and state agencies and their practitioners need to understand clearly the changes in their practices that are required so as to make this possible.

As we have argued, community organisation among GRT communities has been shaped by the intense social networks caused by exclusion and that are part of the social capital of GRT people (Ryder, 2011). The challenge for GRT civil society has been to transfer the unity and solidarity of communities to the NGO sector. This feat, though, has not yet been achieved at a transnational level, where some would argue Roma civil society has at times drifted into 'verbalism', which mobilises community consciousness without matching that with action. Freire (1972) warns that 'verbalism' produces the risk of disillusionment and lethargy returning to mobilised groups. Some scepticism has been expressed recently about the ever-growing verbal emphasis on 'empowerment'. As noted in Chapter Ten, this has been prompted by the Roma Platform, which brings together national governments, the European Union (EU), international organisations and Roma civil society representatives. The Roma Platform in Prague in 2009 established a set of 10 shared principles to address the inclusion of Roma. These included commitments on the 'involvement of civil society' and the 'active participation of the Roma' (European Commission 2011). Such statements imply commitments to forging a dynamic partnership with Roma communities, involving them actively in decision making and policy design. The drive to achieve empowerment has been further spurred by the rhetoric of the EU Framework for National Roma Integration Strategies, which has also emphasised the importance and value of dialogue and partnership between centres of power and GRT communities (Acton and Ryder, 2013).

How can these fine words be made reality? At a service level, the response has been the creation of a growing number of mediator positions by governmental bodies and service providers; the rationale is that the mediators act as bridges between GRT communities and institutions, but they often focus on instrumental efficiency, not empowerment. Cornwall (2008) argues that activists need greater manoeuvrability than do mediators to attempt transformative empowerment that will enable people to make their own decisions and take collective action. Whether sourced from within the community or negotiated from external funders, the tailored and flexible resources do not seem to be there for empowering GRT community organisations on anything like the scale that could radically transform their marginalisation (Acton and Ryder, 2013). In an ideal world, if more community organisers could be funded and allowed to work in the manner outlined, that would play a valuable role in providing the community partners that the EU has rightfully recognised as necessary to help shape institutional change at the local, national and transnational levels (European Commission, 2011). Activism sustained by membership subscriptions could be one means to secure greater independence and community actions that reflect the aspirations of the community rather than of donors, but such democratic and membership-financed structures remain elusive. Instead, GRT civil society sometimes resembles an ethno-business where managerialism and fund raising appear to have taken precedence over activism (Guy, 2013). Chapters Two and Four, which described the early years of the Gypsy Council and FFT, portrayed what could be achieved by poorly funded activist networks, where vision and determination can achieve much. They also made clear the dangers of not having a secure funding base, leading to activists working themselves into the ground and suffering from 'burn-out'.

We suggest that a more inclusive model of community development might yet assist the growth of a more outgoing and democratic local, national and transnational advocacy network shaped by cosmopolitan values, and combining (and moderating) pride in ethnicity with a wider solidarity that addresses other equality and social justice agendas.

Final reflections

In this final section the three editors set down some of their reflections based on their reading and editing of this volume.

Thomas Acton: the power of imagination

The hope of the publishers was that this book would supply practical help for hard-working, hard-pressed community workers. And even though this isn't a cook-book, and we haven't been able to set out a nice, simple set of rules on 'how to do it', we hope community workers will learn from our experiences, and even pick up a few tricks from our case studies; but different readers will learn different things. The reader may, in fact, have intuited that in the editing of this book there has been a sometimes uneasy compromise between the social policy approach of Ryder and Cemlyn and the political science approach of Acton. The discipline of social policy is built around the responsibility of social scientists to put knowledge at the service of government and make the formulation of policy – or the strategy of deserving groups to change policy – as scientifically informed as possible. Value judgements are therefore intrinsic to social policy discourse, and all too easy to confuse with facts (especially if, from some standpoints, they *are* facts). Political science, on the other hand, is more interested to explain policies than to advocate them. When writing as a political scientist I do not consider evaluating policies, or methods of political organisation, any more than a lepidopterist would describe one butterfly as more reactionary or progressive than another, even if a gardener might draw on that work to plant flowers that would attract the more beautiful butterflies, and keep the cabbage whites at bay. Of course, in private life the lepidopterist may also be a passionate gardener, and in private life I have been a passionate activist in many groups, including the Gypsy Council and the Roma Support Group, but I never lose sight of the fact that it is my political science, not my passion, that gives me the chance to influence opponents. Somehow one has to pull off the trick of arguing convincingly from one's opponents' premises, while never angering them by pretending to share their values when you do not. To do this successfully is the essence of both political integrity and political effectiveness, and it requires imagination. So I am somewhat bemused by the tendency of community development writers, from Alinsky on, to think they have found a recipe for success in community campaigning that others can follow, when I see nothing but the age-old predicaments of politics, as clear to Herodotus and Confucius as they are today.

Perhaps I can most easily illustrate this by reflecting on Cemlyn and Ryder's Chapter Seven on the Gypsy Traveller Law Reform Coalition (GTLRC), where the belief of the authors that the GTLRC's success derived from advances in community development techniques shines through. And at one level everything in that chapter is true; but I would still argue that it is not methodological innovation, but imagination, that brought the GTLRC's victories.

In the 2000s the GTLRC painstakingly put back together a coalition as broad as Puxon's Gypsy Council of the 1960s and Mercer's NGEC of the 1980s, and it engaged more Gypsies/Travellers and more women as activists than either of them and it did have a more worked-out philosophy of how to do so, of empowerment, until, like its predecessors, factionalism rent it asunder. And its achievement was enormous; it led to the Labour government adopting an evidence-based approach to site provision, through regional planning, which led to a steady growth in private sites, even if planning permission had to be won on appeal. And this achievement has proved much harder to undo than the Conservative anti-Gypsy spokesman, Eric Pickles MP, had hinted it would be in opposition, because even if under the Localism Act councils can make up their own minds as to how many sites are needed, evidence is still evidence. Councils are not queuing up to follow Basildon down the massively expensive and socially stressful path of the eviction at Dale Farm.

But was the GTLRC's success the result of its organisational method's empowering Travellers? Or can it be seen as perhaps the other way round: that the ideology of the GTLRC was mimicry of the ideology of those in power?

Is it coincidence that those who represent GRT communities in their negotiations with the powerful so often seem to take titles similar to the titles of those in power? In the ages when kings really ruled countries, Gypsy kings and dukes went calling on them. In the Ottoman Empire there were bulibashas; in its feudalised protectorates of Moldavia and Wallachia we also find voevodes. In the Ireland of the 1950s, dominated by the Roman Catholic Church, Tom Doherty called himself the Primate of the Travelling People. In 1960s England, when local councils still had some real power, the Gypsy Council promised them new solutions that would solve age-old problems. That was not the title Grattan Puxon wanted, but it was the one Johnny Brazil stuck him with because it was the one that would work. But once Mrs Thatcher had made local councils part of the enemy within, Peter Mercer and John Day not only described themselves as community workers but were able to gain paid positions as such. The organisations of the 1980s were able to 'hold the line' on accommodation and bank the massive investment in Traveller Education that Ivatts describes in this book. The clear improvements in the positions of Gypsy/Traveller communities perhaps caused resentment that, combined with the racist reaction to Roma immigration after 1989, caused the Major government to adopt anti-Gypsy populism as a strategy to avoid the electoral defeat that the swing of the pendulum was so clearly going to deliver in 1997.

New Labour reacted to Conservative racism by rolling with the punch, instead of punching back. It used the language of 'community empowerment', promising a third-way technical solution. It promised to be even harder on immigration than the Tories (and in office from 1997, amazingly, if incompetently, it was). But the Criminal Justice Act 1994 sent the Gypsy/Traveller organisations into shock. They thought they were being asked to fight the battles of the 1960s all over again, and thought they could do so through the opposition Labour Party and the Labour Campaign for Travellers' Rights (LCTR). They mistakenly thought the racism-lite of Straw and Blair was just a temporary electoral strategy. They were like the Polish cavalry facing the German tanks in 1939, fighting the last war instead of the next one. The Labour Party members of the LCTR were Old Labour to the core, as were their contacts in the Labour and Union hierarchy, shadow minister Peter Pike and Unison leader Rodney Bickerstaffe. But New Labour loathed Old Labour, and the policies LCTR thought it had won were disregarded and discarded.

The genius of Traveller Law Reform was to reinvent the policy of building more Traveller caravan sites not just as the demand of an oppressed minority but as a technical solution developed by a university-based think-tank (Cardiff Law School). Since the New Labour think-tanks were largely historically illiterate, the GTLRC was able to sell its thinking to New Labour as a genuinely new set of policies replacing the failed old policies of the Wilson and Thatcher eras, rather than as the revival of those policies that it actually was.[2] But, even dressed in New Labour language, those policies were still in the interests of the Gypsy/Traveller community, and the GTLRC was able to draw in almost all of the old protest movements and some new ones. This successfully delivered democratic legitimation to a New Labour approach. Appointing Andrew Ryder, a Brownite sceptic of Blairism but still then a true believer in the New Labour project, helped to ensure that slowly but surely the policies were embedded in Labour's regional planning system. As a campaigner not implicated in any of the older factions, Len Smith was able to act as a referee, holding the ring between those older factions. His growing enthusiasm as he realised the constructive effect that his work was having gave him the charisma to keep the show on the road. Eventually, of course, divisions and distrust shattered the GTLRC, not because there is anything especially disunited about GRT movements, but because of the structural divisions of all voluntary ethnic minority movements, as Acton's scandalous attack on Lady Plowden in *New Society* pointed out as long ago as 1974. Ethnic majorities in a democracy would never dream of imposing on themselves the unity that the establishment often demands from minorities.

So, was the GLTRC 'innovative' in its methods? At one level, no; the tactic of using the buzzwords of the powerful to advance the agenda of a sectional interest was as familiar to Confucius and Machiavelli as it was to Mao Tse-Tung or Walter Bagehot (and his descendant Ann, who became secretary of the Gypsy Council), and that does not change. But to do this always requires a fresh imagination.

Why does this book cite various attempts to appropriate the formulations of John Rawls (Saward, 2002) for redistributive policies? Because Rawls has been a pin-up boy for soft, neo or 'woolly' liberal intellectuals, and community development writers use quotes from Rawls to sell themselves to the government as technocrats rather than leftists, with the same dexterity that market reformers in the former Soviet Union ornamented their advocacy of economic competition with carefully chosen quotes from Marx and Lenin and all American politicians quote the Bible.

The successful advancement of sectional interests absolutely requires this tactic but it does not mean that employing it is easy or automatic. On the contrary, it requires imagination, subtlety, diplomacy and narrative skill; and, when successful, it may indeed slightly change the contours of the hegemonic ideology and the composition of the ruling class. And if this Coalition government does not roll out an anti-Gypsy agenda as devastating as that of the present governments of France and Italy, that will be both a vindication of and a monument to the GTLRC.

This volume has argued for grassroots activism, trust and social solidarity and the need to articulate a vision of a society shaped by social justice. But so does the Tea Party in the United States. The powerful can use the buzzwords of the oppressed to confuse them. If this book tells us anything, it is that we have to go beyond the abstract phrases and give them concrete meanings that are plausible and appealing to the great majority. One has to start with counter-narratives that chip away at hegemonic discourses. But to win in politics one needs to go on from counter-narratives to comprehensive narratives, ones that comprehend and incorporate the narrative of one's opponents.[3] There is no recipe for successful community development. It always takes imagination and empathy and taking account of local conditions, current context and capacity.

Andrew Ryder: power and transformative action

The financial crisis of 2008 revealed the full extent of the flaws and contradictions of neoliberalism and has prompted for many campaigners such as myself a re-evaluation of the shape and direction that progressive politics needs to take, based on greater governmental intervention, coupled with radical forms of democracy. However, this realignment has as yet failed to capture the public imagination, as states across Europe still cling to the discredited policies of neoliberalism or lurch even further to the Right, a scenario that leads to Roma communities becoming the perennial 'whipping boy' (scapegoat). The challenge for the Left, of course, is to resist the dilution of its new vision and instead sell that vision. As Acton notes, such a quest may necessitate pragmatism, but also formulating a narrative that is coherent and comprehensible. In that quest it may be necessary not just to invoke the slogans and symbols of political and popular discourse but to reorientate and reinvent them. Hence it was for that reason that the GTLRC (Chapter Seven) invoked the language of 'social inclusion' with a boldness that did successfully prompt governmental action and also stirred within the New Labour project a rare flicker of radicalism and courage that may eventually be seen as one of the few high points in race equality from that period of government.

Different strategies for empowerment and social justice have been at the heart of political debate between Left and Right in the European democracies since 1990. Meanwhile 'local' and 'community' action have become popular terms in British political discourse. Under the present Coalition government there is a perceived danger for Gypsy and Traveller communities that the localist and 'Big Society' (small state) neoliberal political agenda will leave the state and local government as bystanders, while Traveller site provision becomes hostage to parochial and 'nimbyist' pressures stirred up by small oligarchies, so that, as Parvin (2011) argues, the 'greater good' is sacrificed.

It was to avoid and break the log-jam of nimbyist opposition to strategic projects that notions of civic leadership have been accepted in the past, where councillors were expected to face down populist opposition in the interests of a greater good. The Caravan Sites Act 1968 was an example of this. The rationale was to achieve a reduction in enforcement costs and better life chances for a vulnerable minority, and also to reduce community conflict that harmed everyone. The implementation of such policies was often, however, linked to assimilationist agendas based on normative assumptions that did little to change the mind-sets of hostile local populaces. It was also a hierarchical policy approach that led to sites being located in marginal space and subject to harsh management regimes; such sites were referred to as 'reservations' by some alienated residents (Ryder, 2012).

An indication of the 'pendulum' moving away from localism may have taken place with Ed Miliband's assertion that Labour is the party of 'one nation politics' (Cruddas, 2013), which could be seen as an attempt to claim the ground of the consensus politics espoused by both Left and Right in British post-1945 politics and a bid to take over the large initial support for the concept of a 'Big Society', which utilised some of the rhetoric of one-nationism (Hulme and Hulme, 2012). A central tenet of one nation politics has been the concept of a compassionate and strong state. In its post-war consensus form, however, statism could be paternalistic and marginalise minorities in decision making (Richardson, 2000). This was the fate of Gypsies and Travellers in the actual implementation of the Caravan Sites Act 1968, a policy framework that also failed to adequately engage with prejudice and change entrenched opinions. Ultimately it was not robust enough in forms of intervention or sanctions where councils failed in their duty to provide sites. Doogan (2012) has argued that such 'consensus' statism will also fail to muster sufficient resolve to meet present economic, environmental and social challenges without strong state measures being fused with participatory engagement and a strong civil society. Similar arguments and principles can be applied to the realisation of a Social Europe through the EU Framework for National Roma Integration Strategies (Chapter Ten).

Hence, the message of this book is that new relationships and approaches are required from GRT civil society and communities, centres of power, researchers and the wider public to pursue empowerment. This book indicates that those approaches are beginning to take root among activists and the third sector working 'with' and 'for' GRT communities and have prepared the foundations for the new directions we propose through inclusive forms of community development. In sum, there is a need for a more popular acceptance of social justice principles where society moves away from laissez-faire dogma and promotes both redistribution and recognition. This agenda can be advanced through a cosmopolitanism that is firmly rooted in appreciation of our worldwide humanity, through a deliberative democracy coupled with strong political frameworks that mediate between central intervention and community activism.

Confused utopianists sometimes forget that a society based on the primacy of democratic planning is one where 'freedom is the recognition of necessity', namely, a condition that enables society in its entirety rather than a privileged few to fulfil their needs and is reliant on social solidarity and obligation. Rather than utilising liberal or paternalistic versions of consensus politics, transformative action may need to invoke the language of 'inclusive citizenship'. Critical analysis of citizenship has exposed the myriad ways in which marginalised groups have been excluded from full enjoyment of the different elements of citizenship. Certain groups within society enjoy the status of lesser citizens or of non-citizens. The struggles by such groups to redefine and transform 'given' ideas about citizenship provide insights as to what visions of an 'inclusive citizenship' might mean. The four values of inclusive citizenship, which have emerged from the accounts of those at the margins engaged in struggle, are justice, recognition, self-determination and solidarity (Lister, 2008). These may provide a narrative frame for the future struggles facing Roma communities that is post-nationalist and avoids the 'hang-up' of national chauvinism and embraces a conception of a 'Social Europe' (Chapter Ten).

In his advocacy of social justice, Rawls contended that an important foundation for social justice is a social contract based upon the rational evaluation of society and the threats and opportunities within that society, and also means by which the state can maximise equality and opportunity (Rawls, 1971). In other words, 'social justice' is about finding institutional arrangements that satisfy the principles of justice – a system of rules that would result in fair equality of opportunity and would be to the advantage of the least well-off. Acton is sceptical about the notion of citizenship and the development of an updated Rawlsian social contract, but I would argue that Rawls and Marx (or at least a neo version) can be 'bedfellows'. Commentators like Bell have remarked that 'With Rawls, we have the most comprehensive effort in modern philosophy to justify a socialist ethic' (Bell, 1972, p 57). Bell rationalised this statement by noting that Rawls provided 'a fundamental rationale for a major shift in values; instead of the principle "from each according to his ability, to each according to his ability", we have the principle "from each according to his ability, to each according to his need." And the justification for need is fairness to those who are disadvantaged for reasons beyond their control.' It was little surprise that the lead apostles of neoliberalism, Hayek and Nozick, bitterly contested the interventionist arguments of Rawls. Meeting individuals' need should be perceived as stemming from notions of justice rather than charity (Jackson, 2005), thus it is something that cannot be achieved in a free-market, unregulated society and warrants a redistributory and regulatory role by centres of power, which need to work in tandem and dialogue with public constituencies, including the disempowered. The strength and validity of a new, bolder and rejuvenated social contract will be tested by the support, protection and inclusion afforded to Roma communities.

Sarah Cemlyn: community activism, solidarity and gender

Co-editing and co-writing in this book has been a powerful experience for me, particularly the involvement with key women activists for Chapter Nine, and also the insight into activism throughout the chapters. The primary impact is a feeling of awe and celebration of the depth of activists' personal and political engagement and their ability to ignore massive political odds against their communities to advocate for and achieve rights. The backdrop to all the struggles charted is the perennial, extensive and profound discrimination, exclusion and inhumanity faced by GRT communities. The luminous humanity, courage and vision of activists cast into deep shadow the injustice they encounter.

At one level this book is as much about political activism as it is about 'community development'. The historical focus in earlier chapters is on self-starting activism, which may also involve catalysts external to the community (Chapter Two) or with personal connections to it (Chapter Five) but has rarely involved state-sponsored community workers. While community development theorists emphasise the focus on social justice and supporting the empowerment of disadvantaged communities, community development is funded and practised within a contested ideological context (Craig et al, 2011) and may serve the forces of reaction as much as the forces of progress. The absence of GRT communities from 'mainstream' community development discussion has been noted in Chapters One and Seven, and their absence from much of social policy research was raised by Craig in the Foreword. Their scattered geographical location means that they do not fit funding criteria (such as those under New Labour geared at 'regenerating' communities), and conceptions of 'locality communities' may actively exclude groups of Gypsies, Roma and Travellers (Cowan, 2003). The assimilatory potential of welfare and development projects has been noted throughout this text. Under the 'community cohesion' agenda of the early 2000s some initiatives were undertaken with GRT groups, for example to reduce conflict around new site provision, but national policy was about tackling conflict that arose from minority groups being perceived as outside the mainstream (Flint and Robinson, 2008), and therefore even more decidedly than its predecessors was designed to address nonconformity to dominant norms (Flint, 2009).

If community development practitioners are able to find ways of being funded that avoid too much stranglehold by such ideologies, there are some familiar, apparently obvious lessons that have been brought to the fore previously in relation to a range of public services such education, health, even social work (Cemlyn et al, 2009) and that involve a strenuous effort to understand the situation and injustices for GRT communities on their terms and from their position, to challenge this discrimination and to open up opportunities. This book has also shown the centrality of engaging in critical dialogue with the communities to promote radical change. Such principles are embedded in community development theory, but often remain latent in relation to engaging with Gypsies, Roma and Travellers, since 'mainstream' community development (if it can be said to exist still in the current climate of austerity and abdication of government responsibility to under-funded community groups) has not fully engaged with their struggles. Hopefully the book, without setting out to be a manual, has nonetheless provided some insights, inspiration and optimism for those non-GRT community development practitioners who seek to redress the balance. But they may also need to recognise that those who do take up the cudgel on behalf of these communities may themselves experience some of the hostility and marginalisation that is endemic, and they will need to be strategic in building alliances and support networks and identifying chinks in the dominant discourse into which arguments can be driven to support their cause.

Such practitioners may also find food for thought in the examples of voluntary organisations that have developed a multi-layered approach to supporting GRT community development, participation and advocacy, from nurturing individual support through skills training, to establishing intermediary networks, promoting models of good practice, and national advocacy (Chapters Six, Eight and Eleven). Although such organisations are not immune from the tensions between outsider involvement and community self-direction that permeate these pages, they have gone some way to achieving the scaffolded approach to empowerment that was discussed in Chapter One. However, we must also note that all these organisations are specialists within the GRT sector. Examples of wider community development or racial equality organisations that spin off GRT initiatives are rare: they include the Race Equality Council in Devon, through one dedicated staff member; the Quakers, who began the organisation that later became the Gypsy-led Derbyshire Gypsy Liaison Group (Chapter Nine); and some councils of voluntary service that have responded positively to approaches from Gypsy activists.

What is notable is that, despite this ghettoisation of GRT organisations, reflecting the broader experience of the communities, the organisations themselves have championed the development of links with the wider community. They have forged partnerships and alliances that provide opportunities for mainstream organisations, such as local authorities, police and health services, to engage in their own critical reflection and so highlight the need to overhaul policy and practice, and to access increased resources and influence for GRT organisations. Given that there is an ever-present danger of 'outsiders' backsliding, taking over, undermining or deceiving, the generation of trust across boundaries by GRT community organisations is all the more impressive. The National Federation of Gypsy Liaison Groups epitomises such developments.

Throughout this book there are strands of discussion of the impact of gender on community activism, and vice versa. One reservation is that this has remained a somewhat submerged theme, prominent here and there but not as fully developed as it might have been. It is hoped that this can be addressed further in the future. The emergence of prominent women has coincided with the considerable development of activism, charted in later chapters of this book. Despite tensions and difficulties, and often at huge personal cost, there is a great sense of previously untapped activist energy among women. Underpinning and reflecting this is the more prominent theme in this book of the convergence of feminist (for example Harding, 2004; hooks, 1990) and radical (Freire, 1972; Gramsci, 1971) 'standpoint' theories, an affirmation that valid knowledge and understanding to inform and guide the struggle for social justice starts with and in the experience of injustice.

Acton and Ryder have outlined some differences in political analysis, but I think the three editors share similar aspirations. While I am closer to Andrew Ryder, and share his belief that community development can make some contribution to nurturing political activism, it needs to be emphasised that this can happen only where social movements make this impossible to avoid. Struggle is and always has been from below. Solidarity, vision, strategy and alliances are crucial to this struggle, and I hope that the book has opened up increased possibilities for a shared vision of justice for Gypsies, Roma and Travellers.

Notes

[1] The young people used the term 'telep', which derives from 'ciganytelep', which can be translated as 'Gypsy settlement' but which can also hold derogatory connotations and is closer to the term 'slum' than ghetto.

[2] The duty on councils to provide sites was initiated during the Wilson government and there was in fact a large expansion of site provision under Margaret Thatcher. It was the Major government that repealed the duty.

[3] As President de Gaulle did when he told rebellious French soldiers in 1958 'Je vous ai compris'.

References

Acton, T. (1974) 'Charities and the iron law of chaos', *New Society*, vol 30, no 633, 21 November, pp 477–9.

Acton, T. (2013) 'Review of M. Stewart (ed) (2012) *The Gypsy Menace*, London: Hurst', *Slavic Review*, vol 72, no 3, pp 629–31.

Acton, T. and Ryder, A. (2013) *Roma Civil Society: Deliberative Democracy for Change in Europe (Discussion Paper F)*, Birmingham: Third Sector Research Centre.

Ballard, R. and Ballard, C. (1977) 'The Sikhs: the development of South Asian settlements in Britain', in J.L. Watson (ed) *Between Two Cultures*, Oxford: Wiley Blackwell, pp 21–56.

Bell, D. (1972) 'Meritocracy and equality', *The Public Interest*, Fall (29), pp 29–68.

Bíró, A. (2013) 'The price of Roma integration', in W. Guy (ed) *From Victimhood to Citizenship: The Path of Roma Integration*, Budapest: Kossuth Publishing.

Cemlyn, S., Greenfields, M., Burnett, S., Matthews, Z. and Whitwell, C. (2009) *Inequalities Experienced by Gypsy and Traveller Communities: A Review*, London: Equality and Human Rights Commission.

Cornwall, A. (2008) 'Unpacking "participation": models, meanings and practice', *Community Development Journal*, vol 43, no 3, pp 269–83.

Cowan, D. and Lomax, D. (2003) 'Policing unauthorized camping', *Journal of Law and Society*, vol 30, no 2, pp 283–308.

Craig, G., Mayo, M., Popple, K., Shaw, M. and Taylor, M. (2011) *The Community Development Reader: History, Themes and Issues*, Bristol: Policy Press.

Cruddas, J. (2013) *One Nation Labour: Debating the future*, London: Labour List.

Doogan, K. (2012) 'A Fairer Capitalism? DEBATE', *Policy & Politics*, vol 40, no 3, pp 445–50.

European Commission (2011) *An EU Framework for National Roma Integration Strategies up to 2020*, Brussels: European Commission.

Flint, J. (2009) 'Cultures, ghettos and camps: sites of exception and antagonism in the city', *Housing Studies*, vol 24, no 4, 417–31.

Flint, J. and Robinson, D. (ed) (2008) *Community Cohesion in Crisis: New Dimensions of Diversity and Difference*, Bristol: Policy Press.

Foucault, M. (1997) 'Preface to the history of sexuality, volume two', in P. Rabinow (ed) *Ethics: Subjectivity and Truth: Essential Works of Michel Foucault 1954–1984*, vol 1, New York, NY: New Press, pp 199–205.

Fraser, N. (1995) 'From redistribution to recognition? Dilemmas of justice in a "postsocialist" age', *New Left Review*, vol 212, pp 68–93.

Freire, P. (1972) *Pedagogy of the Oppressed*, Harmondsworth: Penguin.

Fung, A. (2002) 'Creating deliberative publics: governance after devolution and democratic centralism', *The Good Society*, vol 11, no 1, pp 66–71.

Gheorghe, N. (1997) 'The social construction of Romani identity', in T.A. Acton (ed) *Gypsy Politics and Traveller Identity*, Hatfield: University of Hertfordshire Press, pp 153–63.

Gheorghe, N. (2013) 'Choices to be made and prices to be paid: potential roles and consequences in Roma activism and policy making', in W. Guy (ed) *From Victimhood to Citizenship: The Path of Roma Integration, A Debate*, Budapest: Kossuth Publishing, pp 41–101.

Gough, J., Eisenschitz, A. and McCulloch, A. (2006) *Spaces of Social Exclusion*, New York, NY: Routlege.

Gramsci, A. (1971) *Selections from the Prison Notebooks*, London: Lawrence and Wishart.

Guy, W. (ed) (2013) *From Victimhood to Citizenship: The Path of Roma Integration*, Budapest: Kossuth Publishing.

Harding, S. (ed) (2004) *The Feminist Standpoint Theory Reader. Intellectual and Political Controversies*. London, Routledge.

Hill, M. (2003) 'Development as empowerment', *Feminist Economics*, vol 9, nos 2–3, pp 117–35.

hooks, b. (1990) 'Choosing the margin as space of radical openness', in S. Harding (ed) (2004) *The Feminist Standpoint Theory Reader: Intellectual and Political Controversies*, London, Routledge, pp 153–9.

Hulme, R. and Hulme, M. (2012) 'Policy learning? Crisis, evidence and reinvention in the making of public policy', *Policy & Politics*, vol 40, no 4, pp 473–89.

Jackson, B. (2005) 'The conceptual history of social justice', *Political Studies Review*, vol 3, pp 356–73.

Ledwith, M. and Springett, J. (2010) *Participatory Practice: Community Based Action for Transformative Change*, Bristol: Policy Press.

Lister, R. (2008) 'Inclusive citizenship, gender and poverty: some implications for education for citizenship', *Citizenship Teaching and Learning*, vol 4, no 1, pp 3–19.

Olsen, K. (2006) *Reflexive Democracy, Political Equality and the Welfare State*, Cambridge, MA and London: MIT Press.

Parvin, P. (2011) 'Localism and the left: the need for strong central government', *Renewal*, vol 19, no 2, pp 37–49.

Rawls, J.B. (1971) *A Theory of Justice*, Cambridge, MA: Belknap Press.

Richardson, R. (ed) (2000) *The Future of Multi-Ethnic Britain – The Parekh Report*, London: Profile Books.

Ryder, A. (2011) 'Gypsies and Travellers and the third sector', University of Birmingham: Third Sector Research Centre Working Paper.

Ryder, A. (2012) 'Hearing the voice of Gypsies and Travellers: the history, development and challenges of Gypsy and Traveller tenants and residents' associations', University of Birmingham: Third Sector Research Centre Working Paper.

Saward, M. (2002) 'Rawls and deliberative democracy', in M. Passerin D'Entreves (ed) *Democracy as Public Deliberation: New Perspectives*, Manchester: Manchester University Press, pp 112–30.

Thompson, S. (2005) 'Is redistribution a form of recognition? Comments on the Fraser–Honneth debate', *Critical Review of International Social and Political Philosophy*, vol 8, no 1, pp 85–102.

Van Baar, H. (2005) 'Scaling the Romany grassroots: Europeanization and transnational networking', conference paper, *Re-activism: Re-drawing the Boundaries of Activism*, CEU, Budapest.

Willis, P. (1977) *Learning To Labor: How Working Class Kids Get Working Class Jobs*, New York: Columbia University Press.

Directory of Gypsy, Roma and Traveller organisations

National

Friends, Families and Travellers – www.gypsy-traveller.org/

The Gypsy Council – visit them on Facebook

The National Federation of Gypsy Liaison Groups – http://nationalgypsytravellerfederation.org/

The Roma Support Group – http://romasupportgroup.org.uk/

Travellers' Aid Trust – http://travellersaidtrust.org/

The Traveller Movement (formerly the Irish Traveller Movement in Britain) – http://irishtraveller.org.uk/

Traveller Solidarity Network – http://travellersolidarity.org/

UK Association of Gypsy Women – see NFGLG website

National Travellers Action Group – see NFGLG website

Walsall Gypsy and Traveller Forum – see NFGLG website

Worcester Gypsy Traveller Roma Partnership – see NFGLG website

Education, culture and history

Advisory Council for the Education of Romany and other Travellers – www.acert.org.uk/

National Association of Teachers of Travellers – www.natt.org.uk/

The Romani Cultural and Arts Company – www.romaniarts.co.uk

Romany and Traveller Family History Society – http://rtfhs.org.uk/

Travellers' Times Magazine – www.travellerstimes.org.uk/

Local regional groups

Brentwood Gypsy Support Group

Canterbury Gypsy Support Group

Cardiff Gypsy and Traveller Project – see NFGLG website

Cheshire Gypsy and Traveller Voice – www.travellersvoice.org

Clearwater Gypsies (Sussex) – see NFGLG website

Derbyshire Gypsy Liaison Group – www.dglg.org/

East Anglia Gypsy Council – see NFGLG website

East Notts Traveller Association (ENTA) – see NFGLG website

Leeds GATE Gypsy and Traveller Exchange – www.leedsgate.co.uk/

Lincolnshire Gypsy Liaison Group – www.lglg.co.uk/

London Gypsy and Traveller Unit – www.lgtu.org.uk/

One Voice for Travellers (East) – www.onevoice4travellers.org.uk

Somerset Gypsy Liaison Group – see NFGLG website

Stableway Traveller Residents' Association (London)

SPARC (North East) – see NFGLG website

Surrey Traveller Community Relations Forum – see NFGLG website

South West Alliance of Nomads – www.gypsytravellerhelp.org/

Southwark Travellers' Action Group – www.staglondon.org/2012/03/05/southwark-travellers-action-group-stag/

TravellerSpace (Devon and South West) – http://travellerspace-cornwall.org/

Legal advocacy

Travellers Advice Team – www.communitylawpartnership.co.uk/our-services/gypsies-and-travellers

Local authority liaison officers

National Association of Gypsy and Traveller Officers – www.nagto.co.uk/

International

European Roma Rights Centre – www.errc.org/

The Roma Education Fund – www.romaeducationfund.hu/

The European Academic Network on Romani Studies – http://romanistudies.eu/

The European Roma Traveller Forum – www.ertf.org/

The International Romani Union – www.internationalromaniunion.org/

The Roma Virtual Network – www.valery-novoselsky.org

APPENDIX 2

The numbers game

Demographic figures depend not only on who will identify themselves, but on whom the statisticians are prepared to count! In Eastern Europe poor, dark-skinned residents of Gypsy ghettos are more likely to be counted than nomads or light-skinned businessmen, while in England, until the 1980s only nomads living in tents or caravans were counted. Not until 2011 did the UK's Census include an ethnic question, inviting individuals to identify as 'Gypsies or Travellers', and about 58,000 did so, 24% of them living in caravans (ONS, 2014). Only 12% were born outside the UK, and it is probable that most of these were born in the Irish Republic. It is understandable that very few of the East European Roma who have migrated here since 1989 would have identified themselves, since most regard the word 'Gypsy' as a bad term. Although we are aware of small numbers of intermarriages between Roma and Romanichals over the past century, it is probably wisest to make separate estimates of 'Roma' and the numbers of 'Gypsies and Travellers' (that is, Romanichals, Kale, Nachins, Minceir, Pavees and caravan-dwelling New Travellers).

The only recent serious attempt to work from the Census and other public data to make a minimum estimate of the number of Gypsies and Travellers in England is that of the then Irish Traveller Movement (2013). It compared the Census with the numbers revealed by local authority Gypsy and Travellers Accommodation Assessments (GTAAs), which in turn take into account the Department for Communities and Local Government biannual caravan counts. Both of these were likely to undercount a little, since they could be used to help determine local authorities' site provision. The English local authority biannual caravan counts have been going since 1979, rising from 8,000 caravans to around 21,000, a growth that reflects both an increasingly reliable methodology and a clear natural population growth. In principle, the forward-looking GTAAs, developed as part of the last Labour government's regional planning strategies, sought to count all those living in caravans now or recently, or possibly desirous of living in caravans. Obviously, Travellers living in houses who would prefer to be in caravans are more likely to have made themselves known to GTAA interviewers than are those perfectly happy to be in houses; but some of the latter were included. Unfortunately, the GTAAs were contracted out to a range of consultants and universities of varying credibility, each of which decided its own methodology; but since the pressure from funders on researchers was relentlessly to massage numbers downward (Niner and Brown, 2011), we can treat the Traveller Movement's (2013) calculation of around 120,000 Gypsies and Travellers in England in 2011 and 2012 as a reliable minimum figure. To that, of course, we have to add an absolute minimum of 5,000 from government figures for Wales, Scotland and Northern Ireland, as well trying to get an idea of how much of an underestimate it is. To do this, we need to go back to the caravan counts and the Census. If we take the most recent caravan counts for each part of the UK in 2013 (Department for Communities and Local Government, 2013), this gives us at least 22,500 caravans, and if we apply the conventional multiplier of an average of three persons per caravan (Niner, 2002; Green, 1991), we have 67,500 individuals. Even if we round this down to 60,000 so as to exclude New Travellers, who do not identify ethnically as Gypsies or Travellers, this is still more than the Census figure of 58,000 (of whom only 24% live in caravans). That tells us that there are some four times as many identifiable Gypsies and Travellers living in caravans as were prepared to identify themselves to the Census. It also means there are at least 44,000 Gypsies and Travellers living in houses who registered in the Census; and if we apply the same multiplier as we know to be the case for caravan dwellers, that will give us somewhere between 180,000 and 190,000 living in houses who (sometimes at least) identify as Gypsies and Travellers whom we should add to the minimum of 60,000 living in caravans. Identifying as an ethnic group, however, is more like an attitude than a physical characteristic such as height! As noted in our text, some people identify very strongly and all the time, and others only occasionally. But we can assert with reasonable confidence that the numbers of individuals in the UK who are prepared sometimes to acknowledge Gypsy or Traveller ethnicity outside of their immediate family are certainly not fewer than 125,000, and probably not more than 250,000. In addition there may be 5,000–10,000 New Travellers.

We find the same variability among Roma communities that have migrated here since the fall of East European communism in 1989. The writers know many middle-class Romani families who are happy to attend, and sometimes even organise, Romani musical or cultural events, but always identify themselves to the authorities as Polish, Slovak, Bulgarian or Romanian. But substantial numbers of poorer families become known to educational, housing or social services. The first serious attempt to enumerate these through a survey of local authorities was by Fremlova, Ureche and Oakley (2009). In a complex but methodologically transparent process, they counted the numbers of Roma known to local authorities and then, by interviewing those families, were led to other families not known to the authorities, and they too could be asked for details of other families related or known to them, and the size of other communities that they knew about. On the basis of this Fremlova et al asserted there were no fewer than 110,000 Roma in England, while the estimates of some of their Roma informants were as many as one million in the UK. Their own more recent estimate of the likely figure by Fremlova and Ureche (2011) was 500,000. In various seminars and meetings in 2009–10, discussing the 2009 work, which was funded by the Department for Children, Schools and Families, government advisers and officials (before 2010) privately conceded that 200,000 seemed a plausible estimate. This has recently been supported by a study at Salford University (Brown et al, 2013), following a similar but more limited and less transparent methodology than Fremlova and Ureche's, which came up with the surprisingly specific minimum figure of 197,705 Roma in the UK. Now, though, the government and officials seem reluctant to support such estimates.

It is on the basis of the above that we make our assertion in Chapter One that in the current decade there are no fewer than 240,000 people in the UK at any one time who normally identify as Gypsies, Roma or Travellers, and perhaps around 350,000 who sometimes do and never more than 750,000.

This may shock some readers who are used to publications and even official reports confidently giving much more precise and consistent figures. But in truth these are based on extrapolations and updating of very limited empirical work. As noted above, from 1945 until the 1980s the only estimates of numbers in the UK were of 'nomads' or of 'people of nomadic habit of life'. The first attempts to estimate the detailed size and character of the GRT community were by Acton and Kenrick (1986, 1991), updated at intervals in response to requests from European projects (Liégeois, 1994). In 1986, using official caravan counts and National Gypsy Education Council data, they estimated the size of the English and Welsh Gypsy communities and the Scottish and Irish Traveller communities using different (and somewhat speculative) multipliers for each to get from the caravan-dwelling numbers to the total numbers including house dwellers. They included an estimate of 1,000 for the number of Roma, based on people personally known to Acton and Kenrick, the largest groups of whom were the so-called 'Old London Kalderash', descended from the so-called 'German Gypsies' who arrived in 1906, and the Romungre, who arrived after the Hungarian uprising of 1956. There were also small numbers of other showmen Romungre (although we have not included Showmen's Guild members in any of our calculations), Rudari, Ursari and South European Sinte. This led them to suggest a minimum figure of 88,000, and a possible likely estimate of 90,000–110,000, which they and others updated in the early 1990s according to increases in the caravan counts and the arrival of new Roma migrants after the fall of the Berlin Wall. Some commentators may also have mistaken the figure of '90–110,000 voyageurs', as they became in European publications, as being for 'nomades' only, and doubled again to allow for 'sedentaries'. Others appear not to have realised that Roma were included in such estimates. The widely cited Campaign for Racial Equality (2006) report seems to make such errors, and while Clark and Greenfields (2006) are properly cautious and sceptical of such estimates in the introduction to their collection, some of their contributors are not. Most recent European statistics for the UK are offered without justification and seem to be extrapolations of previous figures – which are then often confidently cited by UK writers as independent evidence. It is for this reason that we make no apology for making clear at length the bases of our own estimates.

References

Acton, T.A. and Kenrick, D.S. with the assistance of Douglas-Home, G. (1986) 'The education of Gypsy/Traveller children in Great Britain and Northern Ireland', London: unpublished report for the European Communities Commission.

Acton, T.A. and Kenrick, D.S. (1991) 'From Summer voluntary schemes to European community bureaucracy: the development of special provision for Traveller education in the UK since 1967', *European Journal of Intercultural Studies*, vol 1, no 3, pp 47–62.

Brown, P., Scullion, L. and Martin, P. (2013) *Migrant Roma in the UK*, Salford: University of Salford.

Clark, C. and Greenfields, M. (eds) (2006) *Here to Stay: The Gypsies and Travellers of Britain*, Hatfield: University of Hertfordshire Press.

Commission for Racial Equality (CRE) (2006) *Common Ground: Equality, Good Race Relations and Sites for Gypsies and Irish Travellers: Report of a CRE Inquiry in England and Wales*, London: CRE.

Department for Communities and Local Government (2013) *Collection: Traveller Caravan Count*, London, DCLG, www.gov.uk/government/collections/traveller-caravan-count.

Fremlova, L. and Ureche, H. (2011) *From Segregation to Inclusion: Roma Pupils in the UK: A Pilot Project*, London: Equality-UK.

Fremlova, L. with Ureche, H. and Oakley, R. (2009) *The Movement of Roma from New EU Member States: A Mapping Survey of A2 and A8 Roma in England: Patterns of Settlement and Current Situation of the New Roma Communities*, London: European Dialogue/Department of Children, Schools and Families.

Green, H. (1991) *Counting Gypsies*, London: HMSO.

Irish Traveller Movement (2013) *The Gypsy and Traveller Population in England and the 2011 Census*, London: The Traveller Movement, www. travellermovement.org.uk/wp-content/uploads/2014/03/Gypsy-and-Traveller-population-in-England-policy-report.pdf.

Niner, P. (2002) *The Provision and Condition of Local Authority Gypsy/ Traveller Sites in England*, London: Office of the Deputy Prime Minister.

Niner, P. and Brown, P. (2011), 'The evidence base for Gypsy and Traveller site planning: a story of complexity and tension', *Evidence and Policy*, vol 7, no 3, pp 327–45.

ONS (2014) *What Does the 2011 Census Tell Us About the Characteristics of Gypsy or Irish Travellers in England and Wales*, Press release, London: Office for National Statistics, www.ons.gov.uk/ons/rel/census/2011-census-analysis/index.html

Traveller Movement (2013) *Gypsy and Traveller population in England and the 2011 Census*, London, http://irishtraveller.org.uk/wp-content/uploads/2013/08/Gypsy-and-Traveller-population-in-England-policy-report.pdf

Index

Note: The following abbreviations have been used – *n* =note; *t* = table

Delaney, Johnny 120
Delaney, Mary 43
deliberative democracy 10, 178, 179, 220, 231
'deliberative publics' 222
Department for Children, Schools and Families (DCSF) 64–5*n*, 114, 212*n*, 213*n*, 245
Department for Communities and Local Government (DCLG) 210, 243
Department for Education (DfE) 210, 212
Department of Education and Science (DfES) 58, 60–2
Derbyshire Gypsy Liaison Group (DGLG) 45, 161, 163, 174*n*, 234
'designated status': sites 37–8
DfES *see* Department of Education and Science
DGLG *see* Derbyshire Gypsy Liaison Group
Diamond, L. 183
Dion Fund 101
discrimination 35, 100, 111, 207, 220
DIY Fund grants programme 142, 148–9
Dodds, Norman 16
Doherty, Tommy 33, 37, 39, 119, 227
Doogan, K. 231
double consciousness 45
Du Bois, W.E.B. 45
Dunajeva, Katya 217, 219
Dunn, Sylvia 36, 44, 158

E

e-mail discussion groups 124, 125
EAGC *see* East Anglian Gypsy Council
EANRS *see* European Academic Network on Romani Studies
East Anglian Gypsy Council (EAGC) 40, 42, 44, 45
Eastern Europe 12
Easton, Elizabeth 35–6, 41
Edenbridge Travellers 41
Education Act (1981) 39, 43
Education Bill (1906) 15–16
Education, Ministry of 51, 57–60
education services xii, 5, 14, 15, 16, 35, 43, 49–52
  activism and 38–40, 121
  community participation and involvement 62–4
  formalisation of national developments 52–5
  role of Department of Education and Science and Her Majesty's Inspectorate 60–2

role of Ministry of Education and Her Majesty's Inspectorate 57–60
Roma communities 189–91, 201–2, 204, 209–10, 218
state schooling 52, 55–7, 63
Traveller schools 32, 39
electronic communication 124
Emejulu, A. 8, 156
emotional capital 14–15, 161–2
employment 5, 94, 203–5, 208, 211
empowerment 7, 11, 13, 15–17, 95, 217–20
  collectivity and 224–5
  community activism 233–5
  educational success and 14
  imagination and 225–9
  power and transformative action 229–32
  praxis and obstacles to empowerment 229–23
  Roma communities and 177, 180, 181*t*, 186, 187, 200, 202–5, 207–10
  social justice and identity 223
English Gypsies (Romanichals) 33–4, 201, 243
Equalities Act (2010) 101
Equalities Impact Assessments 101
Esmée Fairbairn Foundation 151
'ethnogenic processes' 138
EU Framework for National Roma Integration Strategies 181–3, 190, 191, 210, 224, 231
EUOMC *see* European Union Open Method of Coordination
European Academic Network on Romani Studies (EANRS) 190, 191–2*n*
European Dialogue 197, 198–9, 212*n*
European Roma Institute (ERI) 192*n*
European Roma Rights Center 185
European Roma and Travellers Forum 158
European Union (EU) xiv, 21*n*, 44, 183, 212*n*, 224
European Union Open Method of Coordination (EUOMC) 181
Evangelism 187

F

'Fair Play' statement (Conservative Party) 129, 130*t*
Fakova, Pavlina 201–2
feminist perspective 8, 15, 17, 156, 220
Festival Eye (magazine) 85
Festival Welfare Services (FWS) 140, 141
Filcak, R. 179–80
Firle Bonfire Society 127, 128